Administrative Problem-Solving for Writing Programs and Writing Centers

Administrative Problem-Solving for Writing Programs and Writing Centers

Scenarios in Effective Program Management

Edited by

Linda Myers-Breslin
Texas Tech University

National Council of Teachers of English
1111 W. Kenyon Road, Urbana, Illinois 61801-1096

Staff Editor: Kurt Austin

Interior Design: Doug Burnett

Cover Design: Carlton Bruett

NCTE Stock Number: 00511-3050

Library of Congress Cataloging-in-Publication Data

Administrative problem-solving for writing programs and writing
    centers: scenarios in effective program management/edited by
    Linda Myers-Breslin.
        p. cm.
    Includes bibliographical references and index.
    ISBN 0-8141-0051-1
        1. English language—Rhetoric—Study and teaching—United States.
    2. Writing centers—United States—Administration.   I. Myers-Breslin,
    Linda.
    PE1405.U6A37   1999
    808'.042'071173—dc21   99-12806
                                                        CIP

Contents

Preface

Douglas D. Hesse
Illinois State University

In *Knowing and Being*, Michael Polanyi tells of a psychiatrist leading medical students on rounds. They encounter a patient in seizure, and one student asks for a specific diagnosis. The psychiatrist replies, "Gentlemen . . . you have seen a true epileptic seizure. I cannot tell you how to recognize it; you will learn this by more extensive experience" (124).

Those of us who direct writing programs or writing centers (and I'll use the conventional generic term *writing program administrator* or *WPA*) might be struck by two aspects of Polanyi's scene. First is the implication that some phenomena cannot be understood or taught abstractly; they can be known only by experiencing the phenomena—and a single experience may not be enough. Consider an apparently simple example: a dean asking for "information about staffing in a first-year composition course." The request seems straightforward. Yet a WPA's experience working with deans in general and with that dean in particular ought to reveal the request as complex. How is the information to be used? To examine budgets, to understand the first-year experience, to fit part of an accreditation review, to reassure state legislators? Obviously, the WPA would ask why the information is requested. Even then, she or he must know how to ask in just the right way and how to interpret any reply, as a physician interprets lab results. It is important to have the experience, in some fashion, of working with deans.

A second aspect of Polanyi's example is perhaps less obvious. Even though the psychiatrist says she cannot tell the students how to recognize the seizure, they are nonetheless on rounds. The doctor simultaneously names the phenomenon and abjures providing a mere checklist of its features. But she does so in the presence of the phenomenon. The doctor is there, the would-be doctors are there, the patient is there. Together they form a complex mixture of knowledges and interests, all on different trajectories but coalescing in the exigency of the seizure. Certain kinds of knowledge cannot be analytically transmitted, but the teacher can—and must—direct the students' gazes. Such direction does not occur in a vacuum; before they have seen this patient, the group has visited others, and ever more are yet to come.

In terms of the knowledge that WPAs need and the ways they can and cannot acquire it, Polanyi's example resonates through several harmonics. To suggest how, I'll tell a narrow history.

When I started directing a large writing program in 1988, I was beginning my third year as an assistant professor. Doing this sort of work had never been a career goal, which was probably true for most WPAs of my generation. We had no specialized training, but then little was available or, to be honest, necessary. At forty-one and still in the first half (I hope) of my professional career, I admit it's pretentious to invoke "my generation," but the phrase seems apt. While faculty members have directed writing programs and centers for decades, the professional status of the WPA—anointed by a professional organization, journal, meeting, and graduate coursework—is a recent development. The Council of Writing Program Administrators was founded in 1977, and the twenty years since then provide a convenient way of laying out three generations.

Faculty who were directing writing programs or centers in the late 1970s may have had graduate coursework in rhetoric and composition—but likely did not. More rarely had they completed dissertations in the field. Yet most had an interest in teaching and doing research in writing, an interest often developed on the job after graduate school. Though some WPAs then (and now) probably did the administrative work out of a sense of obligation spiced by extra pay—after all, the reassigned time from teaching has never been commensurate with the job's demands—I suspect for more it promised intellectual and professional reward. Already in the seventies there was sufficient awareness of the WPA's special work to prod a handful of people—Ken Bruffee, Tim Donovan, Lynn Bloom, Elaine Maimon, Win Horner, among them—to form the WPA organization, with Bruffee first editing its journal. Motivations for this movement paralleled those thirty years earlier that had led to the formation of the Conference on College Composition and Communication. At the same time, new courses and doctoral programs in rhetoric and composition began to join the pacesetters.

The Institute on Writing that the National Endowment for the Humanities funded at the University of Iowa from 1977 to 1980 marks a convenient, if arbitrary, generational watershed both for rhetoric and composition and for WPAs. The project, led by Carl Klaus, Richard Lloyd-Jones, and Paul Diehl, brought writing program directors from around the country for an intensive semester's discussion of courses and programs. Most notably, and farsightedly, deans of participating institutions were required to attend some of the Institute.

By the mid-1980s, the period I've claimed for "my generation," increasing numbers of faculty hired to teach writing, rhetoric, and courses in the burgeoning area that came broadly to be known as composition studies had extensive coursework and degrees in rhetoric and composition. Their formal credentials were substantially different from those of first-generation WPAs, especially in large universities. What they still did not have was training in administration per se. Several of them had previous experiences as program assistants or mentors to beginning teaching assistants, but there was hardly a sufficient professional literature in writing program administration to support graduate work. And, to be candid, neither do I think there was the interest. Anything looking too much like "college of education courses in bureaucracy management" seemed tawdry to graduate students and faculty. However, if formal coursework seemed excessive, other kinds of training did not. In the mid-1980s the Council of Writing Program Administrators began sponsoring a summer workshop for WPAs, an intensive three-day experience in which two veteran administrators guided a small group of mostly newer WPAs through several issues. The 1997 workshop in Houghton, Michigan, had over twenty participants, suggesting the continued success of this administrator support model.

We are now at the outset of a third generation of WPAs, faculty members who will increasingly have formal training directly in program administration or directing writing centers. Regularly on the writing program administrators' listserv (WPA-L) there have been requests to exchange syllabi and reading lists for courses focusing on administrative issues. Regularly I see vitae from job applicants who, in addition to considerable graduate work in composition studies, are able to present compelling preparation for administration. Unlike me or others of my generation, many new Ph.D. graduates are specifically pursuing careers in writing program administration, rather than happening into such positions, as most of us previously did.

Why? Why now? Three reasons, I think. The first is that the professional literature on writing program administration has reached a critical mass. Once the professional literature on any academic topic reaches a certain volume and has sufficient numbers of stakeholders, the topic exerts, almost of its own Darwinian agency, a force to create courses to disseminate and, thus, perpetuate and extend the topic.

A second reason concerns the relationship between theory and practice. Even more than the question "What should a writing course be?" the question "What should a writing program be?" focalizes complex issues in theory and research. It does so through a pragmatic lens of institutional philosophies, politics, and financial constraints, all refracted by the needs and interests of various constituents. To ask, "What should a writing program be and how should it be run?" is to enact a powerful heuristic for exploring fundamental questions of writing, learning, and literacy.

Growing out of the second reason is a third, most compelling one. Simply put, the environment in which WPAs must now work is much more complicated than ever before. WPAs must now judge and juggle different and competing interests of various constituents, not only teachers and students, but also colleagues beyond the English department, administrators, and legislators. Let me suggest two related ways this complexity amplifies itself in a synergistic feedback loop. One is financial. Especially for public universities, external funding levels are diminishing even as the expenses of buying new technologies and renovating aging physical plants are mounting. For both public and private institutions, rising costs frequently shape a marketing focus that influences, perhaps minutely, decisions throughout the university. Because of their size in proportion to other entities within the university, writing programs tend to serve as lightning rods for issues grounded in economics.

The second, related engine of complexity is wide public skepticism about higher education, especially those aspects of the university charged with developing "skills." Many people perceive the values and practices of English professors and writing teachers to be at odds with, sometimes dangerously out of touch with, the values and needs of students. Exacerbating the situation, this public perception is often shared by faculty across the university. Space does not permit me to explore these issues in depth. I will simply note that being a WPA is a heck of a lot messier today than it was when I began in 1988. The mess can be exhilarating, but it is still messy.

How, then, should a faculty member near the turn of the century prepare for WPA work? For better or worse, especially in larger institutions WPAs can no longer afford to learn everything on the job, as they could perhaps in earlier, more forgiving environments. Of course, much they can know only by working as a WPA, just as physicians can learn most of the arts of medicine only by being physicians. I choose the term "arts of medicine" deliberately, echoing the tradition of medical practitioners themselves to cast their work as art, in the root sense of *techne*, and not only as science. I don't want to push the analogy beyond reason, but some of medical education's logic applies to preparing WPAs.

Between classroom training, in which information and advice are transmitted via textbook and lecture, and private or group practice, with one's own real patients, there is a vital intermediary stage, the clinical, in which an expert practitioner leads novices through a wide range of cases, many of them complex, helping them learn to read what is presented in various situations and to understand available options. Crucially, clinical training is not reserved for new physicians only, as can be seen through the continued practice of medicine journals publishing case histories.

This book assembles a number of expert practitioners, people who direct or work closely with writing programs or writing centers. Each has a complex case. The scenarios they have provided invite readers to explore problems actively and intricately. Each provides an opportunity for what might be characterized, after Polanyi, as indwelling, the process of examining a framework or situation from within that framework or situation. A book is not a hospital bed (thank heavens), and neither is it a campus. Yet scenarios such as these provide one of the best ways I know to demonstrate and experience the work of writing administration.

Acknowledgments

I thank all authors contributing to this volume for their creative, scholarly excellence and for their conscientiousness regarding submission and revision deadlines. I am especially grateful to my husband Mike, whose advice, assistance, and support encouraged me to produce this text. I also thank Michael Greer of NCTE for his kind, patient answers to many questions and for his continual encouragement regarding this project.

Introduction

Linda Myers-Breslin
Texas Tech University

The relationship of writing programs and writing centers to English departments is administrative as well as intellectual. Although writing programs serve an interdisciplinary service, they need a departmental base. The effort to decide the future of writing programs and centers within the academy raises questions about traditional departmental structures and their effect on education reform. As a result, we need to understand the structure of the academy, how it operates, and the difficulties that administrators and directors face within this structure.

To understand the role of the writing program administrator (WPA) and the writing center director (WCD) is not to uphold a particular pedagogy, theory, or managerial style. It is to understand the academy and how its operations affect programs, positively and negatively, within the larger structure of the academic institution. In the balance, the WPA and WCD roles fluctuate. Is the WPA or the WCD an independent scholar? A managerial executive? An instructor of graduate and undergraduate students? A server within a service? A psychologist/soothsayer/mentor? All of the above? The case studies within this text provide an epistemology of the problem-solving process that guides directors through role fluctuations to the most advantageous decisions. This holistic approach teaches context, meaning, complexity, and interaction.

Administrative Problem-Solving for Writing Programs and Writing Centers uses experience as a teacher. As in all aspects of life, examining the experiences of others provides practical perceptions. Many experienced professors of writing, writing program administrators, and writing center directors have much experience to share. This text presents real-world situations about different aspects of administration, each containing issues for discussion revolving around one key area of contention. Each contributor provides a description of a problematic situation, as well as enough information about the institution and program to resolve the situation. This text is distinctive in that the cases place readers into administrative situations. The text does not merely describe theories of administration nor present a particular problem and tell how to solve it. Instead, each chapter guides readers through institutional, program, and center context, personnel descriptions, problem definitions, and other pertinent considerations. This guidance provides vicarious, hands-on experience in writing program administration and writing center directorship. By the end of this text, readers will develop decision-making strategies, perhaps a problem-solving template, that will assist them once they embark on careers in our ever-expanding field. Thus, the vicarious experience in solving (or at least extensively pondering) these problems will prove invaluable to readers and administrators alike.

The empirical nature of administrative situations, decisions, and repercussions makes the case study quite suited for instructional purposes. There are no certainties, exact answers, or clean results. Thus, readers seeking wisdom about administration will gain much from this approach, an approach that attempts to develop and understand the universal principles by a close examination of particular cases.

The purpose of this text is three-fold: (1) to provide graduate-student readers with decision-making opportunities that will prepare them to assume administrative roles in the future; (2) to invite current administrators to consider these scenarios and in doing so reconsider their own decision-making strategies; and (3) to give instructors at any level the chance to gain skill at administrative problem-solving. The problem-solving approach used throughout the text places readers into situations that provide the opportunity for decision-making. Administrators of writing programs and writing centers confront many challenges that go unnoticed by anyone but themselves. They simply deal with them as they arise. Experience has taught these administrators how to handle various challenges as they arise throughout the days, weeks, and semesters. What about the new administrator who lacks experience, the administrator who is unaware of the daily challenges that must be faced, problems that must be resolved, decisions that must be made? Graduate readers just entering writing programs are dealing with new levels of academic challenge—graduate course work (often while simultaneously teaching first-year composition classes), interaction with faculty as professors and colleagues, competition with other graduates in their field, and the demands of presentation and publication. While each of these challenges is important for introducing graduates into the world of academe, all of the effort and experience does nothing to prepare readers for the duties of administration. Thus far, our teaching and training do not address the multitude of areas that comprise a program or center—training, budgets, technology, attaining authority, personnel decisions, time management, handling complaints, etc. All of these demands exist outside the realm of course work, teaching assistantships, exams, and, in most cases, thesis and dissertation writing. These "outside" demands, however, are what readers will face once they cross the desk and, therefore, are the demands for which readers must be prepared.

Because most graduate students who enter the job market today will perform administrative tasks, it is our obligation (as teachers of rhetoric and composition) to prepare them for these challenges. Most new administrators have not had much opportunity to think carefully about the administrative issues that they will face within the first year or two of employment. College composition has become a huge endeavor. Almost 90 percent of all first-year students must take a writing course. This enormous enterprise encompasses a vast assortment of pedagogies, methods, philosophies, curricular designs, and resources. Effective administration means having the ability to address the often conflicting ideas and make thoughtful decisions about program mission, pedagogy, method, and design.

Readers of *Administrative Problem-Solving for Writing Programs and Writing Centers* can approach the scenarios along two distinct but intersecting routes—type of program and type of problem. Listserv surveys, asking for three administratively problematic areas, were sent to the W-PAL and to WCenter. The results of these surveys provided the areas most vexing for administrators of both writing programs and writing centers: authority/location, budget, technology, creating a theory and mission statement, training, attaining support for the program or center, and time management (balancing administration, research, teaching, and service). The structure of this text associates the type of program (writing program or writing center) to common problems that arise throughout an academic year. Readers can also look at a particular problem area (i.e., budget) and see how it is addressed in a variety of programs at a variety of schools. To ensure approachability and comprehensiveness, various tenured, associate, and assistant administrators from many differing educational institutions—private, public, and community—have detailed scenarios that place readers in the midst of a situation that requires decision-making resolution.

Not all authors use their current school as the model in their chapters. Some use a school at which they previously worked, others combine situations from several schools, and others create schools. The situations described, however, are all quite real and quite current.

The Embedded Design of Each Case

Development across time of a program or center is essential information. The first goal of each case study is to describe the academic institution in order to provide historical context for the situation. One must know the historical and political context in order to make informed decisions. Looking at the past informs decisions for the future.

To enhance information about the past, the second goal of each case is to describe the history of the program or center within the academic institution. Development is a key element of the decision-making process. Authors describe the current political climate, how this climate evolved, the key players, and the key challenges to confront.

The third goal of each case is to detail an intensive description of particular circumstances of an individual situation. The value of such a detailed understanding of a case is three-fold:

1. Understanding one case thoroughly can inform an overall problem-solving strategy. Such a strategy requires simultaneous consideration and combination of many program or center aspects in relationship to one another. For example, resolving a center budgetary problem requires consideration of current and future goals and personnel, and prior strategies, decisions, plans, and budgets—all simultaneously. Plus, readers must try to discern how their decisions affect all sides: the participating instructors and students, the nonparticipating instructors and students, the direct administration, the indirect administration, the directly and indirectly involved departments and staffs, and the community inside and outside of the academy. All who could possibly be affected require consideration.

2. Each case is thoroughly detailed so that problems and decisions can be cross-referenced to each other. The holistic, multiple-case design enables readers to apply problems from one case to the context of another case. For example, if we look at the historical and current description of a large state school which describes budget problems, we can take that budget problem and apply it to the description of the small private school. Likewise, the tutor-training difficulties of the small private school can be placed within the context of the large state school, and we can examine similarities and differences in the potential outcomes of each problematic situation.

3. Resolution is the final goal of each case. An Author's Case Commentary is located at the end of each chapter. In order to assist readers with problem-solving strategies, each Author's Case Commentary describes

what her or his school did or is doing to resolve the situation described. This section is not intended as an "answer key." There are many variables in each situation and thus many solutions. These commentaries are intended only to provide one approach to the given situation and to provoke readers into creating optional means of resolving the problematic circumstances.

Ways This Book Can Be Used

Selection of contributors for this text was based on diversity, experience, and expertise. Contributors have written scenarios situated in small private liberal arts colleges, medium-sized land-grant institutions, large state universities. School locations range from the east to the west coast and in between, and from rural to urban settings. Because the mission of a school and its writing program strongly influence decisions made regarding the program, the programs and centers described also differ in their philosophical and pedagogical orientations. Thus, readers can take a scenario from one school and apply it to another. For example, readers can take the technology scenario described for a small private college, look at the description of the large state school, and consider what the outcome would be for the state school and how this outcome differs from the one arrived at for the private school.

This text will be useful in a variety of contexts including classroom, meeting room, workshop, and virtual settings. In a graduate seminar, readers will gain valuable vicarious administrative experience. The scenarios may provide helpful discussion prompts for current administrators who meet to discuss their programs. Those creating new programs will gain knowledge of problems they may encounter, program types that already exist, why they evolved as they have, and the problems that these programs had and still have. The book will provide new perspectives for those considering program expansion or evaluation of their current programs. Also, more seasoned administrators will find helpful outcomes to common problems as well as strategies that have been instituted and tested. Researchers will discover shared problems that need to be investigated. In all contexts, this text can help open dialogues and support more reflective administrative practice.

An Overview of the Text

To make this book accessible, it is divided into three sections. Each section represents a context for particular decision-making challenges. These sections are arranged chronologically by occurrence within an academic year: challenges that one is likely to meet at the beginning of the term are discussed before those that arise a bit later.

The first section deals with selection and training—attaining a voice in the TA/tutor selection; ways to select from prospective tutors and TAs; and preparing these new TAs and tutors to perform their duties. Within this section, Rich Bullock moves readers beyond conventional thinking on TA preparation; Muriel Harris discusses tutor selection, training, and evaluation; Christine Hult and Lynn Meeks provide scenarios with problematic graduate instructors; Allene Cooper and her teaching assistants describe portfolio assessment, competency exams, portfolios, workshops, and meetings; Paul Bodmer introduces a developmental writing program at a small two-year college; and Howard Tinberg examines our assumptions as gatekeepers.

Section Two addresses several aspects of program development—creating a new program curriculum, pedagogy, and structure; or integrating new elements into an existing program in order to improve the program. Louise Wetherbee Phelps thinks strategically about human resources; Joan Mullin discusses maintaining program integrity in the midst of downsizing; Linda S. Houston explores the requirements of initial funding as well as the problems associated with continued operation of a writing center; Deborah Holdstein considers the many aspects involved with introducing computers into a writing program; Sara Kimball describes what writing centers do with computers when integrating computer services into their program; and Rita Malenczyk helps decide the possibility of productive change in the turbulent atmosphere of a micromanaged program.

The third section contains essays on professional issues of departmental authority and professional development—how one manages relationships within a program, dealing with the conceptual and practical issues that arise among competing elements in a department or other powers in the institution; and how one motivates veteran instructors and tutors to stay current and progressive in the field. Authority and development of faculty are ongoing, relevant concerns. Ben McClelland presents a situation in which a newly arrived WPA attempts to implement a theory-based program in an institution that has been employing early writing process pedagogy (laced with lots of lore); I discuss running a large writing program; Barry Maid explains how WPAs can learn to use power and authority to their own advantage; Ed White and Carol Haviland describe the internal struggles for power as faculty members vie for offices and titles that situate them near desirable centers of power; Dave Healy balances the management of the writing center with that of classroom instruction; Lisa Gerrard challenges faculty to maintain professional activity; and Robert Dornsife offers issues that need negotiation when initiating a peer tutoring program/training into an institution that traditionally prides itself on providing students with "degreed" professional instruction.

The book ends with two lists: one of readings suggested by the contributors and one compiling all works cited in the book.

The sheer number of assumptions, expectations, questions, theories, pedagogies, methods, approaches, complexities, and continual changes relevant to programs and centers prevents readers from easily stepping into an administrative position. Although I hope this text makes clear that there is no one right way to resolve a situation, I also hope that consideration of the experiences, opinions, and fundamental concerns will better enable new and experienced administrators to successfully run programs and centers.

I Selection and Training

1 In Pursuit of Competence: Preparing New Graduate Teaching Assistants for the Classroom

Richard Bullock
Wright State University

How can WPAs give new graduate teaching assistants the knowledge and skills they need to be successful writing teachers? This chapter's scenario outlines a typical situation, in which new TAs, who most likely have neither teaching experience nor any knowledge of composition pedagogy, must be prepared to teach first-year composition in a very limited time; it invites readers to move beyond conventional thinking on TA preparation.

Institution Overview

The university in which you now work is a mid-sized, state-supported one, with about 16,000 students and 600 faculty, several M.A. programs and a couple of Ph.D. programs. Students primarily come to it from the surrounding region, which includes a moderately large city with its suburbs and lots of surrounding farmland. The student body is 85 to 90 percent white, the other 10 to 15 percent mostly African American. As at other "metropolitan" universities, the student body is a bit older than at residential colleges, many students starting their studies after several years of work, many students working full time and studying part time and so stretching their studies out over several years. Recently, though, the number of straight-from-high-school students has been increasing, and this past year just over half of the first-year students lived in dormitories.

The student body reflects a wide range of abilities, since the school's policy is to admit anyone with a high school diploma. Composite ACT scores average 21, SATs 1000. Students who aren't sure whether or not they want to attend college or who aren't sure they have the ability to succeed in college come here to give college a try. At the same time, excellent students are drawn to the school's strong engineering, business, and theater programs, as are good students from the area who must attend for financial reasons. This mix is seen as good, in that the school provides a place for students to succeed on their merits as college students, rather than penalizing them for past mistakes; it is also seen as bad, though, because faculty must try to reach students with many levels of preparation within a single course, and because some students inevitably decide that this school, or any school, isn't right for them: about a third of first-year students do not return for their sophomore year. Retention of students—seen as "student success"—is therefore an institutional priority. Incoming first-year students participate in a two-day orientation program during June and July, during which they are tested for placement into math and writing classes (the writing placement test is a holistically scored essay), advised, and registered for their fall quarter courses.

Courses

One of those courses is likely, of course, to be first-year English: ENG 101 and 102. The courses are part of a fairly traditional general education program that also includes history, mathematics, science, political science, sociology, and psychology courses, as well as some interdisciplinary courses in regional studies and cultural studies. Four of the required GE courses in addition to 101 and 102 are writing-intensive, though the class size (40 or more per section) keeps them from being too writing-intensive. By contrast, the 50 to 60 quarterly sections of 101 and 102 maintain class sizes of 25, 20 in the 8 sections taught each quarter in computer-equipped classrooms. The classes meet each week either two days in 75-minute periods or three days in 50-minute periods.

ENG 101 and 102 are taught by faculty and graduate teaching assistants in the Department of English. The department offers an undergraduate major in literature which has recently been redesigned to downplay period survey courses and emphasize theory, a popular major in creative writing, and a major in professional writing that involves course work in business writing, research writing, and technical writing. The graduate program consists of a two-year master's degree, which can be earned in literature, composition and rhetoric, women's studies, professional writing, and TESOL. There are about 200 undergraduate English majors and 80 to 100 graduate students in the programs, including 26 graduate teaching assistants who teach seven courses over their two-year appointments: three in year one, four in year two.

Faculty

The department's faculty consists of 25 tenure-line faculty, along with 2 to 3 instructors who have master's degrees and limited-term contracts, and 6 to 12 adjunct faculty, most of whom have M.A.'s. The department has several senior faculty who were trained in current-traditional methods of teaching writing and who tend to dismiss current practices as "something we did twenty years ago." Fortunately, there is a large contingent of associate professors, and a few senior faculty, who are aware of current scholarship in the field and who are the leaders in the department. They are the faculty who supported your position and your hiring. Your predecessor in your position as WPA began in literary studies but retooled herself as a composition specialist (though she still teaches literature courses occasionally). She is supportive, but has either moved to a different position, perhaps as writing-across-the-curriculum coordinator, or has left on a well-deserved sabbatical; in any event, your contact with her is limited to occasional conversations due to her schedule and her desire to let you establish your own authority. There are also several assistant professors with various, mostly literary, specialties but some knowledge of composition studies. The instructors, who teach only first-year composition and are ineligible for administrative posts, were hired for their expertise in composition and rhetoric and are very happy that you were hired; they interact with the TAs on a regular basis, since their offices are all in the same place (the basement of the library, a good ten-minute walk from the English department's main office but near the University Writing Center, where tutoring in writing is offered and the WAC program has its home).

History

The two-course first-year writing program you have inherited has an uneven history. For most of the department's history, the literature faculty took turns as WPA, and the rest of the faculty taught as the WPA of the moment suggested. When your predecessor arrived as the first hired-in composition specialist and WPA, the program focused on five-paragraph themes and grammar study; the textbooks were a handbook and a reader. Over the next several years, she changed the program considerably, moving to a mix of expressivist pedagogy in 101 and argument in 102. This program, which you are maintaining in its overall structure, has seen widespread acceptance among the TAs, instructors, and adjunct faculty (mostly former TAs) who teach the vast majority of the courses. Some of the senior faculty who taught under the current-traditional model grumble over the changes in the program (though they do not teach in it), but so far their dissatisfaction has produced little unrest.

Key Charge

Your position as WPA involves many duties. You are in charge of designing the first-year writing program in its overall shape, though there is no tradition here of using uniform syllabi in the courses. You chair the department's Writing Programs Committee, which has jurisdiction over all aspects of the writing programs and courses. You monitor the upper-level writing courses offered to undergraduates, which may lead to certificates in professional or technical writing. You supervise students working as writing interns in area companies. You teach undergraduate and graduate writing and writing pedagogy courses and first-year composition when you can. You advise students on appropriate writing courses to take. And, you prepare new, incoming TAs for the ENG 101 classroom. You have no assistant director, though the Writing Programs Committee includes several instructors who are eager to help you in any way they can, and you do not have to deal with budgets—the chair and dean do that. You receive a stipend of $2,000 per year and one course release each quarter (out of a normal load of seven courses per three-quarter year) for your work as Director of Writing Programs.

Scenario: Preparing TAs to Teach

The ten to fourteen new graduate teaching assistants at your school are very similar to those at other graduate schools throughout the country: their undergraduate preparation is, by and large, solely in literature. Their only contact with composition pedagogy came during their own sojourns through first-year English, unless, of course, they tested out of or were otherwise exempted from it. Their ages range from twenty-two, fresh from undergraduate programs at this school or elsewhere, to forty-five, typically women with grown children wishing to return to school or men who have decided to change their careers. Their goals are as varied as their ages—some want to go on for doctoral study somewhere else, some want to become technical writers, some wish to teach abroad, some simply want to continue to study, read, and write. Most are from the immediate surrounding area, though every year one or two come from out of state. One more thing: they all arrive scared stiff, about the studies they are about to begin, and about leading a class full of students for the first time.

Thankfully, your school has moved from the hoary method of preparing new teaching assistants—which mostly consisted of handing them a textbook and gradebook and showing them their classroom—to a better system. You have inherited from your predecessor the following procedures: new TAs arrive on campus three days preceding the start of fall quarter classes; since classes begin around September 15, but TA contracts—like all faculty contracts—begin September 1, they can be asked to arrive early. The WPA conducts a workshop during those three days, introducing the TAs to basic concepts of teaching writing through activities and reading and leading them to the construction of a syllabus for their course sections (usually based on a model you give them). They all use the same textbook, a popular rhetoric or "guide to writing," and all are expected to follow a similar overall course plan. Then, in the fall and winter quarters, you lead them in a weekly seminar entitled "Teaching College Composition," in which they read more essays on writing and discuss their own experiences teaching 101 in the fall and 102 in the winter.

Here's the problem, though: despite the workshop, many new TAs have fairly difficult and unpleasant experiences in their first quarters of teaching. Full of anxieties, they expend many hours of work preparing lesson plans, grading papers, holding conferences, and reading independently. In some cases they sacrifice their own work—and grades—as students. They try to figure out through trial and error how to behave in their classrooms in ways that feel comfortable and seem productive; they spend hours talking with one another about their problems in the classroom and are often to be seen in your office as well, trying to get help. You visit many TAs' classes several times during the first quarter, trying to help them get on their feet. And yet, students' evaluations of the first-quarter classes taught by many new TAs remain relatively low, and the TAs themselves say that they only begin to figure out how to teach 101 as the quarter ends—and then they have to teach 102 the next quarter, starting over again in many ways.

Clearly, the current situation, while better than nothing, does not work very well, and the TAs learn to teach primarily through immersion, an inefficient and often counterproductive method. What the TAs often "figure out" involves survival strategies that get them through the class but do little or nothing for the students' writing abilities. Worse, they often look back to their own teachers in college or even high school, dragging out grammar worksheets and sentence diagrams and "sneaking" them into the classroom, knowing they are frowned upon but not knowing what else to do. When they run across something that "works," they pass the tip to others, creating an underground pedagogy of sorts that undermines the official, departmentally sanctioned curriculum. And a few of them ally themselves with those disaffected senior faculty, who encourage them in their unwitting subversion.

You, too, feel the pressure. Your own time for program development, scholarship, and other activities dwindles as you spend hours advising and comforting TAs, visiting TAs' classes, and talking with unhappy students who know the TA teaching their class is not doing a good job. The department chair is generally your ally but has expressed displeasure about the poor student evaluations new TAs receive and warned you that the TAs' discomfort provides ammunition for those senior faculty who resist the writing program as it currently exists. And the unhappiness of the students may be noticed by the administration as it pressures all faculty to take actions to improve retention of students.

What You Can—and Can't—Do

Your potential actions are constrained (and enabled) in the following ways. New TAs must teach one course each quarter in order to receive stipends; they must also take at least two courses each quarter—normally 4 quarter hours each—to be considered full time. However, the Teaching College Composition seminars carry only 2 q.h. in the fall, and 2 more in the winter. So new TAs must take three courses in each of their first two quarters.

Together, the two seminars' 4 quarter hours count toward the total M.A. program requirement of 48 hours. You could increase the seminars to the standard 4 hours each, but many faculty worry that doing so would reduce by one or two the number of other courses TAs would take, and many are also reluctant to add to the total number of hours required for the M.A. However, several courses required as prerequisites for other graduate courses do not count toward the degree and end up as "extra" hours; for example, to take Advanced Professional Writing, a 700-level course, students must complete two 500-level writing and desktop publishing courses that cannot be used toward the degree requirement (though TAs can use them to be counted as full-time students).

While you control no budgets as WPA, your chair has some discretionary money—a few hundred dollars at most—that she will probably let you spend on a good cause. Your dean has also been supportive of innovation and of the writing program in the past and might be approached. And, there is a budget line that you can use to deposit and withdraw small amounts. But the budgets are tight, so any plan you make should be as frugal as possible—without cost, if that can be accomplished.

University offices—the Bursar, the Registrar, Student Advising, Conferences, and others—are well-run and helpful, and you have made contacts, through committees and other means, with the heads of most of these departments. The Conferences office regularly runs workshops and special events that involve coordinating rooms, registrations, registration fees, and other logistics. You are lucky in that the school is relatively young and so has not yet encrusted itself with bureaucracy and traditions that together make change difficult and frustrating. You are less lucky in that the school is relatively young and therefore insecure in its position, so it tends to think conservatively; it is leery of being on any "cutting edge"—though it will venture onto one if convinced.

Considerations

A. Your goal, simply and complexly, is to create a procedure that will make first-year TAs better and more confident teachers in ENG 101. What do "better" and "more confident" mean in terms you can define operationally?

B. What does this procedure demand, ideally? What are the best methods for creating excellent teachers? What do other teacher-preparation programs (not just TA-preparation programs) do? What elements of those programs can you adopt or adapt?

C. How can you make changes, and make them work? Think flexibly: what can be accomplished using the people you have available to you (first-year TAs, second-year TAs, instructors, others)? The resources (the various university offices that deal with students or other services, classroom availability when school isn't in session)? The time (the start of contracts, the current pre-fall-term activities in the English department, the teaching seminar time over two quarters)?

D. What are the constraints and difficulties that need to be overcome in order to achieve these changes? Who needs to be convinced to do what? Who needs to be enlisted to help? What will motivate them? If you have no money and need some, where can you get it, if not from existing budgets?

AUTHOR'S CASE COMMENTARY

My solution to this problem evolved over several stages:

1. Lengthen the workshop, reduce the pressure. Since TAs and faculty are under contract starting September 1 and are getting paid for that time, I asked the new TAs to attend a five-day-long workshop. In that workshop we modeled the activities of ENG 101 and then discussed both the reasons for those activities as teachers and the effects those activities had on the TAs as writers and students. I considered my time to be funded through my course release time and my stipend—my contract begins September 1, too. My chair and I also appealed to the Graduate School to bend its rule on the minimum number of hours TAs need to take to maintain assistantships: arguing that TAs in English have greater responsibilities for teaching than other TAs, we suggested that our TAs should be able to maintain their assistantships if they took, not 8 hours each quarter, but 16 over the first two quarters. That way, new TAs could take the teaching seminar and only one other course in the fall (6 hours total) and the seminar and two other courses in the winter (10 hours total). The extra time and reduced course obligations helped TAs, though they still entered the classroom feeling unprepared, as they should have. (This system stayed in place for three years, long enough for the disgruntled senior faculty mentioned earlier to retire; some problems really do go away if you can wait long enough. I was lucky.)

2. Increase credit for the TA seminar. One major source of pressure for TAs was the conflicting demands they felt between their own course work and their teaching responsibilities. The difficulty of distinguishing between the work demanded by the TA seminar and that demanded by their teaching led students to complain that they were being asked to work far too hard for a 2-hour course, even with a reduced fall-quarter class schedule. Once the pre-fall-term workshop was counted as part of the course, though, it clearly met more than enough contact hours to change the seminar to a 4-hour course. Changing this proved simple: I proposed the change to the Graduate Committee, noting that the increased hours would be added to the department's total of "weighted student credit hours," the formula by which the state of Ohio allocates money to its state universities. The Graduate Committee recommended to the department that the change be adopted, and the department agreed. Students now take the seminar and one other course in the fall quarter. In the winter, the seminar is worth only 2 hours, so TAs must take two other courses. The two quarters of seminar add up to 6 quar-

ter hours, so TAs simply end up with two extra hours of credit at the end of their two years—the number of other courses they take still adds up to 11, so the graduate faculty did not "lose" a course to the TA seminar.

3. Add a student teaching component. This was the solution that made the real difference. During the summer orientation sessions for incoming students, we advertise our "Introduction to College Writing Workshop," a four-morning workshop that takes place the week before fall classes start. All students who have placed into ENG 101 may attend, with the idea that they will be better prepared for their fall quarter writing classes, will get accustomed to being on campus and so avoid first-year-student confusion, and will do better in their classes than students who don't—something we didn't anticipate. But in tracking the first-year workshop participants we found it to be true not only in their ENG 101 classes, but across the board. They pay $25 for the four-day workshop, plus room and board if they have to move into the dorm early. And we promise that if they attend the whole workshop, they'll receive a T-shirt. About eighty students attend each year. (This is where cooperation from our administrative units proves crucial, and where contacts show their usefulness. First-year-student advisors promote the workshop to new students; the Conferences office handles their registrations; the Financial Aid office will add the workshop fee to their total bill so that it's covered by their scholarships or student loans; the Registrar provides us with classrooms for the workshop sessions; and the Housing office provides the dorm space for out-of-town students. The Public Relations office even gets us T-shirts at a discounted price.)

I reduced the preterm workshop to three days. During the first two days, usually a Thursday and Friday, the new TAs experience all the activities involved in creating a polished draft: choosing a topic, doing invention activities, drafting, workshopping, revising, editing, and publishing. We follow, in condensed form, a script that they will follow when they teach their sections of the workshop. We discuss the pedagogies of these activities as I model them and they experience them, and during the afternoon of the third day, usually Monday, we meet with the lecturers, instructors, and second-year TAs to discuss nuts and bolts of teaching (what to do on the first day, how to dress, and other tricks of the trade) and to get acquainted. While I have much to say about these subjects, the people who teach first-year comp much more often than I do have much more to say—and I want the new TAs to see them as mentors, models, and resources, rather than relying only on me for advice.

At this meeting, each new TA is paired with a second-year TA or an instructor, and together they will take charge of a workshop class of five to eight students. (The second-year TAs are technically under the same contractual obligation as the first-year TAs, but I've found that they and the instructors participate willingly, rather than out of legal obligation; the TAs tell me they remember how much the workshop helped them in their initial struggle to become teachers and want to share that help with the first-year TAs, and the instructors both echo that sentiment and say that attending the workshop "recharges" them for the new year while letting them get to know the new TAs. So enlisting their help has cost me only the price of a new T-shirt for each of them.)

On Tuesday morning, new TAs, their teaching partners, and the first-year students who enrolled in the workshop meet in a large lecture hall. I welcome them, introduce the workshop, and lead the group in the first few invention activities. Then we divide the students into their individual sections of five to eight students each, the TAs lead their students to their classrooms, and for the next four mornings the workshops continue on their own, the TAs leading the students through the writing activities they experienced the week before, their partners assisting when needed, taking over when asked, or simply being present to provide reassurance. At week's end, they collect the students' revised and edited drafts, which we photocopy, bind into magazines, and send to the students. At the last session, too, the TAs present the students with "Introduction to College Writing" T-shirts as graduation presents. In the afternoons, the new TAs meet with me to discuss the morning's events, go over the next day's, and work on preparing syllabi for their sections of ENG 101.

The new TAs, then, experience over fifteen hours of teaching before they have to take charge of a classroom of their own—the equivalent of half a quarter of normal teaching—and do so with the comfort of a "backup" teacher in the room and a smaller group of first-year students.

The effects of this workshop have been better than we ever anticipated. The new TAs start their first quarter far more self-assured and calm, with a much clearer understanding of the rhythm of teaching and their roles in the classroom than they had before. They have also developed contacts and friendships with experienced teachers that last throughout their careers—and lead them to volunteer to return early the next fall to mentor the next year's group of new TAs. And, most important, they are far more consistently successful in their classrooms than before, with higher student evaluations to show it. The effects on those students—higher grade point averages and greater retention rates than students with virtually identical records who did not attend the workshop—are a bonus that has generated good publicity for the program within the university administration. And the money the workshop generates—about $12 per student, after the shirts, publication, and conference fees for doing the paperwork—gives the writing program a small pot of money to use for books, periodicals, and travel for graduate students who want to attend conferences.

2 Selecting and Training Undergraduate and Graduate Staffs in a Writing Lab

Muriel Harris
Purdue University

To ensure as competent a staff as possible, the administrator has to select, train, and evaluate the staff, and do so within a variety of constraints that impinge on how the training is carried out. Funding may limit the size of the staff and may also limit the length of training—but with a dash of ingenuity, lack of funds isn't an unsolvable problem. The pool of candidates to select from may pose other questions that require some mental barrier leaping, and time constraints for training are always a problem. I propose to deal with these issues here in terms of the concerns that arise in the process of developing effective staffs in our Writing Lab at Purdue.

Institution Overview

The Purdue University Writing Lab exists as part of a large midwestern land-grant university (yes, Indiana really does have two public, land-grant institutions) with a population of 32,000 students and 1,600 faculty. About three-fourths of the undergraduates on our mainly residential campus come from rural and urban areas in Indiana, though we also have out-of-state and international students. Over two-thirds of the undergraduate population are traditional students, most coming from the upper half of their high school classes. About 1,000 are international students, mostly doing graduate work, and there are students of color, nontraditional students, and part-time students as well.

The university is a research institution which rewards research more than teaching, though the state legislature (which has been increasingly stingy with funding) has made known its interest in having teaching stressed more highly. Purdue excels in science, engineering, agriculture, and technology, and while the humanities do not dominate the campus, they are well represented, with the School of Liberal Arts being among the fastest growing. The English department has a large graduate program in rhetoric and composition, which means that many of the graduate teaching assistants are particularly knowledgeable in the theories and pedagogies of teaching writing and are experienced teachers of basic writing, technical writing, business writing, English as a second language (ESL), etc. Among the four hundred undergraduate English majors are students in English education, professional writing, and creative writing, in addition to literature majors, so the potential pool of tutors to draw from in English is quite large. Other large pools include a huge communications department within the School of Liberal Arts as well as an expanding School of Education.

Writing Lab Overview

The Writing Lab exists within the English department and is funded by the department, though we serve the entire university. Being funded by the English department means having limitations on our budget and staffing while trying to meet the needs of a vast university population. No one has ever quite defined our mission in terms of whether we are an all-university service or whether we exist primarily to serve students in the many departmental writing programs (basic writing, first-year composition, advanced composition, English as a second language, business writing, technical writing, and creative writing as well as literature and linguistics courses). As the interest in writing skills expands on our campus, we find ourselves working with more students across campus, both undergraduate and graduate. In the absence of a formalized writing-across-the-curriculum program, we have—like many other writing centers—become the de facto center for writing on campus.

Staff, Space, and Computing

We have a secretary/assistant and a receptionist who are both clerical staff, but unlike at other writing centers of our size, the director, a faculty member, has no additional professional or faculty assistance to handle administrative work and is responsible for most staff training. (The staff of peer tutors who work with resumes and related business writing is coordinated by one of the graduate student tutors in the lab.) Our lab occupies two large rooms joined by a walk-through door, a space far too small to house our tutoring tables, computers, secretary's office, reception desk and waiting area, director's desk, instructional materials, and storage facilities. Space limitations are part of the constraints within which we operate, and one of the survival skills we have to acquire is the ability to squeeze between tutoring tables and step over old couches to get from one side of the room to another. We work with about 3,500 students a semester in a face-to-face setting, which is about 11 percent of the student population. In addition, we have an OWL (Online Writing Lab), our newest set of services, which is growing rapidly. Data on usage from the most recent semester indicates 3,701 users at Purdue and 244,693 Internet users not at Purdue. The vast majority of these uses are by people accessing information available in our e-mail, Gopher, and World Wide Web sites.

The majority of the students we meet in tutorials are working on papers for various writing courses. We also work with students writing papers in a variety of courses in the university (communications, computer science, history, political science, biology, etc.), as well as students working on graduate papers, resumes, job applications, essays for graduate or professional schools, co-op reports, and a variety of other writing projects. Our tutorial theories and pedagogies are informed by current writing center theory and practice, and we have easy access to the *Writing Lab Newsletter* (which I edit). Our collaborative approach is integrated throughout the program so that every staff member is considered as part of a teaching team and has an equal voice in setting policies as well as selecting fellow staff members. This is done in recognition of our collaborative approach and our commitment to working as a community of peers. Our three staffs are as follows:

1. Graduate teaching assistants who work with the general population of undergraduate and graduate students writing papers for any course on campus
2. Peer tutors who work with the Developmental Writing Program
3. Peer tutors who work with resumes and business writing

The Graduate Teaching Assistants

The department funds eleven graduate teaching assistants each semester to tutor in the Writing Lab, and department policy requires that every new graduate teaching assistant teach at least one year in the first-year composition program before branching out to work in any other instructional program, such as tutoring in the Writing Lab or teaching business writing. During that first year in the department, all new teaching assistants must enroll in a credit-bearing training course in the teaching of first-year composition. Thus, when graduate students apply for a position in the lab, they have had at least a year of classroom experience, have been mentored in a course in the basics of teaching writing, have been observed in their classrooms, and have had their syllabi, graded papers, and student evaluations closely scrutinized. This level of expertise and experience influences the type of training they will need when they begin working in the Writing Lab. The department has also instituted a credit-bearing training course for each new writing program the graduate students enter. Thus, when they begin working in the Writing Lab or begin teaching in any of the other writing programs, they enroll in a one-semester practicum during the first semester they begin in that program. The Writing Lab practicum is taught by the director. There is a high degree of competition to become a staff member in the Writing Lab because from the 150 graduate students in the department, there are normally about fifteen to twenty applicants for the two or three vacancies that occur each year (because current Writing Lab tutors normally tend to stay on for at least two years in the lab).

The Peer Tutors in the Developmental Writing Program (UTAs)

We have a group of about twelve to fourteen undergraduate tutors, referred to locally as UTAs (Undergraduate Teaching Assistants). They are funded by the English department and are closely integrated into the developmental composition program that is offered only in the fall semester each year. Each UTA is assigned to a particular teacher and attends that teacher's class one day a week to observe, assist, become familiar with the classwork, and get to know the students in their classroom setting. The UTAs also meet in tutorials with every student from that class every week, in the Writing Lab. Before being selected to be UTAs, students enroll in a credit-bearing course, a practicum in the tutoring of writing taught by the Writing Lab director; the training course is offered in both the fall and spring semesters.

The Resume and Business Writing Peer Tutors (Writing Consultants)

We have a second group of three or four peer tutors to assist with the heavy demand for tutorial help in writing resumes, job applications, and applications to professional or graduate schools. The English department's policy is that because this is not course-related writing instruction, the department is not responsible for funding this group, and so other funding has to be located. The size of the staff is determined by the ability to secure outside funds, and the graduate student tutor who coordinates the staff has several hours released time from tutoring to select and train the staff.

; and Issues to Consider

Selection

ral Staff Selection Issues

ıugh selecting each of our Writing Lab staffs presents its own unıque issues and problems, there are general considerations for any staff selection: How do we identify the available pool of promising candidates? When we have a target group in mind, how do we let them know about the application process? What is an appropriate application process? What procedures will work well to select the best candidates among the applicants, and which skills will we be looking for?

2. Selection of Graduate Teaching Assistants

In our case, the pool is limited to teaching assistants in the English department, all of whom were required to spend a year teaching first-year composition and to take a training course in general composition instruction. Within this context, issues we have to consider include the following:

- With a small Writing Lab staff and only a few vacancies each year, how can we proceed in a way that ensures that the selection process is publicly perceived as fair and unbiased? (There have been some muted complaints that the current staff tends to select only its own friends, thereby discouraging some graduate students from applying.)

- What application procedures should we use? Is a written application sufficient? If not, what else can be done to offer applicants adequate opportunities to indicate their skills?

- What skills should we look for? How important is previous writing center experience elsewhere or classroom experience and/or evidence of good teaching? If we're looking for general tutoring skills, what are these skills? Should we give higher priority to applicants with a broad range of experiences or to applicants with very specialized skills for working with various segments of our student population? In our Writing Lab our tutors are called upon to help ESL students, business writing students, journalism students, etc., and we have an OWL (Online Writing Lab) which requires some degree of computer literacy to meet students online or incorporate OWL into tutorials. Should we try to fill holes in our staff's various types of expertise (for example, find someone with ESL experience when previous tutors with ESL expertise leave) or seek the people with the best general tutoring skills or broadest range of experience?

- Because we want to remain consistent with our philosophy of working collaboratively as a staff, what procedures will ensure that everyone on the staff collaborates in the selection process? Since present staff members are often personal friends of applicants, how does the selection process avoid being a sorority/fraternity blackball session? Should graduate students sit in judgment of their friends? What are the benefits and disadvantages of such collaborative efforts? Or should a director step in and make final decisions in order to relieve graduate students of potentially tension-producing situations?

3. Selection of UTAs (Undergraduate Teaching Assistants)

- In a university with thousands of undergraduates majoring in a wide variety of fields, what is the best pool of applicants? How important is it, for example, to have English majors or students majoring in various areas of teacher training? Or is it better to reach out across the university and try to find, for example, history majors or math majors? Should the pool be limited to more experienced, mature students who are farther along in their studies, perhaps those classified as juniors or higher? Or does that limit the length of time they'll spend on the staff? Are there advantages to including younger students, perhaps those at the sophomore level? Is that too early in their college career, or does that help to provide the kind of continuity that is beneficial for a staff? Are grade point averages good indicators? How important is diversity in the staff? Since few students of color apply and since most of the applicants are white females, to what extent should we weight the selection process to diversify the staff in terms of race, gender, nationality, and so on?

- In a large university, how can we identify and reach the proposed pool of applicants? With limited budgets in terms of time and money, what procedures might help to locate applicants? Is teacher referral a potentially good source, or are teachers likely to recommend students for the wrong reasons? Might you insult teachers and/or create ill will toward the writing center if you reject their candidates? Would they be more likely to send students to the center knowing that their students are there as tutors? What are other useful resources to draw on to help publicize the search for applicants?

- What application procedures should be used? Should applicants, for example, submit writing samples? Teacher recommendations? If interviews are included, what interview procedures help to identify potentially effective tutors?

- What are the skills being sought? Is the ability to write well as important or more important than other skills such as the ability to listen closely?

- Who should make the selection decisions? Should the present UTA staff have a voice in the selection? If so, how do we ensure that their criteria for selection is similar to the director's? Or, to what degree do the criteria have to match?

- If the training program is a credit-bearing course, should anyone be allowed to enroll or should there be restrictions because of selection procedures and because of the nature of the class? Should class size be limited to ensure close contact with all the students? Should all students in the class expect to go on to become tutors after completing the course? If there is a selection process from the class for the tutoring staff, how will that be done? What role will the current staff play in the next step of the selection process?

4. Selection of Writing Consultants

- When a staff with specialized knowledge is needed (in this case, knowledge about writing resumes and job application letters), how can we identify the pool of qualified applicants?

- If the pool is small, how can we encourage more applicants?

- What skills should be sought? Is the specialized knowledge more important than general teaching/tutoring skills?

- What application procedures should be used when the pool of applicants is small and we don't want to discourage applicants who might not bother because they perceive the application process as difficult or time-consuming?

B. Staff Training

1. General Staff Training Issues

Among the general issues to consider for training any staff are the following: When will the training occur—before tutoring begins or during the semester while the tutor is already at work? Will training be in a credit-bearing course, in an orientation session, in weekly meetings, or in some other format? If training is mainly in sessions before the tutor starts working, will there also be ongoing training? How will this be accomplished? Given the difficulties of getting large or busy staffs together at the same time, what alternative methods, such as e-mail discussion lists, are there to keep in touch? How much of a tutor's time commitment can training involve? How much time can reasonably be spent on assignments in addition to attending training sessions?

In addition to the logistical concerns of training, various options for the content and goals of the training course have to be considered. What are the major issues the staff will have to be familiar with? How much theory and background will they need to know? Which aspects of the local situation (procedures, policies, materials, etc.) will they need to know? What kinds of skills will they need? What are some of the common situations they will need to know how to handle? What are their present levels of knowledge, expertise, and skills before being introduced to the content of the training course? What types of activities will lead to the most effective learning? Reading about tutoring? Group discussions? Observations of tutoring in progress? For tutors-in-training who are not yet tutoring, how will they gain some hands-on experience? If writing is used to promote learning about tutoring, what should they write about? Are mock tutorials useful? What role does the current staff play in training? How will the tutors' progress in learning about tutoring be evaluated? What forms of feedback would be most useful, effective, and feasible?

2. Issues in Training Graduate Student Tutors

Graduate students who join our Writing Lab staff are required to take a credit-bearing course on tutoring in our Writing Lab. The person teaching such a course must keep in mind that these graduate students have very busy lives—teaching at least one classroom course in addition to tutoring in the Writing Lab, taking their own classes, doing research, writing conference proposals and preparing presentations, and so on. Preparing a long reading list for the training course or expecting them to write extended papers is unrealistic. In addition, since the course meets during the semester, they have to be at least minimally prepared to begin as competent tutors when classes start and the lab opens its doors. Some tutors come with prior experience in other writing centers, some are very new to the world of one-to-one tutoring, and others think that their classroom teaching skills will suffice. Some are very apprehensive about certain aspects of tutoring, such as working with an ESL student, and others wonder if they'll ever figure out how to find the various resources and handouts in the room or master the tutor's role (and accompanying technology) of online tutoring with our OWL. In short, any group of new tutors comes with a variety of skill levels and a huge tote bag of worries and concerns. But our time together is short, and I have to find ways to help each new tutor. Some questions and issues that arise in structuring a training program to meet their needs are as follows:

- The person in charge of the training has to do some diagnostic work to find out what each new tutor knows and needs to learn. How can this be accomplished, keeping in mind that this hap-

pens in the midst of the hectic pace of the beginning of the semester when the director/trainer also has to attend to a huge
number of other tasks to start the lab off, and the new graduate
students who will start tutoring in the lab will be involved in
other courses they are teaching and taking.

- Since the new tutors have been chosen because they have displayed some level of competence already, and since some of
them are taking graduate courses in composition theory, what
approaches can the trainer use to introduce material without
insulting them or implying that they need to review basics?
What *do* new tutors need to know in addition to their knowledge of teaching writing in the classroom?

- How can the current staff help with the training? What use can
be made of their skills and special areas of expertise?

- Since ongoing training is always helpful for any staff, how can
some of the training be integrated into regular staff meetings?

- How can these new tutors be evaluated, and how can evaluation be done in ways that will permit them to have paper trails
for the portfolios they will eventually be preparing when they
begin their job searches?

3. Issues in Training Undergraduate Teaching Assistants

For our UTA program of peer tutors who work with the basic writers
in our Developmental Composition Program, we have a credit-bearing
training course taught every semester. Students take the course prior
to the time in which they begin tutoring, and vacancies on the current
staff are filled by students who have completed the course. This means
that not everyone who takes the course is guaranteed a tutoring job, and
there is a fairly high level of anxiety about being evaluated in terms of
whether the student will "make the grade" and be chosen to become a
UTA. The students in the class are also aware of our collaborative approach in that the UTAs have a crucial voice in the selection of who will
join their staff. So, because our Writing Lab is also a place to hang out,
as UTAs and class members often do, there is added pressure and anxiety about socializing together and the need for students in the training
course (as some of them perceive it) to ingratiate themselves with the
UTAs (despite my constant reminders that choices are made on the basis of competence, not friendship). Since I view the socializing time as
a time also to build a sense of collaborative team effort, I particularly worry
about how to remove or lessen the competitive undercurrent that is
present. These tensions should not be overemphasized, but they do exist.

Another matter of concern is that the basic writing course is taught
only in the fall semester even though the training course is taught in

both semesters (in order to ensure that there will be enough competent new tutors to fill the vacancies). This means that students in the training course in the fall can observe or sit in on actual tutoring sessions, while students in the spring semester have no such opportunity. In addition, in the fall the UTA staff is meeting regularly, tutoring, and hanging around the lab, but since there is no tutoring in the spring, the UTAs have no official responsibilities or official reasons to be in the lab. Thus, interaction between the class and the UTAs has to be planned. Tight funding means that most of the staff's funds have to be spent in the fall for actual tutoring, though some small amounts of money can be hoarded for spring use, if needed. Given all this, the following questions have to be considered:

- How can class time be most profitably spent? Should all the hours be spent in meeting as a group? What about other alternatives, such as individual time spent in the lab or in small-group work, either scheduled as part of the large-group meeting time or as a separate activity? How much time should be spent in non-class activities such as observing tutors, doing mock tutorials, and completing reading and writing assignments?

- What are the most important concepts and skills the tutors-in-training have to learn about? How much do students need to know about topics such as the following: writing center theory and practice; writing processes; individual differences in writing processes; communication skills; tutoring strategies; paper diagnosis; ESL; learning disabilities; higher-order writing skills such as focus, clarity, and organization; grammar and mechanics; and so on? How can they best acquire such knowledge? If it is necessary to prioritize among these topics, which are more important and which less important? Is practice in a mock tutorial the best—or only—option to pick up such skills? Can recording such practice by means of videotaping or audio recording be effective? How will such recordings be used?

- Since many of the students start the class with misconceptions about the role of the tutor in a writing center (likening it to editing and/or to error hunting and correction), how can such misconceptions best be rooted out?

- Because tutoring involves learning both theory and practice, how can students in such a course best be graded? What assignments or tests would be useful in such evaluation?

- If students learning to tutor are to learn collaborative, nonevaluative practices (basic tenets of writing center approaches), how can a class be structured and the students evaluated in ways consistent with these underlying concepts?

4. Issues in Training Writing Consultants

The students who are trained to work with resumes, job applications, and business writing are typically seniors (because almost all of these students are unable to take the required course on business and resume writing until their senior year). Therefore, because it's not practical to have a training course prior to the semester in which they begin tutoring, the course is offered during the semester in which they start tutoring. This means that there are a number of additional issues which are unique to training this group that do not arise in the training course for the UTAs discussed above:

- Because these writing consultants must have some time to learn local practices and policies as well as knowledge about tutoring, how much time can be devoted to introducing them to their jobs before they actually start tutoring? Should there be an orientation session before classes begin? Should they begin tutoring immediately, or can their tutoring be delayed for a period until they've acquired enough of the basics to dive in? For how long?

- Is there a way to ease these students from pure training to total tutoring? If there should be such an interim period, how would this be set up?

- With a focus on specialized tutoring, what do students need to know about general tutoring theory, practice, and strategies?

For all the questions raised here, there are a great number of possible answers, depending on the emphasis on various issues and on local conditions. In the Purdue Writing Lab we have tried to respond to these concerns with outcomes that, for the most part, work for us, but such outcomes are not necessarily appropriate for writing centers elsewhere. But such outcomes may be useful as starting points for you to bounce your thoughts against.

AUTHOR'S CASE COMMENTARY

A. Selection

1. Graduate Student Tutors

Each semester, graduate students in our English department receive a department memo listing all the available teaching options, and they indicate which they are interested in for the following semester. I contact those who select the Writing Lab by sending them a short questionnaire asking about prior tutoring experience and reasons for their interest in tutoring, plus an open-ended question asking what else they would like us to know about them. Two graduate student lab tutors then meet with each applicant to answer the applicant's questions about the lab and to talk with the applicant about his or her teaching philosophies, methods, classroom work, etc. The lab staff then devotes one staff meeting to reviewing all the candidates, with the two interviewers reporting to the rest of us what they learned from talking with the candidate. While we have no definitive list of selection criteria, the conversation about each candidate concerns such issues as that person's student-centered approaches, communication skills, understanding of writing processes, ability to ask questions and to listen, special knowledge or prior experience, and so on. Factors relevant to our local situation are also likely to come up. While we have never successfully defined the list of characteristics that are important, we seem to come to group consensus about who the strongest candidates are. We then winnow the list down to these candidates and vote.

At these sessions each year, I am constantly impressed (deeply so) by the maturity and professionalism displayed by the staff during these discussions. They show strong concern for the lab and for the students who use it, and they display great insight into their fellow graduate students' skills, knowledge, sense of responsibility, and dedication to teaching writing. Our selection process is truly a group effort—and is one that is educational for the staff as well because these are people who in their future academic life will be doing such collegial selection. They also learn, for their own future job seeking, important insights into successful interviewing.

2. Undergraduate Teaching Assistants

The selection of future staff is a two-step process as students must first be selected to take the training class, and tutors are then selected from among the students in the class. The initial pool of candidates for the course is a collection drawn from several sources in various ways: (1) I ask the registrar's office for a list of all the students who fit a designated profile (are majors in English and some of the communications fields; are in semesters 3, 4, and 5; and have at least a B average) and send letters of invitation, with an enclosed application form, to all the students on this list; (2) we visit a required education course for all high school teaching majors and explain the course and the tutoring opportunities, distributing applications to anyone who wants one; and (3) I send a notice to English department faculty and teaching assistants, asking them to announce the course or to recommend students, and give applications to all interested students. The application form consists of one page of short-answer questions about the student's prior experience and goals and another page which has two tutoring scenarios for which the applicant is to describe what he or she would do in that tutorial. We usually get about fifty or more completed applications and winnow that number down to about thirty to thirty-five students to interview, for a class that I limit to ten to twelve students. (The class requires instructor consent in order to enroll.)

Students invited for interviews are asked to pick up a student paper prior to the interview. UTAs and I then interview candidates in groups of three or four, explaining the course, answering questions, and asking them to talk together for a while about tutoring the student whose paper they read before the interview. As the interviewees interact among themselves, we observe their communication skills, their ability to listen to each other, any undesirable tendencies (such as dominating the conversation, responding negatively to another person's comments, showing a strong tendency to confine their conversation to error hunting in the paper, etc.), their sympathy for difficulties in the writing process and awareness of the characteristics of good writing, their ability to think of strategies to help the writer, their awareness of writing processes (especially in terms of thinking about how the paper can be revised rather than denouncing its weaknesses), and so on. Again, we do not have a definitive list of the traits that are important in the selection process, and again, we still seem to come to consensus easily about the strongest candidates. We have made a few poor choices, and we learn from that, but such mistakes do happen. However, by the time the UTAs and I have interacted with the students in the class for the entire semester, those mistakes become very apparent. Final selection of future tutors from the class is done at a UTA staff meeting at the end of the semester, and the discussion is as mature and professional as that in the graduate staff meeting. Here, the UTAs and I have a deeper knowledge of each student, based on fifteen weeks of class performance and participation as well as the tutoring skills they have displayed in mock tutorials or other interactions with the UTAs.

3. Writing Consultants

The pool of available candidates is necessarily limited to students who have taken the requisite business writing course. Invitations are issued in these classes, and the instructors are invited to recommend students. Applicants submit a resume and letter of application, thereby displaying their command of the specialized knowledge they will need. Potential candidates are interviewed and selected by the graduate student coordinator based on the interview. When possible, writing consultants on the present staff sit in on interviews and take part in the selection process.

B. Training

1. Graduate Student Tutors

Before the semester begins, we meet in an orientation session in which I review some of the basics of tutoring principles and strategies, explain local policies, give them a tour of the lab's resources, and introduce them to some of the practical aspects of paperwork, record keeping, and other matters that they will need to know immediately when tutoring. A major emphasis in that meeting is to remind them that we eye with deep suspicion anyone who thinks he or she knows all the answers and that we expect they'll ask for help—frequently. Then, we meet every other week in a credit-bearing course offered on a pass/no pass basis, alternating our course meetings with staff meetings (which are also every other week). At our course meetings, the focus is on the topics covered in a packet of materials I've put together, though every meeting begins with questions they have. The discussion resulting from such questions often dominates the meeting, and new tutors say that they profit greatly from hearing that they are not alone in being confronted with concerns for which they had no ready answer. We also discuss readings in writing center theory and practice and how this differs from or overlaps with classroom practice, analyze tutorials they've been involved with since our last meeting, talk about individual differences in writing processes, try to come up with solutions to tutoring problems that I introduce, and draw on each other's expertise in learning about specialty areas such as ESL tutoring, learning disabilities, and so on.

In addition, since my desk is in the lab and close to the tutoring tables, I depend on "inservice training," that is, ongoing discussions during the times that the new tutors are in the lab. I ask questions, they ask me questions, and we use opportunities before and after their tutoring to talk about a great variety of writing center and tutoring concerns (mixed, of course, with some enjoyable socializing). I find this individual interaction to be far more helpful than our group discussion, as I have useful and frequent opportunities to get to know each new tutor and respond to questions they raise and to encourage special interests they are developing about tutorial instruction or about projects they might want to undertake in the lab. Often, by merely asking how a tutorial went, I find we can get involved in a probing discussion that often expands my thinking about our work. When invited to do so, I also sit in on tutorials and write an evaluation of the tutor based on that observation. Such reviews are useful records for the tutor's portfolio, and I encourage tutors to acquire a paper trail about all their work as graduate students. However, after all the close contact, I already have a good sense of how effective they are as tutors and what their strengths are. If any problems connected to their tutoring have surfaced, we deal with them informally, in daily conversations.

2. Undergraduate Teaching Assistants

The training course is a two-credit course, with a pass/no pass system (rather than grades). We meet once a week as a group, and each student in the class signs up for two additional hours each week in the lab. During the time they are in the lab on their own, there are a number of options as to how they can use their time: observe tutorials, talk to me or other tutors about questions they have, familiarize themselves with our materials and resources, read books and articles on writing center practice, and explore some aspect of the lab in more depth. From time to time, there are also small-group assignments which they complete during this time. For example, early in the semester, to help them learn how to assess what a student may want to work on with a draft of a paper in hand, they are asked to work in small groups and read a paper in the manual I've prepared. The questionnaire the group fills out asks questions that I hope they are internalizing as questions they want to ask themselves when first reading a paper (e.g., what is the assignment, what is the paper's purpose, what is the main point, how well does the paper fulfill the assignment, what positive comments would they offer the writer, what revisions would make the paper stronger, what strategies would they use in a tutorial, and so on).

For our class meeting, there is a manual of weekly readings and writing assignments to help them learn about writing processes, individual differences in writing processes, writing center approaches, specific tutoring skills and strategies, tutoring problems, learning disabilities, ESL, and so on. In addition to the assignments designed to help them explore these topics, students keep a weekly journal focusing on how they spent their two hours in the lab and what they've learned from that. By mid-semester, students in the fall semester course choose one UTA as a mentor and start sitting in regularly in that tutor's tutorials, eventually taking over some of the tutoring under the UTA's guidance and thereby gaining some hands-on experience. In the spring semester, students in the class have a series of mock tutorials with the UTAs to compensate for not having any of the UTA's tutorials to observe. While informal evaluation goes on all the time as we observe the students' strengths improve, the final assignment in the course is a paper that asks them to assess their own strengths and weaknesses as tutors. During the semester, they have gotten a lot of informal feedback about their tutoring skills, and the students who are our best candidates for joining the staff are usually the ones who, in that last paper, are very aware of what their skills are and what they need to work on. The students who have not progressed sufficiently or who have not absorbed any of the feedback are more inclined to be blissfully unaware of their weaknesses or of what an effective tutor should be able to do.

3. Writing Consultants

The new writing consultants start the semester with an orientation session in the basics that will permit them to understand what they'll be observing for the next month or so. Then they spend one hour a week in a two-credit class (offered on a pass/no pass basis), completing readings from a manual and discussing aspects of resumes, job applications, and other business writing they will be working with. They also read and talk about tutoring strategies and practices. In addition, they spend additional time each week observing the tutorials of the writing consultants on the staff. By mid-semester, they begin to tutor on their own, and class time becomes more of a problem-solving situation in which they discuss the tutorials they've had during the week. There is an extended final project in which they either explore some topic related to their tutoring or develop some materials for future use in the lab. Because this group of students is small, usually no more than two or three students, evaluation is both informal and ongoing during the semester.

3 The Problem Graduate Instructor

Lynn Langer Meeks
Utah State University

Christine A. Hult
Utah State University

Those who administer writing programs are invariably faced with their share of personnel problems—from the abusive student to the complaining parent. However, among the most challenging personnel problems facing WPAs are those involving graduate instructors, most of whom find themselves in front of classrooms for the very first time. In this chapter, we will provide you with some scenarios involving problem graduate instructors, adapted from real cases with details changed to protect the innocent (and the guilty).

Institution Overview

The authors of this chapter are both faculty members in the English department at Utah State University: Lynn Meeks is the Director of Writing and Christine Hult is the Associate Department Head. We often work together on issues of program development, curriculum design, and graduate instructor training and supervision. As the Director of Writing, Meeks is responsible for the day-to-day operation of the program; as the Associate Department Head, Hult is responsible for the appointment of lecturers and graduate instructors and for the writing program budget.

Utah State University, founded in 1889, sits on top of a hill in Logan, Utah, overlooking the mountain-ringed Cache Valley. Logan is about ninety miles northeast of Salt Lake City and about thirty miles south of the Idaho border. Utah State's nearest sister institutions are the University of Utah in Salt Lake City and Idaho State University ninety miles to the north in Pocatello. Utah State is a land-grant university and has been designated a Carnegie Type I Research University. We have

---

Lynn Langer Meeks wishes to dedicate this essay to her mentor, the late Robert E. Shafer, Director of the English Education Program, Arizona State University.

780 faculty members, 3,450 graduate students, and serve approximately 16,300 undergraduates in both on-campus and extension programs. The English department is one of the largest departments on campus—as well as one of the fastest-growing. Our English majors number over 300 undergraduates and 100 graduates, with the professional writing track and teaching track being the most popular (literature comes in third). Consequently, our department as a whole has always placed a great deal of emphasis on the writing program, both the writing track for majors and the service writing program for nonmajors. We also offer a very popular master's program in English, which includes specializations in the theory and practice of writing, technical writing, literary studies, and folklore. The only English Ph.D. degree in the state is offered by the University of Utah in Salt Lake City.

Courses

Thousands of students each year come in contact with the English department through our university-required writing courses. To satisfy the university's written communication requirement, all students must take both a first-year and a sophomore writing course (English 101: English Composition and English 201: Research Writing). Over two-thirds of the departments on campus require an additional third writing course at the junior level. Many of these third-tier writing courses are taught within specific colleges for their own majors, but many others are taught by the English department, which offers English 301 (Advanced Writing) and English 305 (Technical and Professional Writing) as a service to others on campus.

As the number of students has grown, doubling the size of the university over the past ten years, additional pressure has been placed on the service writing program. The department made a conscious decision in the face of enrollment growth (but no new faculty positions) to staff the writing program primarily with graduate instructors rather than with part-time lecturers. Most of the courses in the writing program are now taught by graduate instructors, with an occasional section taught by a lecturer or a tenure-track faculty member. However, most tenure-track writing faculty now teach upper-division majors sections to our large population of English majors. This trend has left the bulk of the teaching in the writing program to graduate instructors working on their master's degrees.

Writing Program Overview

The writing program at Utah State University has established itself as a model program with both a regional and a national reputation. Prior writing program directors, including Bill Smith and Joyce Kinkead, worked very hard and were instrumental in establishing the program as a national leader. Christine Hult brought the *WPA: Writing Program Administration* journal to Utah State University and served as its editor for seven years. The presence of *WPA* on our campus also helped to secure USU's position of prominence in the field. In recent years, work by several of our faculty members in the computers and writing field has again brought us regional and national attention, including a $300,000 technology grant from the state of Utah and the national Computers & Writing conference held on our campus in May of 1996.

Our writing program has earned the respect of our colleagues and administrators on campus as well. Our courses are highly regarded and widely supported. For example, in a recent campus-wide conversation about general education, there was virtual consensus about continuing the two required writing courses for all students in all colleges at Utah State University. In fact, the legislatively mandated switch from quarters to semesters in the fall of 1998 (from 6 quarter hours to 6 semester hours of writing required of all students) increases the overall time spent on service writing by one third. The writing program has maintained the "vertical" sequence for the past fifteen years; that is, students take one writing course at each level of their academic studies rather than taking them all together. In order to enroll in English 201, for example, students must have successfully completed English 101 *and* achieved sophomore standing. The same holds true for English 301 (satisfied 201 *and* achieved junior standing). We have found that this progression of writing instruction helps our students to see the connections between the writing they are doing in English courses and the writing they are doing in their academic disciplines. We also make a considerable effort to ensure that what we are teaching in our writing program is what the professors in academic disciplines value: critical thinking skills, research and documentation skills, library and computer skills, and so on.

Staff

As the university has grown, so has the writing program. The administrative staff includes the Director of Writing, Lynn Meeks, plus three assistant directors (graduate instructors with reassigned time). The teaching staff includes forty graduate instructors (first- and second-year

M.A. students) and a dozen or so lecturers (largely third-year M.A. students and recent graduates). The teaching staff in the writing program is under the direct supervision of the Director of Writing. A large percentage of Meeks's time, in addition to curriculum development, is taken up by the training and supervision of the writing program staff. Each year, Meeks faces a new crop of twenty or so graduate instructors, many of whom are fresh from undergraduate school, and within the space of a few short weeks, she guides them on their journey toward becoming excellent writing teachers.

Graduate Student Teacher Training

The teacher training process begins as soon as new graduate instructors are chosen in early spring. The new GIs (Graduate Instructors) are introduced to the program through a series of communications and are given their teaching materials over the summer. When they arrive on campus in the fall, they are enrolled in a week-long intensive training workshop in preparation for teaching their first English 101 course. During fall quarter, at the same time as they are teaching, they are also enrolled in a teaching practicum taught by Meeks, which continues the work begun in the pre-term workshop. Graduate Instructors also tutor several hours a week in the Writing Center and attend a tutoring practicum taught by the Writing Center Director.

Although they are only teaching one course in the fall, GIs are paid as though they were teaching two courses, which allows us to require of them the additional training time needed. During this additional training time, first-year GIs videotape each other's teaching at least twice and get together in groups to review their tapes and write self-reflective reports. In addition, each GI is observed four times: once by the Director of Writing and once by each assistant director, followed by "debriefing" sessions in which the directors and the GIs discuss their classroom observations and focus on areas of strengths and areas needing improvement. For the practicum "final," GIs show "before and after" video clips of their teaching and report on their personal teaching goals for the next quarter. For both winter and spring quarters, graduate instructors teach two sections of English 101 each. During winter and spring quarters, the new GIs meet for grade calibration sessions and to discuss issues and concerns about the curriculum and their teaching. In order to accomplish this kind of supervision, the Director of Writing teaches one course per quarter; the rest of her time is reassigned to her curriculum, instruction, supervision, and administrative duties. The

Assistant Directors of Writing are paid to teach two courses per quarter but are reassigned for one of those courses to administrative duties which include responsibility for developing the common syllabus.

English 101 uses a common syllabus developed by the Assistant Directors of Writing and the Director of Writing, based on the departmental goals and objectives for English 101. The common syllabus serves as both a support and a guide to new graduate instructors, most of whom have had no formal teaching experience. The common syllabus guides the graduate instructors to a student-centered, interactive pedagogy that values process equally with product. English 101 serves both as an introduction to college writing as well as a time for "pastoral care" of our first-year students. We set the course cap at twenty-three students (which quickly dwindles to nineteen) to allow graduate instructors to give students individual attention. The course emphasizes group work, one-to-one conferences with the instructor, and frequent visits to the Writing Center. Through the pedagogy embedded in the common syllabus, graduate instructors learn to teach writing as they teach writing.

Graduate instructors' training does not end after their first year of teaching, however. Second-year graduate instructors, many of whom will move into teaching the sophomore-level research writing course, are also provided with a pre-term teaching workshop. In this workshop they are introduced to the second-tier writing course, English 201: Research Writing, its goals and objectives, its student population, and its textbooks and syllabus. Second-year graduate instructors are also observed extensively in the classroom by tenure-track writing faculty and one of the Assistant Directors of Writing, and counseled frequently about their teaching. In January of each year, instructors wishing to continue their employment in the department compile an extensive teaching portfolio, which is then evaluated by a committee who decides on reappointment and on merit increases for the following academic year. In addition to the teaching portfolios and classroom observations, instructors are evaluated quarterly through the university's student evaluation of teachers form. These evaluations are but one piece of the information gathered about teaching effectiveness; but we wish to stress that the entire process is modeled on formative evaluation geared toward teacher improvement rather than on summative performance evaluations.

To inform our theory and practice of teaching graduate instructors to teach writing, we drew on the work of several theorists in staff development and assessment and evaluation. We see our process as a recursive cycle of assessment, evaluation, feedback, reflection, practical and theoretical input, and instructor change as outlined by Brian Cambourne, Jan Turbill, and Andrea Butler in *Frameworks Core Course*. When Christine Hult was working on a collection for NCTE (*Evaluating Teachers of Writing*), she was struck both by the complexity of and our lack of understanding of the entire process of teacher improvement. What did become clear, however, was that administrators must be careful to separate the formative from the summative evaluation procedures, which very often have conflicting purposes.

Evaluation

Summative evaluations are generally used for the purpose of accountability. An example of a summative evaluation in our program would be the review of teaching portfolios we conduct each year for the purpose of reappointment and merit raises. Formative evaluations are generally used for teacher improvement. In our program, teacher observations, videotaping, workshops, and so on, are all examples of formative evaluations that provide teachers with valuable feedback that they can use in self-improvement efforts. "In formative evaluations, one gets another chance, an opportunity to 'revise' one's performance. And a serious effort at formative evaluation can mediate the necessity for summative evaluation, because the evaluator is able to see the shaping of a teacher over time, in a rich and varied context" (Hult 5).

It is out of this multifaceted effort at teacher evaluation and improvement that this chapter was conceived. We feel that in our program we are genuinely trying, and usually succeeding, at helping our teachers toward self-improvement. And the numerical statistics from our teaching evaluations in the program bear out our claim: over the course of their first year of teaching, our graduate instructors uniformly improved their teaching evaluation scores. In addition to the Cambourne, Turbill, and Butler model of staff development, we adapted the five steps toward instructional improvement outlined by Maryellen Weimer in *Improving College Teaching: Strategies for Developing Instructional Effectiveness*: (1) developing instructional awareness through self-reflection; (2) gathering information from colleagues and students; (3) making choices about changes from among those suggested; (4) implementing alterations in the classroom; and (5) assessing the alterations through assessment of peer and student feedback (Weimer 34–41). The vast majority of our graduate instructors do genuinely improve through this process, so we know it is working. But what about those few graduate instructors whose improvement is slight or who started out so poorly that even improvement doesn't bring them to minimal teaching standards? We would like to devote the remainder of the chapter to these problem graduate instructors.

Challenges

As our examples, we will focus on four graduate instructors who were all on staff one fall term not too long ago. The problems that we encountered with these four instructors (out of nearly forty graduate instructors on staff) are detailed below. (Names and details have been changed to preserve anonymity.) After reading each scenario, decide how you would handle these problems. Then we will tell you what we did.

Before you start reading, however, here is some additional information to help you make decisions: All graduate instructors receive a "Policies and Procedures Handbook" which details the professional behavior expected of them as teachers and department members. Furthermore, they receive extensive training from the Office of Equal Opportunity/Affirmative Action on what constitutes prejudicial and sexually harassing behavior. Hult and Meeks work together closely because as Associate Department Head, Hult assigns graduate instructors to classes as well as hires and fires them. Meeks is responsible for curriculum and instruction for both the graduate instructors and the courses they teach in the writing program. Graduate students are hired as graduate instructors on a yearly basis as long as they continue to receive acceptable teaching evaluations and perform their jobs in a professional manner. It is possible to remove graduate instructors from teaching and put them on remediation plans. It is also possible to terminate a graduate instructor for cause during the quarter.

Key Charges

As you read these scenarios and try to decide what to do, you need to assume that you have the ability to hire and fire within the above parameters as well as responsibility for curriculum and instruction and that the graduate students have been fully informed about the responsibilities inherent in their teaching. If you decide to fire one of the graduate instructors described below, you need to assume that you can readily find a replacement among the Writing Program's lecturers and third-year graduate instructors, all of whom are excellent and experienced writing teachers.

Scenarios

Scenario #1: "The Phantom of the Classroom"

George is a second-year graduate instructor, forty years old, the father of three young children. He holds a part-time job as a bartender and commutes twenty miles each way to campus. Although the department has a clear policy about never canceling classes, apparently George has been canceling classes whenever he feels like it. You find this out when you read his course evaluations from summer school. George's teaching scores are the lowest in the department that quarter, and student comments on his evaluations are more than hostile:

> "The USU English Department ripped me off. I want my money back."

> "Tell the instructor that he should meet class once in a while."

> "I paid good money for this class and I didn't learn a thing. The instructor rarely held class."

As you reconstruct what happened during summer session, you learn that George has missed class twelve times. As you investigate further, you discover that he has tried to run most of the class through the Internet and has left assignments for his students on e-mail, expecting his students to e-mail their assignments to him. This in itself has not been approved, nor has he stated this e-mail policy in his syllabus. Often his e-mail did not work and students did not receive their assignments. Students became frustrated and hostile, and he returned their frustration and hostility with equal fervor. Furthermore, George has almost completely abandoned the goals and objectives for English 101. His syllabus bears little resemblance to the common syllabus.

Because of a delay in processing the student evaluations, you discover George's problems two weeks into the fall quarter. You decide to talk to George as soon as possible. You go to his classroom to set up a meeting and discover that he is not there. The students say they have been waiting for ten minutes. You wait. After fifteen minutes, another graduate instructor rushes breathlessly in the door and says, "George is having child care problems and will be here as soon as he can. I'll teach the class until he gets here."

You go back to your office and continue to read George's student evaluations from the summer session with growing horror. Just as you are about to leave, George sticks his head in your office and says, "I hear you wanted to see me. Is anything wrong?" He can tell by the look on your face that something definitely is wrong. What should you do?

    a. give him a stern warning and put him on probation

    b. give him a stern warning and work out a remediation program

    c. replace him immediately and work out a remediation program

    d. fire him

Scenario #2: "Knows More Than God and Aristotle"

Katherine is a second-year teaching assistant, in her late forties, a divorced mother of two grown children, who commutes over eighty miles each way to campus. She owns her own technical writing business and travels a great deal. Businesses hire Katherine as a troubleshooter to help teach technical writing to their staff and to design documents. She is assertive and self-assured, but tends to talk to her students in an almost condescending manner. In addition, her GPA is in trouble. She has not made up an incomplete from the previous year, which has subsequently turned into an "F." Furthermore, she often misses her graduate classes, turns in perfunctory work if she turns it in at all, and is disruptive in class, making snide comments *soto voce*.

Katherine's teaching evaluation scores are below average for the department, and in their teaching evaluations students complain about her classroom manner:

> "She talks all the time and never says anything."
>
> "She didn't teach me a thing."
>
> "All she did was talk. She is so stuck on herself, she didn't care about any of us."
>
> "We never knew what the assignment was. She didn't either."

Classroom observations confirm the students' comments. Her English 201 syllabus is sketchy; she is clearly "winging it" in class, and she likes to make fun of or pick on students. Furthermore, she affects a Socratic method of teaching that makes her the center of attention. Students are rarely asked to participate.

And the irony is, she thinks she is a great teacher. When she meets with you to discuss her teaching performance, she is extremely defensive about her teaching methods. In particular, she blames the international students in her classes for her below average scores and the negative comments she receives on her evaluations because they "can't write and they can't understand plain English." What should you do?

    a. give her a stern warning and put her on probation

    b. give her a stern warning and work out a remediation program

    c. replace her immediately and work out a remediation program

    d. fire her

Scenario #3: "Clueless"

Joan is a first-year teaching assistant, twenty-five, single, and living on campus. She has an undergraduate degree in journalism, has spent two years in the Peace Corps in Zambia, and never lets you forget either fact. Joan struggles to relate to her fellow graduate students, who find her difficult to talk to and work with. In graduate classes she often offends or alienates fellow students by her "off the wall" comments. Sometimes she asks completely off-topic questions. Sometimes she talks at length about an obvious point. Sometimes she talks at length about nonrelated issues. Fellow students and instructors begin to cringe when she raises her hand. A talented writer, she often begins a casual conversation by thrusting a draft of an article or letter-to-the-editor into your hands, asking you to read and comment on it.

    Classroom observations confirm the worst. Although extremely confident when speaking in a graduate class, she is at a loss in front of her own students. However, she has meticulously detailed lesson plans which she types and reads from. She often gives students directions, then changes her mind a few seconds later and asks them to do something else. In your post-evaluation conference she reports that she changed her lesson plans at the last minute "because she got a new idea." During one observation, students come late, leave early, read the newspaper, and have side conversations while Joan continues to read from her typed notes. To pull Joan off task, one student asks Joan a question about the Peace Corps and then makes a rude response to Joan's answer. You have been in junior high classes that were better behaved.

    In spite of your immediate intervention, observations, and counseling, Joan's first-quarter student evaluations are the lowest scores in the memory of your department. Students excoriated her on her teaching evaluations:

> "I have never, ever had such a terrible teacher in my life."

> "Joan seems like a nice person, but she should never be a teacher. She doesn't know the first thing about teaching."

> "This class was a total joke. This woman should never have been allowed in front of a classroom."

When you meet with Joan to go over her teaching evaluations, Joan is devastated by her students' comments. She reports that she had no idea that her students were so upset. Joan explains that what she really wants to be is a journalist, but that she has taken the graduate instructorship as a way to support herself in graduate school. If she loses this job, she has to drop out of graduate school. What should you do?

    a. give her a stern warning and put her on probation

    b. give her a stern warning and work out a remediation program

    c. replace her immediately and work out a remediation program

    d. fire her

Scenario #4: "Mister Goodbar"

Brent is twenty-two, unmarried, living off campus, and a first-year teaching assistant right out of undergraduate school with a degree in history. By all reports—both initial classroom observations and teaching evaluations—he is an excellent teacher. However, you become a bit concerned about Brent one day when he makes several pointed comments about how great looking a couple of his female students are. Then he goes on to say he doesn't think it is fair for the department to have a policy about not dating students.

    Your concerns are justified the day that a female student marches into your office in tears and says she "wants something done about Mr. Brown." She tells you a story of subtle sexual harassment—not the overt kind like inappropriate touching or sex for grades—but a classroom atmosphere that makes her uncomfortable. She reports that Mr. Brown starts each class by commenting on her or another female student's hair and dress. She says that, although Brent always makes very complimentary—and what she considers innocent—comments, such as "Looking good today, Tracey" or "Tell your boyfriend I think he's a lucky guy," his remarks make her uncomfortable. Furthermore, other students are beginning to tease her. However, the final straw for her is when Mr. Brown decides to hold conferences in his apartment rather than his office "because it's a more relaxing atmosphere."

    You explain to the student the affirmative action policies in place at the university: that you are required to immediately inform your department head about the student's complaint. This concerns the student, who is worried about retaliation. You ask the student how she would like to have the situation resolved. The student replies, "I don't want him fired or anything. He really is a good teacher, and I don't think he means to be offensive. I just want him to stop his comments, and I don't want to have to go to his apartment for conferences." What do you do?

    a. give him a stern warning and put him on probation

    b. give him a stern warning and work out a remediation program

    c. replace him immediately and work out a remediation program

    d. fire him

AUTHOR'S CASE COMMENTARY

Scenario #1 "The Phantom of the Classroom"

We fired George on the spot and replaced him with another graduate instructor, although it was two weeks into the fall quarter. Even though George had personal problems, the English department has a clear policy on canceling class. We understood that graduate instructors may have to miss class occasionally for various legitimate reasons, but our department policy clearly states that GIs find their own substitutes and instruction continues. Furthermore, the English 101 syllabus is based on the goals and objectives for the course, and graduate instructors are expected to teach the course as it is written, with certain personal variations.

    We had no plans to offer George a second chance, but George himself asked if there were anything he could do to be reinstated as a graduate instructor. Meeks and George worked out a remediation plan in which George read widely in the theory and practice of teaching composition and observed in several different composition classrooms. During winter quarter, George became Meeks's graduate assistant and helped team-teach a first-year-level composition course. By spring quarter, George had made such an improvement in both classroom teaching skills and professional behavior that he was given his own class for spring quarter and continued to teach successfully in the composition program until he graduated.

Scenario #2: "Knows More Than God and Aristotle"

Because Katherine had a low GPA, we, in consultation with the Director of Graduate Studies for the English department, relieved Katherine of her teaching duties for one quarter and placed her on academic probation. During the quarter she was on probation, she was to read widely in the theory and practice of composition, observe in other composition classrooms, and meet weekly with Meeks to discuss her readings and observations. Unfortunately, Katherine continued to miss more graduate classes, turned in unacceptable work, forgot appointments with

Meeks or arrived for her weekly conferences unprepared. During the conferences that Katherine attended, she blamed her students, the Writing Program, and the texts for her poor teaching evaluations. At the end of the quarter, we told Katherine that she would not be rehired. Shortly thereafter, the Graduate School expelled her because of her low GPA.

Scenario #3: "Clueless"

We met with Joan at the end of the quarter to review her teaching evaluations. Even though she had been observed and counseled during the first quarter, there seemed to be no improvement in her classroom skills. Meeks gave Joan the option of participating in a rigorous remediation program or not being rehired for the following quarter. Joan agreed to the remediation program. She dropped one of her classes for winter quarter and began a program of reading widely in theory and practice, observing in other composition classrooms, keeping detailed lesson plans, videotaping herself weekly and reviewing the videotape with a colleague, submitting lesson plans to Meeks and meeting with Meeks weekly. Furthermore, Joan was observed weekly by the Associate Director of Writing, who also spent an hour in conference with her per week.

Although Joan did make progress during winter quarter, we felt that she had not made enough improvement to allow her to continue teaching. Her teaching scores certainly improved, as did her interpersonal skills, but we felt that it was not in the best interests of the Writing Program to continue to use her as a graduate instructor. Instead, Joan was encouraged to get involved with English department publications where she could use her writing talents more fully. Joan did not teach again for the Writing Program, although other graduate instructors often asked her to "substitute" for them if they were ill. She found another job and did not drop out of the graduate program.

Scenario #4: "Mister Goodbar"

Meeks immediately wrote a memo to the English department chair informing him of the sexual harassment complaint. The department chair asked the Office of Affirmative Action/Equal Opportunity to begin an investigation. Brent was put on a "leave of absence with pay" until the end of the quarter and the completion of the investigation. The investigation confirmed the female student's complaints. Brent received a stern written reprimand in his permanent file from the English department chair. However, since this was Brent's first sexual harassment offense, he was not fired, but was required to attend affirmative action training during the next quarter. He also met several times with the department chair and Meeks to discuss his understanding of what constitutes sexually harassing behavior. His teaching was also observed regularly, and he met often to discuss his teaching with Meeks. Brent worked hard to understand why his comments constituted sexually harassing behavior. Brent made excellent progress and was given a full teaching load the next quarter. There were no repeated incidents.

4 What Happens When Discourse Communities Collide? Portfolio Assessment and Non-Tenure-Track Faculty

Allene Cooper, Martha Sipe, Teresa Dewey, and **Stephanie Hunt**
Boise State University

The Authors

At the time of this writing, Allene Cooper is Writing Program Director and assistant professor. Martha Sipe is the Assistant Writing Program Director and is a full-time non-tenure-track lecturer. Teresa Dewey and Stephanie Hunt are teaching assistants.

Institution Overview

Local

Your university is located in the state capital and center of business of a northwestern state with traditional industries of forestry, mining, agricultural crops, and cattle. Today's economy is increasingly being built on high technology and light manufacturing. Two other well-established state universities are each three hundred miles away in different directions. Your university began as a junior college and retains some of its community college function. Some students in English composition are enrolled in two-year technical certificate programs and associate degree programs, while others are traditional first-year students. The university currently has several master's programs and a newly instituted doctoral program in educational administration.

Students

Fourteen thousand students attend the university. About 92 percent of the university's new students (including first-year students and new transfers) come from within the state. Most come from the capital city, nearby communities, and farming areas. Fifty-two percent of the new students are female; 9 percent are people of color. The average high school GPA of new students is 2.74. They average 18 on the ACT and 868 on the SAT. (Nationally, first-year students average 20.6 on the ACT and 896 on the SAT.) A study conducted in 1985–87 found that the average age of first-year students was twenty-two years.

Generally, the students at your university are conscientious, serious students who are eager to please their teachers and a little anxious about the university and about writing.

Key Challenge

A seemingly "unending conversation" (to allude to Michael Oakeshott's discussion of "*the* defining human characteristic") is going on in your department concerning assessment. The conversation has included questions about assessment such as "Why are we doing it?", "Who are we assessing?", and "What's the best way to assess?" The answers have been hard to come by, even though many voices have contributed to the discussion.

For some time, your department has been focused on the question, "What do we do about the MCE?" The Minimal Competency Exam (MCE) has been in place since 1981. It is a graduation requirement that every student, including transfers and returning students, has had to take in order to receive grades in English Composition 101 and 102. The E101 exam is a computer-scored multiple-choice test of mechanical correctness. The E102 exam is an impromptu writing on an assigned personal topic. Both are given in the fifth week of the semester to test entering competencies.

There were originally several objectives of this type of assessment, including verifying that university students were competent in English skills and that courses throughout the department would become more consistent. After much consideration, talk, and review of other programs, your program has begun a pilot using portfolios of student writing to replace the MCE exams.

The Portfolio Pilot has lasted four semesters. The first semester, six instructors participated with their classes. The next semester sixteen participated. In the third semester, twenty-six teachers participated. In the fourth semester, although your department ran out of pilot funding to pay the participants to read the portfolios, nine instructors volunteered.

You, as Writing Program Director, see three goals for the Portfolio Pilot:

- First, to develop an instrument to replace the outdated Minimal Competency Exam as a graduation requirement (or better still, help the department eliminate the need for such a barrier test).

- Second, to foster collegiality and a dialogue about your courses and program among the twenty-five full-time and part-time adjuncts and twelve TAs who teach E101 and E102. You hope a dialogue among them will promote more consistency in expectations and practices in your courses.

- Third, to meet the outcomes assessment requirements imposed upon your program by the administration as a result of accreditation recommendations.

Not everyone understands or has agreed upon those goals, but in coming to address them, your department has joined an ongoing conversation outside the department. You and other composition specialists have provided much reading material for department members. You have invited guest speakers to campus, attended assessment sessions at conferences, and talked by phone or e-mail to many people across the country about their assessment vehicles. The original pilot group presented your experiences and learned from others at an NCTE Regional Conference on Portfolios held in a nearby state.

As a result of joining other discourse communities, your program has made several major paradigm shifts concerning assessment, shifts which have included moving from thinking of minimal competencies to exit proficiencies; from thinking about what students *can't* do to what they *can* do; from thinking about student assessment to program assessment.

These paradigm shifts did not come easily. The unending conversation in your department has included a lot of "creative conflict." Here you will read about one event that could happen when you enter what Mary Louise Pratt has called "the contact zone" where conflicting expectations, assumptions, and beliefs about assessment collide.

Other Challenges

When your new assessment project began, adjunct faculty were reeling from widespread change in the university. The president, provost, department chair, and writing program director (you) were all new. The president had come to a department meeting and had commented on the adjunct faculty situation on campus. At that time, over 40 percent of university instructors were adjuncts and over 70 percent of the composition courses were taught by adjunct faculty. The president indicated that he was aware there was a problem, but that adjuncts were, in his words, "a dime a dozen." Perhaps he had not meant it the way it sounded, but that meeting had been the beginning of a long slide of adjunct morale. Erosion of adjunct spirit was exacerbated when the department quadrupled the number of TAs. When the number of graduate students teaching composition jumped from three to twelve over a two-year period, long-time adjuncts feared they would no longer be able to teach the courses they loved. They felt displaced and isolated.

Further problems developed between the two groups because TAs taught from a common syllabus, emphasizing writing-across-the-curriculum subjects and pedagogy. Adjuncts became apprehensive that their teaching styles and expressive ideologies would no longer be valued and that they, too, would have their classroom performance prescribed. Their professionalism felt threatened.

When TAs joined the portfolio pilot, adjuncts again felt displaced. A small group of adjuncts, along with tenure-track faculty members, had planned and carried out the first semester of the new assessment program. TAs joined during their second semester of teaching, which was the third semester of the pilot. The TAs were enthusiastic both about the pilot and about their new experience as teachers. They were eager to learn about how to teach more effectively. The portfolio project was an opportunity to interact professionally with others in the department. While their teaching curriculum was based on a model developed by you, the writing program director, during their second semester, they wanted to learn about other philosophies as well.

They knew that differences existed among the composition instructors in the department. They not only sensed tension in the hall, but they heard adjuncts talking about their frustrations. TAs felt powerless to change the attitude, but hoped they could glean information to improve their teaching by observing a wide variety of teachers working in different contexts in the department.

One TA said that she "came to the portfolio hoping the differences I'd heard about could be overcome." But that hope was dashed when the conflict, smoldering until then, came out in the open discussion during the midterm assessment session.

At midterm, as part of the pilot, students collected and submitted materials in a preliminary portfolio. One of the aims of the preliminary portfolio was to prepare students for the final portfolios which when scored would affect their course grade. Another aim was to give instructors a "practice" scoring session. Instructors met for a day, exchanged portfolios, and scored them, writing suggestions for revision on students' papers. A TA recorded her reaction to the session this way:

> I was absolutely shocked at the comments written to my students [by one adjunct faculty reader]. These comments reflected no analysis of my students' writing but conveyed only anger and sarcasm towards the teaching model I had used. Comments told my students such things as "you did a good job given such a boring assignment" and "This was—it seems to me—an awful assignment—considering that, I think you did as well as could be expected." I was to give these back to my students and tell them that this is a tool that we used to either pass or fail them from the class. I was angry. I did not know who to hold responsible, and felt frustrated. My idealism was eroded. I felt distanced from the adjunct faculty as a whole.

Considerations

Through the vehicle of the portfolio assessment project, several issues have been brought into focus. Your adjunct faculty, like their counterparts at other colleges and universities, have traditionally faced problems of low pay, no job security, no benefits, and no upward mobility within their profession. In addition to these issues of professional insecurity, they have faced the more subtle problem of isolation. They teach at odd hours and odd sites. Many feel almost invisible—it's not uncommon for other faculty members not even to recognize them as fellow teachers.

It was thought, both by you as director and by others in the administration and faculty, that the portfolios would not only provide a more valid assessment tool than the Minimal Competency Exam, but would also lead to greater camaraderie and a sense of peer professionalism among the non-tenure-track teaching staff. However, such claims by portfolio advocates across the composition professional community have not been realized in your department. Instead, the problems that arose during the midterm portfolio readings proved that camaraderie and peer professionalism do not spring up automatically with portfolio assessment of student writing. The personnel and pedagogical problems you have experienced are problems that most universities in this country face.

The adjuncts formed one discourse community, and the new teaching assistants formed another. (In another university, the division may be between adjunct and tenure-track faculty or between composition faculty and literature specialists.) These discourse communities ran aground on issues of theory, pedagogy, hegemony, and economics;

issues that became concrete and personal when students' work and teacher's assignment were assessed and discussed in an open forum which allowed for injured egos.

Key Charge

So what happens when two discourse communities collide? One or the other can crush the opposition, or both can gain new ideas and new friendships from the experience. Your midterm scoring session, because it has brought the disparities and insecurities of department members out into the open, has identified areas of conflict between two legitimate points of view. These conflicts are exactly the points that you, as writing director, must help the department open to scholarly, reciprocal discussion so that you can study and resolve them on a professional level.

Where do you go from here? The portfolio pilot successfully eliminated the MCE. Your department seems to be shifting away from gatekeeping, student-centered assessment to program assessment. Because funding large-scale portfolios has become impossible in your department, you might use random sampling of student portfolios to gather data needed to tell you what the program is and to decide what you want your program to be in the future. You and your department must continue to answer questions about assessment of student writing:

- Why are we doing it? Ensuring student proficiency? Unifying teaching goals and methods? Ensuring quality teaching? Appraising curricular practices and goals?
- What are we assessing? Students' writing abilities? Teachers' performance?
- What is the best way to assess? As part of a course? A freestanding, departmental exam?
- Who will have access to the results of evaluations? Administrators? Teachers? Students?

You no longer have a budget for grading sessions, and the portfolio pilot has ended, but the issues which surfaced are still a source of conflict and division in your program. You must look for other ways for the adjuncts and graduate TAs to meet to discuss curriculum and teaching strategies. Might they form mentoring teams? Have faculty development meetings? Teach collaboratively? How will you work to set the terms and research questions of your own program assessment? How can you overcome the personnel and pedagogical problems you have experienced when assessment allowed you to see underlying conflicts and the contact zones of several paradigm shifts?

At stake are not only morale issues of isolation and insecurity, but also the quality of the writing courses you teach. If non-tenure-track faculty, both adjuncts and TAs, can blend their disparate voices, then assessment can lead to better teaching. Writing director, faculty, and students will be the ultimate winners if the various discourse communities are willing to learn from each other.

AUTHOR'S CASE COMMENTARY

This example represents several common challenges faced by WPAs: adjunct professionalism, TA training, large-scale assessment, and programmatic morale.

Issues related to contract faculty include proper training, fair remuneration, scheduling, and course assignments. The teaching of service courses, including first-year composition and mathematics, has for many years been underfunded. The many issues and perspectives surrounding this condition are discussed in some of the readings listed in the bibliography. And prospective WPAs would do well to understand the historical development and probable future of the problem and the reactions by the professional community of composition organizations. The movement toward part-time help in other professions in our country lets us know that the issues we face will not likely go away or be solved in the near future. What should WPAs do? The WPA is the person with the responsibility to provide adequate teaching of writing skills to the students of her school. She should perform with that responsibility in mind. Where part-timers are her faculty, she should provide training for them and, whenever possible, require their attendance at inservice meetings.

She should speak out and act against their exploitation, however. For example, where tenure-track faculty are probably hired with expectations that they will contribute service to the program, department, and college, adjunct faculty are typically hired with no expectations and no funding to reimburse them for their time. In addition, many contract faculty must work more than one job. Whenever possible, the WPA can schedule their courses at times which make this possible.

New programs aimed at solving problems associated with part-time teachers are being tried across the country. At some universities adjunct faculty are being let go and tenure-track faculty are being assigned composition classes. At other universities, qualified adjuncts are being promoted to full-time lecturer positions with primary responsibilities of teaching and programmatic service. Other approaches may be tried as well. Change involves tension, and so with any of these approaches the WPA will face concerned and threatened regular and contract faculty.

Another responsibility often entrusted to the WPA is the professional training of TAs. That issue is more fully addressed elsewhere in this book. Here it is important to note that the WPA must perform something of a balancing act. The WPA is the supervisor of two very diverse groups: the part-timers and the TAs. TAs are often less mature teachers and might require more supervision and training. But TAs are often enthusiastic and very willing to learn. Both groups, however, often are composed of teachers from backgrounds other than composition or rhetoric. In addition, the groups may be alienated from each other due to age, experience, and individual ability to spend time on campus. The WPA must treat all of the instructors with respect and understanding of their backgrounds and goals.

The example in this chapter also brings up issues of large-scale assessment. Issues involve whether we should do it at all; if we do test the writing skills of all our students, what is the best way to do so; who will score the exams, how will they be reimbursed, how should the results be used for program development and student progress? Many of these issues are addressed in the readings listed in the bibliography.

Turning now to the issue of program morale, the WPA will come to call often on the old adage that "Time heals all." If she stays in the department for several years, she may see that the changes that seemed so onerous when they happened will eventually become traditions for which faculty will fight. Past tempests may seem in retrospect as minor drizzles. If she "rides it through," she may learn many administrative techniques which will make her a better adminstrator. She will learn that people who are foes on one battlefield are allies on another, and so she must not take differences personally. If on the other hand she moves on, she should carry with her the learning experiences afforded her, even in tough situations. The adage "Time heals all" is one the WPA could apply to most problems.

This is not to say that the WPA should be a passive bystander in cases of morale difficulties. The WPA must learn to encourage her faculty and be their advocate whenever situations allow. She should provide opportunities and, when possible, funding for faculty to develop their skills, talents, and interests within the scope of composition instruction. She should provide occasions for faculty members to become an effective and happy working community. She will need to develop a frank but caring perspective and manner. And most important, she will need to develop the art of imparting that perspective to others. The WPA must be a leader in every sense.

In all these experiences, the WPA must have the support—moral, financial, and practical—of the administration. And she must cultivate it if she is to do her job. The chair of her department and her dean play a large role in the success of the writing program and in meeting its goals. In the case being discussed here, where adjunct faculty and TAs were called upon to work together in a time of change, administrative agendas affected the outcomes.

While dean and chair hoped to be rid of the MCE, the mandated exam of mechanical correctness which had kept the writing program and entire English department fruitlessly busy for over twenty years, neither wanted to finance another test to replace it. Neither wanted to keep adjunct faculty at a high profile in the department. And both wanted to promote the practice of using TAs in the composition class-room and to augment the graduate program. Their goals were at odds with the tradition in the department, which had never had TAs before and which had relied chiefly on adjuncts and tenure-track faculty to teach writing classes. Times were changing. Faculty were upset. Administrative edicts and agendas, even if forward-thinking, can be problematic.

The WPA is often caught in the middle of these changes. Unfortunately, that is a fact of life, especially for a new assistant professor assigned as WPA. Typically, if a program hires a new assistant professor as WPA, that indicates a young, underdeveloped program where there will be many necessary but often unwelcome changes. Sometimes, even supportive administrators can do little to resolve differences in the contact zone.

Although some of these issues seem insurmountable, the WPA, perhaps as much as any person at a university, has the opportunity to grow as an administrator and as a person. When she comes to see and value the talents and contributions of the people—administrators, faculty, adjuncts, and TAs—with whom she works, she will develop her own talents and will be able to make a positive difference, not only in her university but in our profession.

5 Introducing a Developmental Writing Program at a Small, Rural Two-Year College

Paul Bodmer
Bismarck State College

This chapter presents the problems you, as new WPA, face while introducing a developmental writing program that is based on solid understanding of the writing process to a rural community college where the administrative staff of the college and other faculty members do not understand the pedagogical requirements of developmental classes and a writing center.

Institution Overview

Bismarck State College is a comprehensive two-year college with a student population of approximately twenty-five hundred students. BSC offers the traditional transfer programs of the Associate in Arts and Associate in Science degree for about 60 percent of its students, and the Diploma, Certificate, and Associate in Applied Science degree for the 40 percent taking technical programs to enter the workforce immediately after finishing at BSC. Most students (approximately 75 percent) are between the ages of eighteen and twenty-two, although the other 25 percent are distributed fairly evenly between twenty-five and fifty years of age. Bismarck State College is part of the North Dakota University System, a public system of eleven campuses across North Dakota that includes two universities that offer doctoral programs, four four-year universities, and five two-year colleges.

The total student population of the North Dakota University System is about 38,000 students. The eleven institutions are connected with an interactive video network that allows audio-video delivery of courses across the state. Through this cooperation, BSC coordinates two baccalaureate degrees—criminal justice and business management—delivered to our campus from one of the four-year universities. There will be other bachelor's degrees through another of the four-year universities in the next few years. The University of North Dakota offers graduate degrees in public and educational administration on the BSC campus as well.

Local

Bismarck is the capital city of North Dakota, located on the Missouri River. Across the river is the sister city of Mandan. The combined population of the urban area of the two communities is approximately sixty thousand. While there is some manufacturing and industry in Bismarck, the primary economy of the area is agriculture. Because it is the capital city, much of the workforce is occupied in government work. Bismarck is a major rural medical facility, with two hospitals, both supporting nursing training programs.

Bismarck State is the only public higher education institution in the area. There is a private, church-supported university, the University of Mary, with about nineteen hundred students, and a tribal two-year college, United Tribes Technical College, in the community. The University of Mary is a four-year, liberal arts institution that offers some graduate programs at the master's level. They also offer a nursing degree program. One of the hospitals also offers a nursing degree program in cooperation with BSC. BSC provides the lower-division general education and science courses, and the nursing program offers the upper division nursing course work. The closest university offering master's degrees in English is two hundred miles away, and the closest offering a doctorate in English is two hundred and fifty miles away.

Computing

BSC has a full network of computer labs, and part of the degree requirement is computer literacy. Some of the first-year composition courses require all written work to be done on the campus computer network, and all of the composition classes strongly encourage students to use computers for their writing.

Library

The library has a collection of fifty thousand volumes. It is staffed with a head librarian, a research librarian, two library technicians, and student help. The card catalog is electronic and connected to all the libraries in the North Dakota University System.

Mission

The mission statement of Bismarck State College was revised over the past two years. It was developed following a campuswide process of assessing our goals and commitments in relation to educational and economic trends for the campus. It reads:

> Bismarck State College, a member of the North Dakota University System, is the area's comprehensive two-year college. We encourage intellectual inquiry, individuality, and responsibility, and provide an atmosphere for students to attain their goal of learning and the satisfaction of achievement in an open and safe environment. We are committed to maintaining a learning community by providing affordable quality education and training opportunities for life-long development and employability in an increasingly technological environment through transfer, technical, and continuing education supported by student services, administrative coordination, and fiscal management. As an area-based institution, BSC utilizes research and planned change to stimulate academic excellence, student success, and economic development.

Faculty

There are approximately ninety full-time tenured or tenure-track faculty members and seventy part-time instructors. The faculty has been very stable, with very few new hires until the past few years. Most of the senior faculty have been on staff for more than fifteen years. Unfortunately, some of the tenure-track positions, particularly in the liberal arts, are being filled with adjunct instructors. In most cases the adjunct instructors are trained professionals in their fields, for instance criminal prosecution, social work, money and banking, who come on campus and are expected to *deliver* their expertise rather than *teach* the discipline.

It is important to remember that there are no graduate assistants, ABDs, or graduate students in the area, not to mention graduate students in composition and rhetoric. This is not a university community with scores of people who have had experience teaching composition and who would be willing to invest much time for little pay to accept this position. There is no pool of people with training and experience in composition to staff extra sections of composition. And particularly there is no pool of people who have experience in writing centers and with developmental classes. However, the pressure remains from the administration to hire adjuncts. The vice president has said on more than one occasion that positions would be filled regardless of the pool of applicants.

Students

Over 75 percent of the students come from the immediate area of the Bismarck-Mandan community, and about 90 percent come from within a seventy-five-mile radius of Bismarck. While primarily a commuter campus, BSC does have men's and women's residence halls as well as a small unit of student apartments. While the primary service area is south central North Dakota, students from all over the state and nation do attend. Because North Dakota borders on Canada, most of the students classified as international would be from Canada; however, there are occasional students from other areas of the world as well. The primary student population is native North Dakotan, specifically from the greater Bismarck-Mandan area. The ethnic background is primarily northern European, specifically Scandinavian and German. Most students are three to six generations away from immigration, and more than half are first-generation college students in their families.

Program/Center Overview

All students receiving the A.A. and A.S. degree take a year of first-year composition (Composition I and Composition II) and a semester of speech. Students receiving the Associate in Applied Science degree take either one semester of first-year composition or a semester of speech. Until the present time there was no course that preceded first-year composition such as basic or developmental writing. North Dakota has, since early in the twentieth century, had a high degree of literacy. North Dakota still has the highest number of high school graduates per capita, the highest percentage of high school graduates who attend college, and the highest percentage of high school graduates who receive some sort of college degree. The result has been a very homogenous high school graduating class across the state. The campus has discovered, however, that even with a high school degree, there is a growing percentage of students who are not prepared for first-year composition. As a result, a pre-composition course, College Writing Prep, has been introduced this fall.

An attempt was made to pursue writing across the curriculum about ten years ago. Unfortunately, the wrong presenter was chosen, and many faculty members were more turned off than opened up to the possibilities. Faculty in other disciplines than English who assigned writing would tell students to "write a paper" on a particular subject, with no further directions, and then be upset with the English department when they received inadequate papers. In general, the dean supported the other disciplines in fostering a mood of "blaming" the English department because students were not writing good term papers in their introductory courses.

Bismarck State College has always been an open-door community college, with no required assessment examination until 1990. At that time the State Board of Higher Education in North Dakota established a requirement that all entering students in all public higher education institutions must take the ACT exam. The results of the exam were used for minimal advising, but until this fall there was no placement in English classes based on the ACT scores.

Five years ago, recognizing the need for more help for students with writing problems, the English department conducted research into the nature of the problems students were having. The conclusion reached was that there were not yet enough students to warrant a separate, pre-first-year composition course, but that a writing center could handle those few instances while also addressing the much larger number of students who needed some tutorial help. The department presented a proposal for a writing center to the administration, but the administration replied that a writing center would be too expensive and that a remedial course in grammar would solve the problems. The department declined to develop the remedial course at that time, insisting that the writing problems they identified are not solely grammatical problems of remediation. The department asked for but did not receive support for appropriate research to more clearly identify the problems and find the right solution.

Once again the department argued for a scaled-down writing center, explaining how the center would be for all students, all faculty, all disciplines, and that the writing center would help develop assignments, clarify writing prompts, and provide the support necessary for improving student writing. The department also explained how the writing center could be a resource for faculty for various kinds of writing assignments (outside of the traditional paper) that would effectively improve student learning. The answer from the dean was the same as before—a remedial grammar class would fix the problems.

In the interim the department began working more closely with the tutoring staff in the skills center who, previously, had been available only to technical program students. The department began testing students for basic skills in usage and syntax and assigning students to the skills center for tutorial help. This was, at best, a stop-gap move to try to develop a writing program philosophy based on research of student needs.

When a new president was hired two years ago, her background supported developing student skills centers, or student success centers. She was very well aware that research precedes development of a program, and she gave full support to the needs of the English department in developing its own set of programs to meet the student needs. With the necessary administrative support to get information about students, the English department was able to predict, based on the ACT, probable student failure, as well as a range of ability where there would probably be writing problems, and that a writing sample would determine the nature of the writing problems.

The research the department conducted revealed that entering students fall into one of three categories:

1. Students scoring 12 and below on the ACT would almost certainly fail Composition I.
2. Students scoring 13 to 20 on the ACT could succeed, but would probably have problems with their writing.
3. Students scoring 21 and above on the ACT would, more than likely, have no problem doing well in Composition I.

These numbers are all within the national averages, verifying the local research. The English department recommended that the first group would be automatically assigned to the College Writing Prep course. Research of present students indicated that there would be no more than fifty students in this category. Students scoring 13 and above would enter Composition I. All students in Composition I would be required to write an initial assessment essay. Those who showed, through their writing, that they would not succeed in Composition I would be replaced in College Writing Prep. Those students who demonstrated problems in some areas of their writing, but not serious enough to warrant re-placement, would be assigned to various seminars in the writing center. Students who did not demonstrate any particular deficiency in their readiness for Composition I would not be assigned to the writing center. However, all students would be encouraged to use the writing center for any of their writing concerns, regardless of the origin of the writing assignment.

The department plan would include three sections of developmental writing, called College Writing Prep, as well as an extensive tutoring program in a writing center that would be housed in the new Student Success Center. It would require hiring a full-time tenure-track faculty member to develop the College Writing Prep courses, the seminars in the writing center, and the coordination of the writing center with the composition classes as well as the rest of the disciplines on campus.

The proposal was presented. BSC would need to hire one full-time tenure-track, qualified faculty member who would develop the program. There would be tutorial help (two part-time people were already on staff for tutoring writing, and more would be hired as needed). With the completion of the new student success center, there would be full computer access in the writing center. The campus assessment committee accepted the proposal and assured the department that what they asked for would happen. The dean assured the English department that it would work, and that a tenure-track position could be advertised. The department chair wrote the job description and turned it in to the personnel office.

Then word came that the administration had decided that a tenure-track, full-time faculty member was not a high priority for the developmental classes and writing center director. In fact, there would be no funding for a full-time tenure-track position in the near future. The department was instructed to find adjunct instructors for the classes, or present department personnel would each pick up one of the classes. The department wanted to put the program on hold for another year, or at least a semester, to adequately search for a solution. The administration held firm—hire anybody you can or use present faculty to teach the College Writing Prep classes. When asked what would happen if competent faculty could not be found, the vice president's answer was that we would be able to find adjunct instructors—after all, these were not difficult or advanced classes. He argued repeatedly that there would be no problem finding a qualified person to teach the College Writing Prep classes; after all, those students did not need as much skill as the more "advanced" student. There had to be people in the community who could do it. It was just slower and louder than a regular class, wasn't it?

Your Charge

You have been hired, either as a part-time instructor or as a tenure-track, full-time instructor, to teach the College Writing Prep class and coordinate the development of the writing center. You will be responsible for developing the Writing Center as well as coordinating the tutorial work in the center.

Questions

1. How do you show the value of writing as a tool for thinking to an administration that does very little writing?

2. How do you show the value of writing as a necessary academic tool to a faculty that does very little professional writing?

3. How do you show that developmental or basic writing instruction is more complex than just first-year composition at a slower pace?

4. How do you demonstrate that the writing center is for all students, not just the basic writers and those having problems in first-year composition.

5. How do you show that, in the long run, investment in a properly staffed writing center, coordinated with the campus learning environment, is a high priority?

Key Challenges

- There is an administration that pays lip service to the value of writing centers, but does not understand the writing process or the work of a writing center, and, therefore, does not see the need for strong financial support.

- There is no WAC program on campus. However, there is potential to develop one, particularly with recent hires.

- The pool of tutors is limited. The possibility exists to develop student tutors. However, a two-year campus does not always have a pool of available students skilled in writing and tutoring.

- As BSC coordinates the offerings of more baccalaureate and graduate degrees on campus delivered from other institutions, the writing center will need to address the needs of upper-division and graduate students as well.

- The climate for professional writing is not very intense. However, the faculty senate is reviewing the present faculty rank system, and there will be scholarship requirements for advances in rank. This may increase faculty interest in academic writing.

AUTHOR'S CASE COMMENTARY

We did advertise for and find an adjunct instructor to teach the College Writing Prep classes. Luckily, a person from the community is in the process of receiving her master's degree from one of the two universities, and she has studied composition theory for basic writers. We were able to convince the vice president to hire her at approximately three-fourths contract for her to develop the writing center. However, we have no assurances except the obligatory "we are doing all that we can with the resources we have" that this will become a permanent, tenure-track position.

The adjunct issue has not been resolved. We could easily use one more full-time tenured position for composition as well as the full-time tenured position for the writing center. The vice president has told the faculty senate that "if a position opens at BSC, administration will look at filling that position with qualified adjunct faculty. If [the] position cannot be filled with qualified adjunct, administration will have to decide whether or not to hire full-time faculty or look at other alternatives" (Bismarck State College Faculty Senate Minutes, October 2, 1997).

6 Examining Our Assumptions as Gatekeepers: A Two-Year College Perspective

Howard Tinberg
Bristol Community College

What standards must writers for whom English is not a first language meet in order to "mainstream" both into the standard writing course and into the college-wide curriculum? How do we determine such competency? I would like to narrate the story of one such writer, a story which caused many of us who teach and tutor writing to re-examine our assumptions about writing competencies, exit exams, and, more profoundly, the very nature of our gatekeeping roles.

Institution Overview

This scenario takes place at a thirty-five-year-old comprehensive, open-access, public community college, located in one of the most ethnically diverse and most economically undeveloped regions of a northeastern state. With its unemployment and high school dropout rates among the highest in the state, the community looks to your college to provide a way to a better life. The college offers a full range of transfer and career programs, as well as developmental and lifelong education and specialized and short-term certificate programs.

Local

The city which the college serves was once the site of powerful textile and fishing industries, both of which have long since declined. While some high-tech firms have entered the area, joblessness remains high and wages depressingly low. These demographics, from 1992, tell a good part of the story:

- income of 13 percent of families in the city falls below the poverty level, compared to the state average of 7 percent
- unemployment in the city is 12 percent, while the state's average is 6 percent
- the average grade level achieved for adults is 8
- the city is multicultural in the truest sense, with over 50 percent of Portuguese descent and growing African American, Asian, and Hispanic communities

Students

In the grant proposal that initiated the Writing Lab, students were described as follows:

> Most students at the college are first-generation college students. Eighty-seven percent (87%) of their fathers and 90 percent of their mothers do not have college degrees. Since their parents did not attend college, they often receive neither the family understanding nor the emotional support they need to encourage them to continue their education. . . .
>
> Predictably, the dropout [rate] is higher than that experienced at other colleges. The two-year dropout rate for day students is 50.7 percent. This means that less than half of the day students who are admitted in a Fall semester will remain enrolled four semesters later. Forty percent (40%) of day college students do not continue their education from one year to the next, and disadvantaged students enrolling in the college's developmental program drop out at a rate of 70% over four semesters. . . .

To meet these students' needs, the college continues to improve support services, as well as assessment and intervention measures.

Courses

The college offers thirty associate degree programs and more than ten certificate programs. It also offers a range of academic support services, including a tutoring center, a writing lab, and L2 or English as a Second Language courses. All students who enter the college are tested for their reading, writing, and math skills, prior to enrollment in their courses. Students who score below the cutoff score on the writing sample are placed in developmental writing courses. Students who fail the Iowa Silent Reading test are required to take a course to develop reading strategies. Students who do not pass the math test must enroll in basic computation courses before taking higher-level math courses.

Writing Lab Overview

History

The college's Writing Lab began five years ago under the Strengthening Institutions Program of the federal Title III Act of 1965. The Lab was but one component of Project Success, a collegewide effort to increase student success through an improvement of students' writing and critical thinking skills, an enhancement of academic support services and faculty/staff development, and an improved administration decision-making capability.

Mission

The Writing Lab, from its inception, had a complex and comprehensive mission aimed at providing much needed help to developing writers, promoting writing across the curriculum while enhancing faculty/staff development at the college, and, significantly, acting as gatekeepers for L2 students wishing to take the mainstream writing course. The lab's goals, as stated in the grant, were:

- improve the writing proficiency of the students using the Lab
- offer faculty training in teaching writing across the disciplines
- through workshops, increase the number of courses in which writing is at least 20% of the course grade
- score the exit exams of ESL students who seek to mainstream into the standard composition course

The lab's mission statement reads as follows:

> Offering an open-door policy to all members of the college and the community at-large, the Writing Lab assists all writers regardless of the subject that generates the writing and the writer's level of experience and expertise. The highly-trained staff listens to the writer's concerns, establishes a dialogue, identifies the writing problem, and offers encouragement either to begin the writing process or improve by revision. Staffed by the faculty representing a wide range of disciplines and by accomplished peer tutors, the Lab provides an impressive depth of experience and expertise.

The lab is staffed by a team of faculty tutors, representing the six academic divisions of the college. Faculty serve for a year, during which they receive one course released time for each semester's worth of tutoring. When the year is completed, faculty return to their divisions to be replaced by another team of faculty. So far, some forty full-time faculty (out of roughly ninety) have served as Writing Lab tutors.

Training

Faculty receive training as tutors in a two-day workshop prior to their first semester of work in the lab. In the summer marking a midpoint in their lab service, faculty attend an intensive two-and-a-half-week workshop on writing in the disciplines, during which they consider what it means to write and think in our particular disciplines as well as how we can best respond as tutors and teachers to student writing.

During the school year, faculty tutors attend weekly staff meetings to discuss problems that arise in the lab as well as to screen the writing of ESL writers who wish to move on to the mainstream composition course. It was during one such staff meeting that the case which you will be concerned with occurred. But before we delve into the nature of the case, you need to know something of the role of the lab faculty in writing assessment at the college.

The Writing Lab as a Site for Writing Assessment

All students who walk through the college's doors must sit for a forty-minute placement exam which consists of responding to a single writing prompt designed and scored by English department faculty. Scored holistically on a 6-point scale, the writing samples must demonstrate competence in the following areas:

- establishing a clear perspective
- employing a clear and logical structure
- marshaling useful and appropriate evidence for support
- demonstrating a sense of audience
- showing a control of diction, grammar, and mechanics

Students who receive scores above 3 are allowed to enroll in the required, mainstream composition course. Those with a score below 3 are placed in one of two kinds of courses: developmental writing or English as a Second Language. Successful completion of the developmental course with a C or better allows students to move on to the standard first-year composition course. Those students who are placed in the ESL course can pass out of the course only when they have submitted writing to the Writing Lab staff that receives a passing score from the staff. The Writing Lab reads such papers and urges, simply, a pass or a fail.

Scenario: Breaking the Rules

It is Thursday at 1:50 P.M., and you have every reason to wish you were somewhere else. The lab's weekly staff meeting is about to commence and you know that today's agenda calls for scoring of ESL writing. To-day is the day that you play the "keeper of the gates," deciding who shall pass through and who shall not. You take no issue with assess-ment per se: each of us as teachers and tutors must obviously evaluate the work that students bring us in order to offer them the help that they need. Nor do you feel discomfort in sharing the burden of assessment with the group. Indeed you welcome the opportunity to review student writing with colleagues, especially with colleagues outside your own department (the English department).

What troubles you has in part to do with the tensions inherent in assigning a college assessment role to the Writing Lab. Shouldn't the lab maintain its independence as an extracurricular site of student sup-port? When we assess in order to promote students within the curricu-lum, do we not compromise that lab's vital role as intermediary or trans-lator between the classroom teacher and the student? When students come to us for help, should we not expect them to ask us what *we* want them to write?

But there are other issues as well that trouble you about this pro-cess. Although all of us who serve as faculty have plenty of experience reading and grading student writing, you fear that precious few of us have training with this particular kind of student writing, namely that done by L2 writers. More and more of these students are coming to the lab for help with their work and you wonder how prepared you and the other tutors are to deal with the complex array of cultural and lin-guistic issues such students bring with them. How exactly does tutor-ing such students differ from the tutoring we do for native speakers and writers of English?

Moreover, you are troubled by the obvious double standard at work here. Those students who are taking the developmental writing course need only receive a grade of C or better to move on to the stan-dard first-year composition course. They need not sit for an exit exam, as the L2 students must. They need not submit their writing to faculty who have little knowledge of their in-class work. The unfairness is com-pounded when you consider that the L2 students do not receive col-lege credit (and therefore financial aid) for their course, while those tak-ing basic and first-year composition courses do.

Challenges

Make no mistake about it: you and the others sitting around the table have been carefully "normed" and "calibrated" as holistic and accurate readers of student writing. Hours of shared reading both during the year (it is now late in your second and last semester of duty) and during the intensive and extensive summer workshop have made you confident in your ability to perform group assessment well. But this is not a generic assessment, nor are these students' concerns as writers so easily categorized or resolved.

To top it off, you are upset, as are many of the two-year college faculty with whom you work in the lab and in the department, with the all-too-obvious policy among transfer institutions at the four-year colleges to cede responsibility for the teaching and assessing of such students (indeed, of developmental students in a variety of skill areas) to the two-year colleges. As more and more students are encouraged by four-year colleges to take their developmental courses at the local community college before continuing with their university studies (or even as they take courses at the university), two-year colleges must scramble to handle this most difficult teaching assignment. Given the comprehensive mission of most two-year colleges, energies needed to meet that mission may very well be sapped by such teaching.

But there you are, nonetheless. And this meeting will proceed, nonetheless. The lab director, who is also a member of the English department, offers the group an interesting case for you and the others to consider. You will learn nothing about the student's background before reading the sample but will, you are told, be given some information about this interesting case after you have accomplished the scoring of all the papers for that session.

The scoring goes smoothly, producing little disagreement or discrepancy—that is, with one exception. The prompt, as you know, asked the students to describe who they were. Students were urged to be "creative" in their response but had to produce writing that was "well-organized" with a clarity of language and purpose. Most of the responses play it very safe, presenting in essay form students' testimony as father, son, mother, or daughter. But one writer does not play it safe. In fact, she persistently writes against the assumptions of the prompt. "Who am I? I know what I am not" is the paper's continual refrain. This is not an essay, nor is it obviously predictable in structure. It seems more like a meditation and a playful manipulation of the prompt.

Two staff members regard the piece as not sufficiently strong to pass, in large part, they say, because of random difficulties with idiom and because the writer simply does not demonstrate a control of formal academic prose as required by the prompt. You and two other colleagues take issue with that assessment, citing the student's willingness to take up the challenge of the prompt to be "creative." Furthermore, you argue that in fact that writing does reveal form (if only in the insistence of that refrain, "I know what I am not") and the language a special kind of power.

Key Charge

The director then lets us know that this student's teacher's colleagues in the ESL area are convinced that the writer is not yet ready to pass on to the mainstreamed course. The student's teacher feels otherwise but a majority of her colleagues disagree. Although the ESL faculty routinely discuss the capabilities of their students, we in the lab rarely get wind of these conversations. This case is different, says the director. It raises a whole host of difficult and complex issues, not the least of which is the case of a student whose approach to a writing prompt simply does not fit the categories of assessment specified by the prompt and by those whose job it is to score the response. It speaks volumes, he says, about the limits of standardized assessment measures. When someone does not fit the pigeonhole, what do you do?

Considerations

For you, this case raises the following additional questions, questions which you need now to consider:

- Do writing centers have a role to play in collegewide assessment?
- If so, what is that role?
- If not, why does the nature of writing centers exclude such a role?
- In an open-door institution and open-access writing center, what consequences does such testing have for the student, for the institution, and for the center?
- How do tutoring practices change when ESL writers enter writing centers?
- Who is the ESL or L2 writer, anyway?
- What markers, if any, do we need to be aware of as tutors?
- What training needs to take place to render writing centers more amenable to such writers?

AUTHOR'S CASE COMMENTARY

Clearly, many issues emerge from the case study that I have offered. Perhaps the most fundamental among them—at least as affecting the status and roles of writing centers—has to do with the relationship of a writing center to writing assessment generally. In performing a gatekeeping role, do writing centers forfeit their mediatory role inevitably? In other words, if tutors now have an institutional responsibility to demote or promote student writers, can they as effectively and as credibly facilitate the improvement of student writing as they would merely as tutors?

Such a question assumes, of course, that writing centers actually occupy a space free of classroom and institutional pressures in the first place. An argument can be made that writing centers, like classrooms, do not and cannot operate free of such pressures. Moreover, if writing centers can bring to bear their special expertise to the matter of writing assessment (perhaps proposing the use of portfolios, for example, instead of the high stakes timed writing sample), then such gatekeeping can become more thoughtful and more productive than at present. Beyond the broad concern over the writing center's gatekeeping role is the interesting and important problem of how a college views the work done in L2 classrooms. In the scenario that I describe, the writing of L2 students is set apart from the work done by native speakers/writers in developmental classes. In terms of the scenario itself, certainly writing center tutors ought to be trained to read the writing of L2 students effectively. Workshops can be organized by campus specialists for just that purpose.

But a more thorny problem laid bare here is the institution's unwillingness to integrate fully L2 instruction with writing instruction generally. Indeed, our scenario touches upon a long-standing issue at my own campus: the great divide between the courses taught by developmental education specialists and the mainstream (read "college ready") academic offerings taught by departmental faculty. Perhaps here, too, writing centers can play a significant role in altering college practice and structure by playing a mediating role between those faculty who teach, in this case, L2 courses and those who teach departmental sanctioned writing courses.

II Program Development

7 Mobilizing Human Resources to (Re)Form a Writing Program

Louise Wetherbee Phelps
Syracuse University

You are newly hired in a tenured position as a writing program director at a mid-size private university in the Northeast. Cicero University is adapting itself to changing economic and demographic conditions by shrinking its size 20 percent and improving the quality of undergraduate education. This case fo-cuses on effective management of human resources within the framework of strategic planning. Your specific challenge is to develop and mobilize the human resources to reform writing instruction *on your campus through a cost-effective, intellectually sound plan compatible with the institution's new mission of providing "student-centered learning" in a research environment.*

Institution Overview

A University in Transition

After a national search, you have been hired as a tenured associate pro-fessor and writing program administrator at a mid-sized private uni-versity set in a small northeastern city, located in a region that is thick with private and public institutions of all types. Cicero University, which has nine professional schools along with a college of liberal arts and sciences, offers regionally distinctive professional programs in creative arts and design, communication, business, engineering, and health sci-ences. Although Cicero markets itself as a national university and meets the criteria for a Research II institution, in fact it draws 78 percent of its undergraduate students from the Northeast, about 45 percent from the state, and is dependent on undergraduate tuition for 70 percent of its budget. Its endowment is not large, providing about 2 percent of its annual revenues. Cicero has a relatively compact and well-maintained campus, a library of over two million volumes, and three hundred desk-top computers in fourteen public clusters, linked by a fiber-optic com-munications network.

History

Cicero is undergoing major reforms, undertaken by a new president in response to significant threats to the health of the institution. During the 1970s and 1980s Cicero grew in size as it improved in perceived quality, based on increased attention to research and publication by its faculty. At peak, it enrolled over 12,500 undergraduates and ran a conservative, comfortably balanced budget. In the early '90s, however, Cicero began to experience the traumatic impact on higher education of widespread economic, demographic, and technological change.[1] Multiple factors interacted to exacerbate student and parental resistance to the rising cost of private higher education. These blows hit the Northeast particularly hard, especially the state and local region from which Cicero draws many of its students, suffering from a weak economy and declining population with little prospects for quick recovery. In order to compete for a shrinking pool of its traditional (eighteen- to twenty-two-year-old) undergraduates, the university faced the need to hold down tuition costs and increase the tuition discount it offered in the form of financial aid from a low 10 percent to (by 1995) 35 percent.

Cicero's new president, anticipating that these conditions would not change substantially before the next century, decided on a strategy of controlled downsizing. The university is now about halfway through a multiyear plan to reduce its size by 20 percent that will decrease its undergraduate enrollment to about 10,000 and cut its faculty by about 15 percent. It has undertaken a major restructuring of its budget and finances in order to manage planned deficits over this period while working toward a surplus by the year 2001. Simultaneously, Cicero has launched initiatives to give it a strategic edge in the crowded northeastern academic marketplace: raise academic and admissions standards through targeted recruiting and financial aid, improve its quality of education and services to undergraduates, increase retention and graduation rates, and create a distinctive new image. Taking advantage of its professional schools and research faculty in arts and sciences, the university proposes in its new mission statement to "combine the liberal arts with research and professional studies in an innovative, student-centered learning environment with many opportunities for multidisciplinary and interdisciplinary courses of study." The president's vision emphasizes the reciprocal responsibilities of faculty and students for effective learning.

Mission

Except for selected graduate and professional degrees, the president has refocused Cicero's mission sharply on undergraduate education. (The university will continue to add some related professional master's degrees that draw full-paying students.) Faculty research and creative activity, in this vision, are most significant for their contributions to undergraduate learning, creating opportunities and motivation for students to explore, create, and apply knowledge themselves. One strategy for carrying out this mission is to emphasize the possibility for students to enroll in double majors or combine majors and minors in liberal arts (humanities, physical and social sciences) with professional studies or vice versa. Another is to develop project-centered learning in both traditional and nontraditional course and credit arrangements. The president has called for the faculty to facilitate undergraduate participation in research and applied projects, improve pedagogies through innovation and assessment, offer greater flexibility for combining courses of study, and provide demanding but rewarding academic programs.

A university committee is in its third and final year of work on an innovative, university-wide general education program that emphasizes learning "over time and across contexts." Requirements, including expectations for communication skills and information literacy, are spread out over all four years of the undergraduate curriculum and organized thematically, allowing both liberal arts and professional faculty to contribute courses to multiple categories. The committee is seeking ways to incorporate interdisciplinary learning and integrative experiences at all levels.

To promote the new goals for multidisciplinary learning, the president has taken a number of specific steps in the last three years to break down internal walls that separate the schools and colleges (historically autonomous, competitive, and territorial) and encourage easier movement of faculty and students among them. He has directed that new accounting metrics and budget processes be developed to support rather than penalize units and faculty for participation in interdepartmental or intercollege projects, programs, courses, and curriculum. He has required every dean to sit in on strategic planning in several other units over the last three years and, in appointing new ones, emphasized their role in a team of deans cooperatively effecting change. And, despite the complexities of such appointments, he has approved hiring some faculty members who are shared among colleges and departments.

Students

Because of demographics in the Northeast and its own history, Cicero is not anticipating major changes in the near future in student diversity. Presently about 80 percent of the students are classified as "white, non-Hispanic." Seventeen percent of the undergraduates are American "minority" students, about 8 percent African American. Foreign nationals comprise about 4 percent, but Cicero is recruiting these more intensively and hopes to increase their number, already high in some graduate fields. About 20 percent of the undergraduates are transfers. The university hopes to stabilize annual new undergraduate enrollment at 2,800, but realizes it may not achieve this goal: the 1995 entering class was 2,400, with enrollment variably up and down in different schools and colleges.

Several years into its multiyear plan, Cicero has made substantial progress in recruiting, improving student retention, and controlling its budget, but it has a long way to go in changing the institutional culture to achieve the president's vision of a more interdisciplinary, collaborative, and student-centered learning environment.

Creating the University Composition Program: Recent History

Until three years ago, Cicero had no identifiable writing "program." Writing instruction was scattered and uncoordinated, with divided responsibility for its components. A combination of TAs and part-time faculty taught a very traditional two-semester first-year English sequence dating from the late seventies. A veteran associate professor in literature had administered these courses without significant change for over ten years. The English department also offered three to four writing electives and an occasional theory course in composition and rhetoric. These upper-division courses mainly served majors in English and English education and met writing requirements in professional schools like engineering and business. They were taught by a few of the most senior part-time faculty along with four professors: a tenured creative writer who also teaches and publishes in composition; an associate professor specializing in professional and technical writing; a young applied linguist (jointly appointed in English and linguistics); and an assistant professor in composition and rhetoric, who has since left the university. These professors eschewed teaching first-year English, with its required text and rigidly controlled pedagogy; in any case the director did not welcome faculty participation that might disturb her well-grooved administrative practices or loosen her tight rein over the teachers of these courses.

When the new president took office, he promised that cuts would not be across the board and that investments would be made in innovation or quality improvements that fit his priorities for reform. Seizing this opportunity, the dean of Liberal Arts and Sciences (LAS) persuaded the provost to direct attention to the quality of writing instruction as an important contributor to the dramatic changes planned. As a common denominator of all students' academic experience, she argued, effective writing instruction could become a hallmark of student-centered learning and a potential tool for recruiting and retention. It was decided to create a University Composition Program (UCP) from the scattered pieces and personnel of existing writing courses, to seek a tenured faculty director through an outside search, and to prioritize very limited instructional innovation funds to LAS for this initiative (conditional, however, on the merit of specific proposals to be made by the new director).

To fund a new senior faculty position and find basic program support funds would take at least two years, perhaps more. Cicero needed to implement its plans for restructuring budgets and reducing the faculty (through an early retirement program) in order to reallocate funds for new faculty positions and reinvestment, while the dean needed to stabilize her own budget and flesh out her strategies for quality improvement. However, the director of first-year English was one of the first to sign up for early retirement at the end of that year. The dean decided that, rather than wait, she would appoint an interim director for two years to set up the new program and conduct the search.

She appointed as interim director a respected senior professor of linguistics well connected in the institutional power structure. His substantial record of administrative experience at Cicero (program director, department chair, assistant dean) included a stint as acting chair of a department in crisis, where he dealt with a large contingent of part-time and adjunct faculty. Having no previous experience with composition instruction, he did not undertake to change curriculum or pedagogy during the transitional period. As head of the interdisciplinary search committee, however, he encouraged members to educate themselves about recent developments in the field of composition and rhetoric and helped brief the dean on the qualifications appropriate for a writing program administrator. The interim director worked closely with the three upper-division writing professors; he sought their help in the search and program planning, invited them to become the core of the new UCP faculty, and negotiated their new appointment arrangements. During this transition period, two of the professors became mentors for a few first-year English instructors and advanced TAs who had taken one or two of their graduate courses; they formed a reading group in composition theory and encouraged some pedagogical experimentation.

Most important, the interim director worked with the dean during a turbulent period of restructuring at Cicero to establish and secure much of the infrastructure of the new program: faculty, budget, space, staff, and improved working conditions for teaching. You are very lucky, you discover, that he has done his job so well. The following summary concentrates on what you learned in your interviews, visit, and reading of institutional documents about *personnel:* who teaches writing and how it is budgeted, what faculty and staff resources are provided for the new program, how its members will be housed and supported.

The University Composition Program has been defined as an autonomous academic program, with a tenured faculty director reporting directly to the dean of Liberal Arts and Sciences. In addition to regular part-time faculty (wholly reassigned to the UCP), it now has a professorial faculty drawn from English, linguistics, and (in the future) other departments and colleges, for whom the director serves as a quasi-department chair.[2] They normally teach 2/2 loads, with released time for administration. Besides yourself, there are four professorial faculty members: the creative writer/compositionist (who will teach also in the creative writing MFA program); the professional/technical writing specialist, whose upper-division courses are now incorporated into the UCP; the young applied linguist (who will teach also in linguistics); and a new assistant professor in composition and rhetoric, hired at the same time as you. The dean holds out the possibility of reallocating two more faculty lines for the UCP in several years, but that will depend on many factors, including progress in fulfilling your mission, demonstrated need, and the future state of the university.

The number and mix of teachers in the UCP is in flux. The interim director sharply reduced the number of part-time faculty, many of whom were teaching in several institutions, by consolidating loads (to 3/2 or 3/3) for the more experienced instructors, enabling those remaining to receive for the first time prorated health and tuition benefits and to make a stronger commitment to the UCP. In addition, the LAS dean is making mandated, graduated downsizing cuts in instructional budgets while at the same time reducing teaching assistantships for most graduate programs. About forty-eight TA lines (at three courses/year) are assigned this year to composition instruction, scheduled to drop to forty-five in the next two years. The UCP currently employs between fifty-five and sixty part-time instructors, but scheduled section cuts will reduce the number further as the planned downsizing of the student body proceeds. Of this number, close to half have taught at Cicero for ten years or more.

Significant changes have occurred in the teaching assistant population, a mix of doctoral and master's students. Many of Cicero's graduate programs have been reduced in size, and a few have been eliminated. The large graduate programs in English, which supplied almost all the TAs for the old first-year English, are being cut substantially. Some TA lines from the English graduate programs and others cut from Ph.D. programs across the institution are being reallocated to the UCP as open lines, for which doctoral students from any program in the university can apply. You have only a few such students now, but the proportion of them to traditional appointments will increase. At present, the program offers new TAs only a minimal one-day orientation, then provides a textbook and syllabus that students are expected to follow with little variation. (Graduate students teaching more than two years have a bit more leeway.)

The dean has consolidated the instructional budget from its various sources and placed it in the University Composition Program. Requirements in place throughout the various schools and colleges mandate that undergraduates take two lower-division writing courses: this provides your primary, guaranteed budget base. Because most of the teaching is done by part-time faculty and TAs, the instructional budget is planned annually by the section (twenty students) rather than in dollars. It is presently base-budgeted for an incoming class of 2,100 students; additional "one-time-only" sections are added by the dean's office each year as needed for additional new students or transfer students taking required writing courses. A constrained number of additional sections is budgeted for upper-division instruction (four different courses, with sections of at least three offered each semester). These meet additional writing requirements in a number of other colleges and provide some electives—not nearly enough to meet demand. The number of students taught in UCP courses this year is 6,250, down from 6,865 the previous year, reflecting not only the phased multiyear decline in new student enrollment but also additional restructuring cuts.

An operating budget was created by the dean since none existed. It is modest to begin with, and operating budgets for instructional units will receive no increases at all in the next four years. Given the ruthless slashing of administrative and clerical positions, you are fortunate that the interim director has managed to hang on to two professional staff lines carried over from first-year English: a full-time academic coordinator who handles registration, scheduling, and budget; and an assistant directorship (vacant). Because the program's space is distributed on several floors, it has two full-time secretaries and a half-time receptionist.

The interim director has made certain decisions with positive budgetary implications. He abolished placement and exit tests from the old first-year English program and took the stipends that were paid to the teachers who designed and read the exams to create a discretionary fund or "bank" for your future use.[3] He also preserved the half-time staff position formerly held by a teacher acting as exam coordinator. These savings have a hidden social cost, however. Composing and grading the exams in the old system provided its only formal mechanism for bringing teachers together to work on a joint task that provoked discussion of students and curriculum. The exams therefore served serendipitously to enable some sharing of pedagogical lore and foster social relations among teachers, albeit a privileged few.

Although Cicero's population is relatively homogeneous, the placement exam was used to sort the lowest-scoring students into a basic English class preceding first-year English, taught by a special group of experienced instructors. (These students have now been mainstreamed.) Because the same instructors also provided one-on-one tutoring sessions for a percentage of their time to students enrolled in first-year English (in lieu of teachers' conferencing with students), they were known as "tutors." For no obvious reason, tutors had higher status and pay than regular classroom instructors. The interim director has erased the pay and status differential between tutorial and regular instructional staff and announced that tutorial appointments per se will be eliminated over the next two years. These changes will yield the equivalent of fifty-six sections that the dean has agreed to "bank" for new initiatives or functions.[4] Until the new curriculum is planned, it is unclear how much of this reserve might be needed for continuing tutorial functions, which are presently carried out in instructors' shared offices and scattered in small classrooms around the building.

The interim director could not, under present conditions, do a great deal to improve base part-time pay. (TA stipends are determined by the Graduate School for the home departments.) However, the dean and provost have agreed to reinvest and supplement some savings from consolidating part-time positions and scheduling students more efficiently into sections to provide professional writing instructors with a small percentage increase above the standard (3 percent) raise pool for each of the next two years. Section rates, now average in the area, will then compete favorably with those at other local institutions.

A vice president has consolidated office space for the UCP, including full-time faculty, part-time faculty, and teaching assistants, on several floors of a conveniently located if rather crowded building. There is no physical space for a writing center and none will become available for several years. All instructors now have shared offices and access to copying facilities as well, and a few phones have been installed on each floor for their use. Some space has been renovated for a reception area, administrative offices, and two small meeting rooms divided by a movable wall. A student computer cluster in the building can be scheduled for the use of writing classes.

The New Mission and Your Charge

The broad mission of the new University Composition Program is to offer theoretically sound, effective, and cost-efficient undergraduate writing instruction distinctively adapted to the university's mission, students, and programs of study; to support and coordinate composition instruction and writing practice with the faculty in other disciplines; and to coordinate its own instructional programs with relevant staff initiatives (e.g., academic support and retention).

Upon your appointment, the LAS dean gave you the following specific charge:

- Update and *modernize methods* of writing instruction to contribute to the president's vision of a student-centered learning environment.
- Create *philosophical coherence* within and among UCP course offerings (i.e., a curriculum, a common pedagogy).
- Tie these improvements to developing a cost-effective instructional plan to *"add value" to other degree programs* so that effective writing instruction and practice can serve as a strategic tool in their recruiting and retention.

The LAS dean has made it clear that in the present climate Cicero cannot afford to make further major investments in the UCP. In fact, the program is still subject to further cuts scheduled by the multiyear restructuring plan. Moreover, the dean has indicated that she distrusts plans, like certain forms of writing across the curriculum, that depend heavily on soft money and cannot be sustained or institutionalized in the long term. However, she does not micromanage, and she has promised you maximum flexibility in making internal decisions and reallocating funds cleverly within your budget. You can compete for university funds set aside for presidential initiatives such as those for instructional innovation, assessment, and interdisciplinary cooperation. Cicero closely controls opportunities to seek grants from alumni or corporations through the University Development Office, according to priorities it sets with the deans. Your dean has put major funding for a writing center on her list of requests for the upcoming Capital Campaign and high in her priorities for fundraising by LAS, but there is no immediate prospect and no guarantee of getting such gifts.

Your Key Challenge: Mobilizing Human Resources

The strict limits on your financial resources may seem daunting, but the most formidable problem you face involves a different kind of resource: people. Your background in the discipline of composition and rhetoric has prepared you well to tackle the challenges of modernizing the theory and pedagogy of the UCP and designing imaginative ways to deliver writing instruction. The problem is, you are not a one-person show. Who would actually implement such plans? Is the present teaching faculty both capable and willing? What role will the faculty, staff, and campus constituencies play in helping to develop the new plans? Who will work with faculty and administrators in other disciplines on cooperative ventures? Your ability to fulfill your charge depends ultimately on your abilities as a leader to marshal and deploy human resources effectively in service of your complex and sophisticated mission.

Human resources in a literal sense may refer to the number of personnel lines or dollars you have on budget, the types of employees, or the person hours you can tap for some task. But more fundamentally they are the talents and human potential represented among people who work for or with the program. Like any resource, these can be cultivated, expanded, and deployed efficiently and ethically; or they can be squandered, misdirected, underestimated, or diminished.[5] Human capital is a more crucial resource than dollars, technology, or even time. By investing energy, pride, and commitment in their work, people provide the knowledge, imagination, motivation, and skill without which the program cannot use other types of resources effectively, or at all.

When you first take stock of the program's human resources, you are somewhat daunted. At first sight, the composite teaching staff inherited largely from the old first-year English courses is wholly unprepared to deliver, much less plan and develop, the modern curriculum and innovative pedagogy called for in the dean's charge. Teaching assistants turn over constantly and require (without necessarily welcoming) intensive teaching and supervision. You can expect very few TAs to have a primary career interest in composition and rhetoric. As graduate students, their first loyalty and sense of obligation is to their home departments and their own graduate programs. They have little contact at present with the part-time instructors.

The part-time writing faculty has been teaching in an outdated paradigm with little scope for choice or experimentation in teaching and no role in governance or curriculum development. Most have master's degrees in creative writing or literature; only a few are familiar with composition as a discipline. Many are disaffected. Typically dedicated to their students, they have long felt undervalued and isolated, coming to campus only to teach their courses. Changes by the interim director have left them feeling ambivalent. They welcome improvements in working conditions and increased loads, but are anxious about the new demands and risks of unknown change. With numerous positions already lost from downsizing and the formation of the UCP, many of those remaining are angry and scared about their insecure future. Yet for both humane and practical reasons they can't simply be swept out and replaced en masse. They are your faculty.

The professorial faculty members have diverse disciplinary backgrounds, only one (the most inexperienced) a generalist in composition and rhetoric. They are likely to have major philosophical differences with you and one another. Although they helped to initiate the program and joined its faculty, they are uncertain what this will mean for their academic duties and future prospects; and they too have mixed feelings of enthusiasm, anticipation, fear, and doubt about what is to occur. Some who have been encouraging instructors to experiment are worried that an incoming director will simply impose a new "theory" on everyone, replacing one arbitrary paradigm with another.

The key challenge that faces you is to create strategies for melding this disparate group of people into a community of teachers with the skills and commitment to plan the changes, adapt to them, and work together to successfully implement new goals. As a leader, what steps can you take to enhance and mobilize the program's human resources? As a manager, how can you reallocate your base budget and tap into other accessible funds to enable these actions? As a program designer and director, how can you reorganize work roles and redeploy the program's human resources in an instructional plan to maximize their effectiveness? What complex responses can you expect from people in the program to these profound changes in their tasks, goals, qualitative expectations, and environment . . . and how might you handle such responses?

Strategic planning requires you to juggle multiple factors in a complex, dynamic environment and to think relationally, as a designer does. Too often, faculty administrators first decide what they want to do (a utopian vision or wish list) and then put their hands out for the money. In this case you are asked to work back and forth between two poles: *goals and possibilities,* on the one hand, *budget, resources, constraints, and conditions* on the other, focusing on the workforce available to carry out the functions of the program. In such relational thinking the conditions of the problem become generative; unexpected ideas and feasible plans will emerge from the interactions among all these factors. Seek synergies!

AUTHOR'S CASE COMMENTARY

This essay draws on ten years of writing program administration by myself and others at Syracuse University, but also on other sources including an administrative fellowship with the American Council of Education, to create an imaginary institution and its current situation. This fictional case captures an ambiguity between creating a "new" writing program—the ostensible task—and reforming one. Despite the institutional lack of a centralized, coherent "program," the workforce providing writing instruction has been in place for many years and must now adapt to the new situation. That fact makes human resources the central challenge in this case.

Cicero University is not Syracuse, but the two schools share many institutional features, including some typical problems among private universities with enrollment, tuition, faculty size, financial aid, and budget. I have borrowed or freely adapted a number of Syracuse's problem-solving strategies, especially Chancellor Kenneth Shaw's financial decisions, to characterize Cicero. For comparison, institutional information on Syracuse, including a history of its downsizing, is available. (See the Web page at http://www.syr.edu/aboutsu).

The program history and scenario are, however, heavily fictionalized: simplified, idealized, and reinvented for my purposes from the materials of my own experience and knowledge. Besides highlighting a cluster of problems around human resources, I wanted to locate the case firmly in today's academic scene, which is dramatically different from the one I myself faced as a WPA hired to develop a writing program in 1986. Composition and rhetoric has evolved further as a discipline, including shifts in its political and institutional relationships to English. But the most important change is that higher education itself is now well into a crisis whose severity has inaugurated deep, wrenching paradigmatic changes, utterly transforming the contexts in which any WPA might confront a similar challenge. As fiction, of course, this case has no ready-made solutions or "real-life" outcome. Instead, here are some concepts for analyzing the problem, followed by some corresponding strategies and tactics you might use.

Framing the Problem

To tackle such a complex challenge, it is often helpful to formulate the problem in a way that "selects things for attention and organizes them, guided by an appreciation of the situation that gives it coherence and sets a direction for action" (Schon 4–5). Such a frame (often metaphorical) allows you to organize the problem as a set of tasks for the program to accomplish under your leadership.

Task 1: Create Intellectual Capital and Make It Accessible

The program's knowledge base and practical expertise, as collectively represented in its members and sustained over time, comprise its intellectual capital. (Historical archives and libraries of program materials are also forms of intellectual capital.) You need to build intellectual capital by continually encouraging development of the abilities, knowledge, skills, and initiative of the workforce. At Cicero the part-time faculty, being the largest contingent of continuing teachers, is a key source of intellectual capital, but your plans must incorporate opportunities for TA, staff, and full-time faculty members all to both learn and contribute. To make the program's intellectual capital accessible, you need to develop policies and mechanisms for sharing it widely. Balance the proportion of new to continuing members in order to achieve and maintain a critical mass of expertise. But ensure that this collective knowledge remains dynamic by creating mechanisms for veterans, newcomers, and outsiders to challenge, assess, revise, refresh, and update it.

Task 2: Create Social Capital

Robert Putnam has recently analyzed the significance of social capital as "civic engagement" in the public life of a democracy. Similar ideas are influencing the corporate workplace, where they are tied to reorganizing work roles and work processes. Putnam defines social capital as "features of social organization such as networks, norms, and social trust that facilitate coordination and cooperation for mutual benefit" (67). You can foster the growth of social capital by planning structures and events that link people in common tasks and form social networks, primarily through face-to-face interactions where they can work together, express feelings, disagree and argue, and cope with the traumatic impact that accompanies any transformative change, even a positive one. Develop structures and channels of communication to extend and support face-to-face networks.

Task 3: Reorganize Work Roles and Work Processes to Fit a New Instructional Plan

The mission of a program must take concrete form as a flexible instructional plan that responds to your charge, taking into account current obligations, constraints, and future possibilities. Such a plan (always subject to negotiation, revision, and—after approval—continued evolution) encompasses the kinds of courses and academic services the program will offer or could provide, including whom they seek to serve and in what general formats. To be effective, such a plan can't be developed simply as a function of curriculum theory or ideals of pedagogical practice. Your plan must from the beginning take into consideration the human resources needed to develop it and incorporate the requisite changes in faculty and staff work roles. Developing the plan requires human resources in the form of collaboration and input from all faculty (including teaching assistants) and staff, as well as extensive consultation with campus constituencies, which they can help you to carry out. As program administrator, you will need to redesign faculty and staff work roles to address the greater range of tasks generated by the new mission; and restructure work processes more horizontally around diversely constituted, flexibly deployed teams. Diversify the roles and responsibilities of individuals (based on specific talents and investment in the program, rather than on their designated "status" or titles) to capitalize on the variety of human resources available. These measures will offer all members new freedoms and greater fluidity in their roles and their place in the social architecture of the program.

Task 4: Determine How to Fund Solutions

Imagine the UCP as relatively self-contained but interdependent with and adaptive to a larger environment, like a national economy within a global one or a regional ecology within a planetary ecosystem. The interdependencies are significant (e.g., alliances, trade, investments, a shared global environment), but you cannot simply tap resources freely from outside. You must budget for professional development and fund the curricular plan, augmenting internal funds only with those the program has explicitly acquired or been promised. You may also seek funding from known institutional sources and consider making proposals to the dean for initiatives that would depend on foregoing future scheduled reductions in your instructional budget. However, your plans, strategies, and proposals must be demonstrably fundable in the long term; reserve soft money for pilot projects and experiments.

Strategies, Tactics, Plans, and Possibilities

The following suggestions include some ideas I have used or seen used and others invented specifically for the case. Although arranged roughly in order of the four-part problem formulation, most strategies serve multiple purposes. Notes on human and financial resources for implementing these strategies are enfolded throughout. Choosing among these multiple possibilities (and funding and staffing them) requires you to make and justify difficult tradeoffs.

Intellectual Capital

Building It

Make an explicit, permanent, base-budgeted commitment to a continuing investment in *professional development*. Much else flows from or synergizes with this decision. A professional development (PD) program should involve and serve everyone in the UCP: graduate students/teaching assistants, part-time writing instructors, staff administrators, secretaries, and—not incidentally—the professorial faculty, whose mentoring and professional development are often neglected. Their needs (and your obligations to meet them) will be different in each case, but many PD opportunities can serve most or all groups. Often these learning benefits are a primary reason that people are working in the program at all. If you didn't have tuition benefits at Cicero for all employees, you'd have to fight for them.

The skills, knowledge, and experiences the UCP can provide its members include these and more:

- knowledge of composition/rhetoric as a discipline
- pedagogical theory and varied teaching practice
- research skills, e.g., archiving, interviewing, analyzing data
- assessment theory and skills, e.g., portfolios
- editing, grant writing
- advanced secretarial skills
- apprenticeship and experience as a leader/administrator; managerial and administrative skills (budgeting, supervising, etc.)
- access to and training in technology (likely, if not certain, from the facts of the case)

In investing time, energy, and money into PD that is more intensive and specialized (for groups), you will have to make hard choices. For example, what is the impact on the program's intellectual capital of time invested in intensive supervision of a TA who leaves the program in one to two years? What are the various costs of *not* doing it? How is this different from time invested in more advanced training (or travel) for a long-term part-time instructor? For a Ph.D. student with professional interests in composition and rhetoric? How will you balance the goal of maximizing intellectual capital in the whole program against other goals, like delivering effective instruction to students in the short term or supporting full-time research travel?

Some professional development options include:

- local travel to other institutions—exchange of visits; attending conferences
- in-house workshops, "conversations in composition," reading or study groups
- guest speakers
- graduate or undergraduate courses on campus
- conferences and special events put on by the program faculty and students
- "publishing" program members' writing in an in-house journal, occasional papers, Web site, etc.
- training and apprenticeship in special roles
- cross-training of staff
- teaching mentors, peer teaching partners
- workshops and mentoring to support professional presentations, writing for publication
- travel support for national conferences in composition/rhetoric
- electronic conversations and lists

Making It Accessible

The goal is to spread information and ideas as broadly as possible, in a timely way, to provide context for individuals' decisions and prompt their judgment, feedback, or input to programmatic decisions (improving these by multiple perspectives). Here are some ways:

- Follow an "open information" policy on program business, even budget (to the extent possible)

- Set up mechanisms like newsletters, a director's journal, a Web site, in-house conferences, and team presentations for regularly reporting activities and decisions by or about the program

- Create multiple channels of communication and exchange (see Social Capital)

- Provide easy access through centralized collections (or electronic means) to archived program materials, especially writings by teachers, to supplement or replace copying

- Work with librarians to increase the university's collections in composition and rhetoric, and put teachers in touch with the library's human resources; create your own small resource library

- Circulate and publicize program members' published writing

A professional development program must be complemented both by a system that rewards learning (and risk-taking) and also by assessment of teaching or other work (part of comprehensive program assessment). Each has major cost implications (allocations of human and financial resources; social costs and benefits). Consider, for example, the economic and social costs and benefits of a merit pay system for part-time instructors in conjunction with a system of assessing teachers' performance that incorporates peer review.

Implementing It with Human and Financial Resources

Who will carry out the work of professional development and how will you afford it? For such a central function, you need oversight from someone on your administrative staff. You have a half-time, undefined staff position (possibly upgradable to full-time in the future) and an assistant directorship; either can be used to appoint someone as a "professional staff development coordinator" to manage the programwide PD planning and coordinate an event calendar. You might want to divide more specialized PD duties between the two positions, e.g., PD for part-time instructors vs. TA orientation, teaching practicum, supervisions, etc. Other staff members may also play important roles in professional development, especially as they acquire new skills themselves.

The professorial faculty will be crucial to professional development, playing a unique role in connecting the program to developments in composition/rhetoric and their professional fields. But there are only a few of them, and they have other responsibilities as teachers and scholars. You need also to cultivate and draw on the talents of the rest of your faculty—professional writing instructors and advanced TAs—as leaders of PD initiatives and peer teachers of others in the program. Try to define and justify for the UCP a critical mass of personnel (total number); an ideal ratio of professorial faculty to TAs and part-time instructors; an ideal balance between veteran faculty and fresh, but inexperienced ones.

Other potential human resources for professional development include:

- undergraduate students (e.g., teaching technology to the faculty, making presentations on their learning experiences)
- faculty in other units at Cicero with relevant expertise
- experts at local educational institutions and in public schools
- professional staff on campus, including those in support units for academic computing, improvement of teaching, etc.
- Cicero's Human Resources department (offers workshops, seminars, etc., to staff, sometimes faculty; has experts you can tap for help)
- regional consortia or national networks of friends and colleagues in higher education
- consultants or speakers solicited from local corporations, nonprofit organizations
- electronic mentors
- national guest speakers (cost-shared with others on campus or at nearby institutions, borrowed when coming to the area or campus anyway, announced when appearing elsewhere)

Many of these people are available without cost or are willing to trade visits or services.

Travel to conferences is often the most difficult form of professional development to fund. Starting with a percentage of your operating budget provided by the dean for travel that doesn't account for nonprofessorial faculty, you must trade off with other expenses, consider how to lower its cost, cost-share with other sources (e.g., dean, Graduate School, Office of Research), and allocate it among program groups to balance goals (exposing teachers to the field, program visibility, research needs of faculty, etc.).

In general, prioritize your existing discretionary funds and seek soft money for heavy investments in PD up front, tapering to a steady commitment allocated from base budget some years into the program.

Social Capital

Fostering It

Creating social capital involves setting a delicate balance among rights, roles, rewards, and responsibilities that are both formal (contractually or organizationally defined) and informal. You need to maintain a certain level of program-sponsored activity to which all groups have obligations. For example, you could contractually require one hour per week from all part-time teachers and advanced TAs spent in a group format to discuss teaching or participate in professional development. Leaders from these sectors of the program can head the groups. For beginning TAs, this time commitment would be higher than that of advanced teachers, while professorial faculty would have different obligations associated with their generic mentoring or leadership roles. In addition, require something at regular intervals that involves the whole program: e.g., a teaching conference or professional development day once a semester. Other activities (e.g., task forces, curriculum groups, reading groups) that involve face-to-face meetings or other forms of communication and association need to be either paid (e.g., by a "section" or stipend), invitational and voluntary, or organized by the participants.

Both PD activities and the normal processes of planning, implementing, and assessing the program curriculum, pedagogy, and services should enhance social capital, if pursued in a team-based organization. Examples of structures, customs, or professional events that bind a teaching community include co-planning and co-teaching in various arrangements; peer teaching observations; participation in a curriculum team or WAC initiative; reading portfolios for teacher or student assessment; writing and editing a program journal or document; and making joint presentations at local or national conferences or other institutions.

Funding

Funding for social capital is already committed because the activity serves other purposes. It is, in that sense, a beneficial side effect of purposeful, interactive activity that should be deliberately cultivated. Exceptions (which you can't afford much of) are the occasional party or social occasion, and even those can be potluck, BYO, or hosted at homes. However, one large expense needs to be negotiated and funded by other levels of the university: habitable space and facilities (you can add small things like a microwave oven or coffee pot) that welcome and afford personal interactions among program members and with students. Check out the space you've been allocated to see what you have or might get.

Work Roles and Processes

Redesigning Them

New work roles will emerge from new goals and in conjunction with instructional plans (see below). These are anticipated in the list of skills and knowledge under intellectual capital and the group/team functions mentioned under social capital, which translate into roles like grant writer, editor, interviewer, group coordinator, portfolio reader, task force leader, and so on. In diverse teams that combine sector representatives as needed (professor, staff member, graduate student, undergraduate student, part-time instructor, outside faculty member, etc.), different people will have the talents to lead or co-lead and to play specialized parts.

In reorganizing work processes around functional, mixed teams, favor ad hoc groups with defined terms over standing committees. Basic program functions need continuing structures (e.g., the weekly teaching groups), but these change personnel regularly and can evolve constantly in their specific focus. Ad hoc groups planned for one to two years enable you to move your funds around regularly among different priorities and to respond quickly to opportunities and initiatives. Priorities can be articulated in a yearly "program agenda"—determined through a spring strategic planning process inviting proposals from all members and announced, discussed, and revised each fall. A program agenda has a conceptual theme, sensitive to current program issues and linked to higher-level university priorities; it organizes a list of planned activities, groups, and problem-solving loosely around this theme.

Funding Them

It is difficult but imperative to find ways to pay for nontraditional roles that directly serve the purpose of improving teaching and coordinating with others for related goals (see your mission). Unfortunately, institutions rarely recognize this need or facilitate it through their accounting procedures. In actual fact, you are very cost efficient, but you don't get back much of what you earn to make investments in quality. Look to your fifty-six-section bank to fund such functions: for example, to pay one section per semester for those leading the weekly teaching groups in a supervisory and professional development role. Look to your operating funds (including your small discretionary fund) and possible grants from institutional innovation or assessment funds as other, known sources for stipends. Ask the dean to push Cicero's Development Office to work with you on corporate and foundation grants. Scrounge: for example, save money by increased efficiency in using operating funds, or by "packing" sections to ensure that they are fully enrolled; and consider trying to earn money, e.g., by charging other units for special services they request.

The general principle is to maintain (despite downsizing) some discretionary edge above and beyond the tightly budgeted sections that Cicero doles out each year and to persuade the dean's office to accept this principle rather than "sweeping" every penny you save.

Instructional Plan

An instructional plan, which lays out the kinds of courses and instructional services you will offer, in what formats to what audiences, may create new teaching categories and functions in addition to the sorts of additional work roles already discussed (e.g., curriculum development, assessment). Both types of changes imply the need to redirect current instructional monies to new ends and to compensate your nonprofessorial faculty for duties beyond direct classroom teaching.[6]

Below are sketched some ideas and alternatives that are suggested by institutional facts and allocatable funds in this case, keeping particularly in mind your goals for building intellectual and social capital and the dean's charge to "add value" to other degree programs.

1. Reallocate the "bank" of fifty-six sections to create two new program roles:

   - "Program coordinators" (two sections per semester, assigned by application to part-time instructors or advanced TAs) to lead small weekly teaching groups (one coordinator per seven to ten teachers) and become a corps of program leaders; some can be paired with professorial faculty advisors for a TA teaching workshop/graduate practicum

   - "Writing consultants" (one or two sections/year, assigned any program teacher) whose consultative responsibilities are broad and flexible. Turn your lack of writing center space to advantage by making them roving "consultative teachers" and program ambassadors with specialized expertise. They constitute a versatile teaching corps with great potential for flexible deployment: they can provide teaching services directly to students (tutoring, workshops) or to other UCP teachers (visiting classes, co-planning courses, providing demonstrations, helping new teachers learn specific practices, etc.); they can be assigned to special funded projects or participate in pilots and teaching experiments; they can offer WAC services; they can mentor new teachers.

2. You have enough courses in writing and composition/rhetoric theory that by redefining and sequencing them (moving the second required writing course to sophomore year) you could construct a minor, which could be very efficient for other units since it would build on requirements students already fulfill. Credits could accrue also from projects like a culminating portfolio in the discipline, writing associated with co-op programs and field-specific internships, and so on. The minor or, alternately, a "certificate in writing," could be generic (LAS) or specific to a professional school or major.

3. A variation would be to construct various possible interdisciplinary programs:

   - a UCP "writing arts" major, in cooperation with creative writing faculty and faculty from public communications

   - joint minors or majors built around literacy, communication, or language arts, allowing students to combine writing with English literature, creative writing, reading (education), speech, visual arts, and/or public communications

   - five-year degrees that yield a professional master's with a minor or certificate in professional writing/rhetoric or a second, professional writing MA

4. Despite the dean's suspicion of writing across the curriculum, the new general education plan offers some possibilities, especially if that plan carries the potential for redirecting instructional funds to the UCP. If endorsed by the general education committee, you might be able to argue effectively to the dean and provost for keeping the UCP instructional funds currently planned for reduction as the student body shrinks, shifting them to interdisciplinary courses, support for writing-intensive courses, links, or UCP services (e.g., faculty workshops) that will encourage incorporation of writing skills throughout the curriculum. (See Louise Wetherbee Phelps, "Exploiting Synergies" at http://wrt.syr.edu/synergies.html) Two elements can make the plan more persuasive. Can you demonstrate that professional development and cross-training make your entire faculty versatile and multiskilled, ready to be redeployed to new tasks as Cicero's needs evolve? Can you design

a plan for writing across the curriculum that is permanently cost-contained, for example, by designating a pool of sections for a capped number of rotating, three-year projects?

By now you should have figured out—and perhaps even persuaded your dean—that human resources are scarce and precious, and not only because funding for them is limited. You need not just sections (funded slots you can put toward different instructional purposes), but a critical mass (headcount) of skilled people. Without it, when you have unexpected opportunities or windfalls of new monies, there is no one to capitalize on them because your teaching staff is fully deployed at the maximum load they are permitted . . . or because available personnel lack the needed skills. This is why developing human resources is a wise investment: it grows intellectual and social capital and adds value.

Notes

1. Among the forces transforming the climate for higher education were a national economic recession; rapid development and spread of new information technologies; industrial and government restructuring in the United States to adjust to a global economy; a sustained, severe decline in public funding for higher education (affecting both state investments in education and also federal student loans and research grants); and changing demographics, including a dip in the birthrate affecting eighteen year olds going to college.

2. The provost has approved in principle a plan to place faculty lines partly or wholly in major, stable academic programs (often interdisciplinary) like women's studies and the UCP. Some may also be assigned to such programs as part-time "affiliated" faculty for varying periods of time. The LAS dean serves on a university committee set up by the provost to develop revised guidelines, procedures, and contractual arrangements to protect such faculty members from the potential negative impact on promotion and tenure decisions of their nontraditional appointments. However, these new arrangements will require time for planning and negotiation, particularly those reassigning current faculty. Meanwhile, UCP faculty have tenure-line appointments in a regular department and are reassigned for 50 to 100 percent of their time to the UCP.

3. This money constitutes "operating" funds and can be reallocated flexibly.

4. The dollars represented by these sections can be reallocated only as "salary" for instruction.

5. Like all metaphors, the strategic frame that treats personnel as "human resources" has significant practical and moral limits. For example, by itself it cannot account for academic freedom, motivate or suggest shared governance structures, define appropriate authority, or help an administrator to deal sensitively with sexism or racism in the workplace. Administrators there-

fore need to employ and integrate multiple, simultaneous frames if they are to make effective use of what any one metaphor can teach them. Viewing people as resources makes sense in a bureaucratic (corporate or managerial) frame. But leaders need to balance this perspective on faculty or staff with others (e.g., collegiality, campus politics, diversity concerns, laws, governmental regulations, unionized labor).

6. Full-time professorial faculty already have contractual obligations for service, which need to be specified for this type of academic unit. Further administrative duties would affect load. See, for example, Syracuse University's Writing Program Promotion and Tenure Guidelines (http://wrt.syr.edu/wrt/pub/miscpub.html).

8 Writing Across the Curriculum

Joan A. Mullin
University of Toledo

While some students may have the opportunity to meet challenges associated with establishing new writing-across-the-curriculum programs, it is more likely that a new director will be taking over an existing program, one that has already gone through several phases of development. Such programs offer unique challenges that need to be met by tapping into institutional memory, reconstructing the context in which decisions were made and in which they are currently being made, and by negotiating the delicate balances between administration and faculty positions, morale, and goals.

The Problem

In this case, a thriving WAC program that had been established through fairly collaborative agreements between administration and faculty, and which had eventually been supported by both groups over years of budget cuts, union votes, and pressures for accountability and increased production, hit a potential breaking point: Beset by more cuts, by a top-down decision to move to semesters and its concomitant directive to do so by recreating the entire university curriculum in less than a year and a half, with animosity rising over what will be dropped from the curriculum, which disciplines will lose and which will win, the WAC program had to prove that it was worth keeping. Your task is to study the context, sift through the pieces of information, and devise a plan which would convince department faculty representatives to vote in favor of including a strong WAC requirement as part of the new semester curriculum. The problem is complicated by the fact that any program favored by administration is in danger of being voted down by a continually demoralized faculty. You want a vote in which faculty demonstrate their continued commitment and support—elements instrumental to WAC's success on this campus.

The Site of the Problem (Ten Years Ago)

The University of Toledo, part of the state system in Ohio, is a comprehensive, urban, research university in northwest Ohio. The main campus has six colleges—Arts and Sciences, Business, Education, Engineering, Pharmacy, and Law—along with a sister community college located five minutes away. Detroit is forty-five miles to the north, the University of Michigan forty miles to the northwest, Bowling Green twenty miles to the southwest, and Ohio State about one hundred fifty miles due south. The geography is important here because during the time this case study begins, UT, though long considered a second-tier school unable to maintain competition with the surrounding institutions, had grown beyond everyone's expectations. Long neglected financially by the state, considered the not-so-friendly college-up-the-block by Toledo residents, and slated for no more than 17,000 students, at the time of this case study UT enrollment exceeds 25,000.

Several factors make UT the choice of presidential scholars and students from across the country: faculty who engage in public and prominent research; the large university in a small city (urban) setting; the convenient geographical location (between Midwest and East Coast), and the cost of the school. The 7 percent international student population, largely from the Middle East, Malaysia, and China, and 11 percent overall students of color population adds to the cultural diversity and multiple backgrounds represented in classrooms. Many of the UT students are first-generation college students. Of those, a good number are from rural areas in northwest Ohio or around the country; many more (22 percent) are nontraditional students. The city of Toledo offers these students a town environment without the big-city confusion and congestion, as well as the ambience of neighborhoods, a world-class museum, symphony, zoo, and extensive river and Lake Erie waterfronts.

By far the largest college with eighteen departments, Arts and Sciences felt the press of increased diversity in student populations and the problems that result three years before I came on campus. General education requirements did not seem to sufficiently prepare students for advanced work, and students at all levels seemed equipped with widely varying skills. When faculty researched the problem on campus and across the country, they targeted two areas to investigate: critical thinking and writing across the curriculum. After inviting leaders in each field to campus, faculty agreed that while WAC included critical thinking, the reverse was not necessarily true. They moved to lay the groundwork for a WAC program. The state board of regents, not sympathetic to supporting UT, did not readily part with funds for new programs, and only grudgingly trickled money into the existing programs that were burgeoning with students. Thus, much-sought-after resources were vied for and coveted: faculty lines, clerical staff, physical space, supply budgets, travel funds. In this 1987 environment, I was hired to start a writing center within the College of Arts and Sciences, with an eye toward eventually expanding it into a writing-across-the-curriculum program. My letter of confirmation from the college office informed me that while my salary was built into their base budget, there were, unfortunately, no additional funds for office space, supplies, clerical personnel, or tutors; I was to be, my letter suggested "a presence on campus" for the first year. I took the job anyway. I figured, since they hired me, they must want a successful writing center and would provide for one. I was naive.

The Program

History

In 1987, the College of Arts and Sciences (CAS) voted for a writing center because of an enthusiastic faculty and a supportive, forward-looking dean. The CAS faculty council voted unanimously to establish a WAC program after a writing center was in place to support all the writing that would result. When I was hired (straight out of graduate school), I already knew that the writing center/WAC program would be freestanding within the college. Any attempt to locate it—or me—in a department would be seen as favoritism: a bid by that department to obtain funding, faculty, and resources. By remaining freestanding, I avoided the day-to-day politics of jealousy, disciplinarity, and suspicion that most writing center, WAC, or writing program directors experience in departments. As it was, there was no consideration of writing as a discipline within the department, and it was the dean and sympathetic English department chair who, behind the scenes, enabled me to teach the first writing theory course on campus that winter.

However, though avoiding intradepartmental competition for funds, hires, and space, I did not avoid suspicion on the college level. While the CAS voted for the writing center and WAC, that did not mean faculty wanted to see dollars go to "another new faddish program"— dollars which might otherwise be spent for a new faculty member in their department, or on computers or travel funds. While faculty were openly curious about who I was and what I promoted, and while many met with me and listened to what I had planned, just as many were, in the words of a later WAC convert, "prepared to fold my arms across my chest and watch you fail."

Through the grace of the college dean, upon my arrival I was given an office in the Honors Program suite to share with an emeritus faculty member, and was fortunate to be mentored by the then-head of the Honors Program and his secretary. They, along with the college office, scrounged up a chair, desk, and a box of basic supplies for me. Since the job started in June, I spent all summer tracking down and talking to every administrator on campus, every department chair, and any faculty who would chat. The purpose was to find out

- what culture I had stepped into,
- what their expectations about writing were,
- how they perceived their students,
- how they talked about their students' writing abilities,
- how knowledgeable they were about current WAC practices and theory.

The answer to this last question proved easy to formulate: Faculty knew very little about WAC. As a whole, they expected me to magically come in and fix all the writing problems—without their involvement or effort. These conversations emphasized the importance of my primary directive to establish a writing center (WC) since it was clear I would have to prove that such an office could "do the job." However, since I was hired to do so with an eye toward beginning a WAC program, I never separated the objectives of the new office from those of WAC. During these many initial conversations, I began to casually talk about some of the new WAC practices used in the particular discipline of the faculty member with whom I spoke.

After the summer and several conversations with the dean in which I outlined my plans, hopes, and wishes about the writing center and WAC, I got a typewriter, then a computer, and, by September and the start of school, found myself with

- the entire suite of Honors offices (they moved out),
- a temporary budget through the college,
- a half-time secretary,
- a graduate assistant through the College of Education,
- permission to teach a writing theory course to train tutors during the winter quarter, and
- permission to open the writing center in the third week of the course.

I didn't know how impossible all this was—so it happened as planned. During that first year, with the assistance of only a graduate student to whom all this theory and practice were new, I

- designed publicity (brochures and bookmarks),

- sent memos and explanations about the writing center to faculty and administrators; solicited students for the new, second-quarter writing theory course (at least those who would make good tutors),

- taught an introduction to literature course (though teaching was not part of my contract) and taught the first writing theory course on campus,

- designed a protocol for the tutors,

- developed forms for tutor reports and for students who use the center; developed a database to collect information; collected, copied, and created tutor materials; and visited classes to explain the writing center.

All of this was done by talking about writing as discipline specific and about using writing as a pedagogical tool to improve critical thinking and learning. Thus, even when I gave class presentations in composition classes, and while they were geared to students, they also served to educate the faculty member about why writing was important in every discipline. That first year, I began giving college-sponsored presentations about writing in many other disciplines besides English. I asked faculty whom I had contacted during the summer who already were incorporating writing into their pedagogy to join me during these talks so that their colleagues would see that someone they knew found these methods successful. Some chairpersons (whom I had met during the summer) encouraged their faculty to ask for a class presentation, or to send their syllabi to the center or to consult with me about new departmental courses. These activities went a long way toward establishing a WAC program and a set of supportive colleagues.

By the time the dean asked the chairpersons in Arts and Sciences to draw up a WAC proposal—my second year—a lot of groundwork had been established. That year, in addition to working with thirteen (male—but that's another story) chairpersons on the proposal, I also linked my first tutor to an education class. The faculty member wanted to experiment with journals and writing as pedagogy, but was wary of the increased workload; so I gave her a tutor who sat in the class, worked within the class, tutored outside the class, and acted, as the faculty member noted, as her "teaching mirror." In addition to sitting in on the Arts and Sciences dean/chairpersons monthly meetings—and getting to know the politics and personalities within the college—I also began to serve on various committees across campus, thus making more faculty contacts. By the third year, in addition to a busy writing center (with a new full-time assistant director, two more computers, and a full-time secretary), the college had a WAC program with implementation steps in place, a tutor-attached program, and a WAC committee with representatives from the three areas (Natural Sciences, Social Sciences, and Arts and Humanities—we later split the last category in two). Part of the implementation plan developed by the chairs (at this point in our history, still considered faculty advocates) included two volunteered or appointed faculty members from each of the eighteen departments to act as WAC liaisons. This was the first program that included faculty representation at all stages of its development: from the original investigation of writing centers and WAC within the college, to the consensus to start a writing center by the Arts and Sciences council, to my interview by faculty groups across campus, to the creation of a plan by faculty/chairs, to the final education of liaisons who would then help shape the rest of the WAC program within their own departments.

Liaisons consisted of faculty curious about or sympathetic to WAC, but they were also chosen because they proved to be influential voices in their departments. To facilitate their understanding of WAC, I concentrated on:

- providing workshops with these thirty-six faculty (two from each department),
- working one-on-one with them to establish writing-intensive classes for their departments (each department had to have an upper- and lower-level course in place), and
- developing through them working relationships with the department.

This was not always easy. The former chair of the art department still recalls how "nasty" (her word) her department acted when I came in to answer their concerns. By then, having spent time going from department meeting to department meeting, I was used to being challenged and knew most of the objections that would be raised (although one never quite gets used to academic nastiness). At another faculty presentation on WAC, one of the biology liaisons, "Peter," said, "Prove this works." The problem was that at that time, there weren't a lot of quantitative or qualitative studies which did prove WAC encouraged critical thinking!

Another problem came from the statisticians—including those in the English department—who worried that a WAC requirement might be constructed which would place a burden on the departments' ability to offer classes for their majors. They bluntly asked, "Now we have to offer WAC classes too?" In addition, since proposal committee members wanted to require students to complete composition classes before reaching junior status, the composition staff panicked. A common myth circulated in the English department that too many students put off taking composition until their junior and senior years. Faculty claimed composition classes would be swamped with such a WAC requirement, and that there wouldn't be enough (part-time) instructors or a large enough budget to offer courses to meet the demand.

It was also argued that since we were proposing that WAC courses be capped at twenty-one students, faculty teaching other courses would have to "pick up" the students who would be cut out of the WAC classes. Departments claimed they could not offer enough courses to meet this proposed cap and the expected student demand for WAC courses without ignoring their own departmental course needs. Two rejoinders to these arguments were easily constructed: (1) I always asked that WAC courses not be *new* courses, but already established, in fact, *required* courses, which were differently taught, thereby putting the burden on no one person and on no department; (2) I admitted that faculty teaching non-WAC required courses would have to make room for students needing the classes; however, ideally, they too would teach WAC classes some day and, on a rotational basis, the faculty loads would eventually average out. While this is not a strong argument, it is difficult to protest against publicly.

To gain more ammunition against these objections, I asked the statistically gifted sociologist on the WAC committee to run some numbers with the Office of Institutional Research. He found out two valuable pieces of information: *When we ran the figures for who put off taking composition until their junior or senior years, we came up with—over five years—fewer than two dozen students.* All were either transfer students or international students working on their language skills. We also looked at the current enrollment and divided that over time, figuring out the total number of WAC courses needed for that number of students. Then, based on the number of majors in departments, we determined how many courses each department would have to offer at each level (lower-division and upper-division) in order to provide range and opportunity for those students. *It averaged out to one course at each level for most departments, three to four courses for larger departments, and five courses for two departments: psychology and communications.* That seemed "do-able."

After answering the objections in meeting after meeting, after sitting through two Arts and Sciences Council meetings—one of which included a personal trial by fire that instilled in me more patience than I ever wanted, and one that contained a twenty-minute argument over whether to use *shall* or *will*—the WAC requirement passed as follows:

- each student would have to complete Composition I with a C or better;
- each student would have to pass Composition II;
- after completing his or her writing courses, each student would take two writing intensive courses—at least one of which had to be in his or her major;
- courses would be capped at twenty-four students per class.

The purpose behind these requirements proved sound: students would, theoretically, take two writing courses their first year, and one each year thereafter. Faculty did not insist upon a senior-year writing requirement because capstone courses were being instituted; these would, by their nature, be writing intensive.

Assessment and Production

Initial assessment of WAC courses involved writing-intensive course approval (carried out by the WAC committee—to which members were committed on three-year rotating schedules). Disciplines developed their own classroom evaluations for students. Evaluations were collected in the writing center and compiled at the end of each quarter. As the number of writing-intensive courses increased, so did use of the writing center and the use of tutors linked to classes. Tutor evaluations, as well as the faculty evaluations of tutors and the student evaluations of tutor-linked classes, were collected at the end of each quarter. With encouragement, faculty began to do in-class research on the effectiveness of WAC:

- a qualitative study, complete with pre- and post-tests, was performed by the College of Pharmacy showing that WAC made a significant difference in students' attitudes toward writing;
- a political scientist showed a positive relationship between those who used the writing center for her WAC class and the grades each received;
- faculty cited tangible improvement in students projects, test scores, and writing skills;
- a modest multiyear portfolio project began which aimed at collecting and assessing students' writing over a four-year period.

In addition to these forms of evaluation, evidence of WAC's influence existed in the form of publications in various disciplines by our faculty who wrote about WAC strategies and theories. There also resulted a growth of interdisciplinary WAC courses, and a culture of faculty development grew around WAC. Free lunches were given for faculty at which colleagues would discuss how they developed, taught, and evaluated their writing-intensive courses. Six years after the initial WAC discussions began, the program was recognized by administration and faculty alike as a success.

Over the Years

The WAC program flourished. At first only the faculty liaisons taught the writing-intensive classes, but gradually other faculty became curious. Students spoke positively about the classes, and the faculty who taught them didn't complain. Biology is a real case in point. Peter begrudgingly taught the first WAC class in the department—and loved it. He can speak more eloquently about his transformation than I can, but that is exactly what he considers it—a transformation. He gained a new enthusiasm for his subject and his students within the student-centered class; he also gained a new respect for their knowledge and abilities as he opened his classroom to their voices. Alas, Peter was having too much fun. A colleague—one of the department's star researchers—decided that if Peter could teach these classes, so could he. So Fred asked to teach the courses—and was an instant convert to WAC. Both he and Peter began to share techniques and conversations about teaching—and they began to develop a second upper-division required class for their majors; Fred decided that the graduate students needed a WAC requirement too. The next I heard, there were six biology faculty standing in line to teach the WAC course!

Each department was to have developed at least two writing-intensive courses; for the college that would be a total of thirty-six classes. By the sixth year of the program, the committee had approved 145 classes and the list continued to grow. Likewise, it was thought that only thirty-six faculty would ever teach WAC courses, but by the end of the sixth year, over one-third of the four-hundred-plus college of Arts and Sciences faculty had taught a WAC class. We began developing an online "WAC-STACK" of syllabi, commentary, and activities.

Faculty support was as evident as student support: both groups sought more WAC courses, recognizing the positive effects on learning, critical thinking, and communication. One math professor notified me that since he was going to have a tough quarter one year, he would not teach any WAC courses. He then called me up and asked if I offered a twelve-step program for those addicted to WAC: In planning his courses, he found he couldn't help himself from inserting writing activities throughout the syllabi.

Contrary to earlier fears—that departments could not provide enough WAC courses to ensure that students would be able to complete their degree and WAC requirement in four years—few students ran into that difficulty. Those few who achieved senior status without taking a second WAC course were found to have ignored their advisor's advice; they often were able to be "grandfathered" because they had taken a course which, while taught as a writing-intensive course, had not as yet been officially approved as a WAC course by the committee. Needless to say, the program was claimed a success in the College of Arts and Sciences and was already working its way unofficially across other colleges. The administration set up a university committee to institute WAC across the entire university curriculum. Unfortunately, within a few months, another decision came down from the administration: Our institution would join a growing statewide trend and move from quarters to semesters. Administrators gave faculty less than two years to completely change the curriculum.

The Problem: Ten Years Later

Actually, we had almost two-and-a-half years, but the first year sent everyone into shock, and faculty protested the fast track. Not only that, but others' experience told us that schools which switched to semesters lost students the first two years. We could not afford this, quite literally. Gutted again by the legislature and suffering like other schools from changing demographics, UT's student population in the last six years was reduced from 26,000 to barely 21,000; predictions were that next year we would be lucky to hit 20,000. After conversion, we might well go as low as 17,000. Such figures affect state support, faculty load, salaries, and hiring. Already every department was down a minimum of two faculty members; some departments had not had as many as eleven faculty members replaced over the past several years. No massive hirings were promised for the future.

So began a series of "dark years" pitting faculty against almost anything administration wanted: increased workload for current faculty was the sore point. Everyone complained that we were already down to the bone and had every drop of blood squeezed out two years ago during budget cuts. We could no longer do more with less; yet that is what we were asked to do. Everyone began scrambling to avoid increased assignments, and everyone began hungrily looking at each others' programs and budgets.

Departments which never worked together found commonality as they argued over workload. The word *strike* surfaced too often. Worse yet, because semesters would offer fewer opportunities for students to take a course, more general education courses would have to be taught by faculty who, over the years, had developed their own specialty courses and areas: these specialty courses would now be subject to intense scrutiny. Each department had to review its general education requirements, and the word finally came down: All course offerings would have to be reduced by one third. Therefore, each area (e.g., social sciences) formerly requiring three courses would only be allowed to require two. Those course requirements are the bread and butter of every department, besides, of course, being curricularly appropriate for a well-rounded college student.

The WAC program always fell somewhere in between a supported faculty program and an administrative idea. The official calendar conversion document offered comfort in that it stated that the process "should not be used to reduce the university's commitment to initiatives already in place such as WAC, Multi-cultural Studies, and Women's Studies." Nonetheless, everyone's discipline, course, and program was at risk, and loyalties were taxed.

"Discussions" broke out among the sciences, humanities, and foreign language faculty—each logically defending the need for their course requirements. I was informed by the Calendar Conversion Committee of the Arts and Sciences Council that since all course requirements had to be reduced, and since the requirement for WAC was two courses beyond composition (which would not be reduced—two semesters would be required), the WAC requirement should be reduced by one-third. However, since we couldn't ask students to take a fraction of a course, the WAC requirement would be reduced by half. The committee regretted the decision, but they had no other alternative, fearing that, with a cap of twenty-four students on WAC classes, we would not be able to provide enough courses for students so they could complete the requirement in a "timely manner." This issue—completion of degree in four years—was being used as a student recruitment tool by our competitors at other universities who promised that students would graduate in four years—thus saving the time and money they might spend at other institutions. Since administration sees us as an enrollment-driven university (i.e., our state subsidy depends on how many full-time students we enroll and retain), faculty feared that requirements which prolonged student matriculation would eventually hurt departmental budgets and faculty lines.

If this proposed cut to the program went through, the heart of WAC would be ripped out; the program would never grow, nor even continue to be supported. It would be an easy step from reducing the requirement to saying the program was now ineffective and should be scrapped. I called the chair of the Curriculum Committee, and committee members (most teachers and supporters of WAC); they were sorry but saw no alternative. Since the entire (seventy-five-member) Arts and Sciences council must vote on every decision, I asked to speak to the council. My request was granted:

If, as I did, you had only five days to prepare and ten minutes to talk to the faculty, what would you do?

> Would you enlist the help of administration? How?
>
> Of faculty? How?
>
> Of other campus populations?
>
> Would you approach the executive committee?
>
> What role might the WAC committee play? The liaisons?
>
> What would be the central focus of your talk to faculty? The importance of the program? The numbers? The money? The effects to date of the program?

Plan your ten-minute talk.

AUTHOR'S CASE COMMENTARY

The objections to WAC continuing in its current form seemed not to be related to whether the faculty supported the program or whether WAC "worked," but whether in retaining the program in its present form enough WAC courses could be offered. Three concerns emerged:

- that semesters would tax the course load of each department's full-time faculty;
- that, since departmental course requirements had to be compressed, faculty would have to give up content in order to concentrate on writing;
- that if courses couldn't be offered often enough, students wouldn't be able to graduate in four years and would thus go elsewhere for their education.

The second claim especially concerned me because I thought we had long ago won the battle over content versus writing by convincing faculty that they should incorporate writing *into*, not in addition to, their teaching of content. So one strategy I could have adopted was to explain again that WAC courses should enhance the teaching of content, not be a burden to the course. I considered choosing a couple of courses from each area (sciences, social sciences, humanities, and fine arts) which demonstrate this by passing out examples of syllabi from before a course was part of WAC and after it was made writing intensive. I thought that by attacking this objection, the first concern would also be cleared up: there wouldn't be a workload issue if writing were made *part* of those courses normally required in the department.

I called the WAC committee and explained our situation to them, asking that they be present to support my argument during the council meeting. I contacted all the WAC faculty I could, asking them to do the same, and contacted the dean of Arts and Sciences who fully supported the continuation of WAC, asking for her presence at the meeting (though I realized that administrative support could also ignite faculty anger at being asked to do more). However, the more I thought about arguing for the efficacy of the program, the more I decided I would be preaching to the choir: clearly, a majority of the faculty supported WAC. However, if the numbers didn't work out, any pedagogical, theoretical, or ethical argument I offered would be moot. I decided to run the numbers.

With three days left, I asked the college office to give me the number of students in each major, including the number of undecideds, first year through junior year. I also asked institutional research to give me the number of students enrolled in each WAC class during an average quarter and the number of students projected to enroll in Arts and Sciences over the next three years. I used these numbers to answer the following questions:

- Faculty were afraid that the twenty-four-student cap would prevent students from finding a seat in a WAC class: Were all WAC classes taught over the last two years filled to capacity?

- Given the present number of students in the college and the projected enrollment, how many WAC courses would the college have to offer in order to meet student demand?

I was ready to concede defeat if the numbers showed that we did not have enough faculty if we could not offer classes with current resources. I would then resort to the pedagogical, theoretical, and ethical arguments—and plead.

Much to my surprise, I saw that few WAC classes were filled to capacity; in fact, according to records, many WAC classes had imposed departmental caps of twelve, fifteen, or twenty students, and these courses were still not necessarily enrolled to capacity. Given the actual caps set by departments, 16 percent of the seats were not filled. If each of those classes had a twenty-four-student cap, 37 percent of the classes would have been available for more students!

Curious about the other data I had collected, I averaged the total number of WAC classes taught over the last three years, and then, because in the semester system course availability would be reduced by one-third, I reduced that number by one-third, assuming this would correspond to the number of courses departments could be expected to offer. I multiplied that number of courses by two separate figures: twenty-four (the number of seats that should be available in every WAC class) and by the number of seats available if every department kept their own current caps on the WAC classes. Given the projected enrollment for the next three years, it was clear that if a cap of twenty-four were maintained, we would have more than enough seats available in WAC classes—without offering any more classes than a one-third reduction of current offerings would produce. I then played with the caps currently imposed by departments and discovered that even if these were to be maintained, given the projected drop in enrollment, we would still have just enough seats in every course to accommodate students (though, admittedly, it might be a scheduling nightmare for students). All of the above numbers were put into bar graphs, pie charts, and line graphs for the presentation.

That day, I began by explaining to the faculty that I was not going to argue the pedagogical or theoretical benefits of the WAC program—that their enthusiasm and support were evidenced by the number of courses approved (I gave the number) and the number of faculty participants involved (I gave that number). However, while we agreed that the program proved beneficial, I said, they had a right to their concerns about whether students would be able to complete the WAC requirement in four years and whether maintaining the requirement would produce faculty overload. Then, with the help of an overhead projector, I launched into my explanations of the numbers I had cranked over the last few days. Time went all too quickly and only a few faculty had the opportunity to respond (positively) to my plea to maintain the two-course requirement; the chair reminded them to discuss the issue in their department and to be ready to vote in two weeks.

During the following two weeks, I sent a memo to chairs, WAC liaisons, and supporting faculty enumerating the number of courses their departments would have to offer on the semester system. On the day of the vote, the chair of the Arts and Sciences curriculum committee complimented me for mustering all the forces—and didn't believe the blank look I gave him in return. Nonetheless I was not prepared for the overwhelming faculty support at the meeting: testimonials to the improvement WAC made in the quality of thinking and writing; explanations of how WAC made our students competitive in job markets; a suggestion that we establish a *more* stringent requirement, not reduce the current one; and, finally, letters from students claiming that "not only are WAC courses valuable for their own sake, their benefits enrich other courses as well"; that in WAC classes, "I've formed rewarding relationships with faculty who served as writing mentors." The vote, not quite unanimous, was overwhelmingly in favor of maintaining the current requirement.

9 Budgeting and Politics: Keeping the Writing Center Alive

Linda S. Houston
Ohio State University Agricultural Technical Institute

The Writing Lab at The Ohio State University Agricultural Technical Institute started as a table in the Math Lab. It now houses fifteen computers and a central study table, and is run by ten to fifteen peer tutors. You have just been hired as the director. A new set of guidelines will need to be established as, while the Writing Lab is not networked, the addition of a main server to the system at the college will require the Writing Lab to connect in order to have access to software used at the university. The key challenge will be to continue strengthening the peer tutoring and the sense of the lab as a place where students feel "at home," while at the same time finding funding and expertise to keep up with the pedagogy and technology.

Institution Overview

History

The Ohio State University Agricultural Technical Institute (ATI), established in 1969, is a two-year technical college accredited by the North Central Association of Schools and Colleges, with a statewide mandate to provide comprehensive agricultural education. The college, an administrative unit of The Ohio State University College of Food, Agricultural and Environmental Sciences, offers an Associate of Applied Science degree (A.A.S.) and an Associate of Science degree (A.S.) which is designed to prepare individuals to transfer to a Bachelor of Science degree program. The A.A.S. program requires students to complete 49 hours of general and basic courses which include the sciences, mathematics, social sciences, and English, while the A.S. degree requires 55 hours of general and basic courses which are directly transferable to The Ohio State University. ATI has a population of 850 students and is located in Wooster, Ohio, a small town of 22,000. There are thirty-six full-time faculty and thirty-nine part-time faculty. Each year the number of part-time faculty increases while the number of full-time faculty remains the same or decreases because the administration believes that a part-time faculty is "the way of the future." There are two full-time faculty members in the English program for 850 students; one of them is a reading specialist, and fall and winter quarters she does not teach the writing courses, so there are seven adjuncts who are supervised by the Writing Lab/Writing Program coordinator while she teaches courses and coordinates the tutors in the Writing Lab.

While students are required by the Board of Regents to complete course work in the sciences and the humanities, the Writing Program and the Writing Lab had not necessarily been the priority of the thirty-six full-time faculty nor the administration. The importance of the Writing Program, and more recently the Reading Program, is continually emphasized through assertive requests for budget considerations, and thus the program becomes a political issue. In 1988, the administration appointed a committee to define the "attributes of a graduate" of ATI. The section which reads "each graduate should be able to comprehend, to write and speak with clarity, and to read and think critically" served to increase the support of faculty and staff for communications skills. While budget issues still plague the Writing Program and the Writing Lab, writing across the curriculum and the introduction of English and reading courses have been supported by the faculty in recent years. For example, after faculty lobbied for twenty years for a mandatory reading course, a required reading course was established for students testing 60 or below in the Degrees of Reading Power inventory.

The focus of the two-year college is undergraduate education. As mentioned earlier, there are two programs: the Associate of Applied Science degree, which has been developed for students preparing to enter middle management careers in agriculture; and the Associate of Science degree, which prepares individuals to transfer to a Bachelor of Science degree program. Regular faculty have a 100 percent teaching appointment, but since ATI is part of a larger system, faculty are required, in order to secure tenure and promotion, to engage in scholarly activity (which includes publications and presentations) and service which includes professional organizations.

Mission

The mission of ATI is to serve people by providing educational programs leading to the associate degrees with primary focus in the business and science of agriculture, horticulture, and the environment. The emphasis is on applying technology for related jobs within a technical area; developing skills and abilities in interpersonal relationships, leadership, communications, problem-solving, and critical thinking; and improving human relations and global understanding. Therefore, the challenge for the Writing Lab is to stay current technologically as well as pedagogically.

Computer Facilities

For a small college, there is an abundance of quality computer facilities, the least of which is the Writing Lab. While there are sixty-eight networked computers in various locations, the Writing Lab has fifteen IBM-compatible computers, usually moved to the lab when abandoned in other areas, with eight dot-matrix printers which jam regularly. At some point, when all the computers are networked to a main server, the Writing Lab will be connected. At this time, as a result of the tutors who are empowered to make decisions for running the lab, the Writing Lab is not connected to the Internet or e-mail since tutors believed that providing access to such features would make the lab less of a "writing center" where students could receive assistance in their college assignments. The Writing Lab is the only computer lab with qualified peer tutors and thus, for writing purposes, continues to have 2,000 visits each fall and winter quarter, with fewer visits during spring when students are on internships. The challenge of the lab coordinator regarding technology is to advocate for improved technology and trained tutors.

Students

The student body at ATI is composed of approximately 850 students. There are no graduate students on campus; therefore, there are no teaching assistants or Writing Lab assistants besides peer tutors. Unlike the student body at other two-year colleges, 80 percent of students are twenty years old and younger. The student body is 99 percent white, 26 percent female, with 97 percent from Ohio. Sixty-eight percent of the students are considered at-risk and over one hundred students have documented learning disabilities. There is very little diversity on the campus.

For a small campus, there are excellent student services, most supplied by Title IV grant money. The services include personal and academic counseling, tutoring in all courses through individual work and study groups, the Writing Lab, the Math Lab, computer labs, and disabilities services. The Library Learning Resources Center at the college is 6,864 square feet housing approximately 19,000 volumes, 595 periodical subscriptions, 558 films and videos, and thousands of vertical file items and microform pieces; patrons also have access to millions of other sources through the online catalogue of The Ohio State University.

Funding

Revenue for the college comes from a state subsidy based on enrollment; performance funds based on meeting Board of Regents guidelines for two-year colleges; student fees, including tuition; and federal and state grants. The Institution is a line item in the state's higher education budget. The Writing Lab is housed in the Arts, Science and Business Division, and while funds to buy and repair the computers in the lab or pay tutors do not come from the Division budget, little funding, in comparison to the need to ensure quality equipment and staffing of the lab, is set aside in the larger college budget. Each year during spring quarter, the cry goes out to cut lab hours and the number of tutors. The difficulty in cutting the number of tutors is that the tutors rely on the income from the wages or work-study program. If the peer tutors were employed only during the fall and winter quarters, it would be difficult to recruit qualified young men and women into the tutoring program. Once again, how can adequate funding be established?

How did the Writing Lab begin in the climate of a technical college and how is it kept alive through budget struggles and power struggles? With the requirement to network to a main server and the Internet and e-mail, how can the Writing Lab improve its programming, train tutors for searching capabilities, and still retain the one-on-one process writing techniques for which tutors are trained? With no direct funding, with little administrative support, and with other faculty and staff marginalizing the need or importance of the Writing Lab, the challenge continues to be to work with the budget and the politics of the Institute. How can that be done without compromising some of the unique qualities, especially the peer tutoring and the "at home" atmosphere?

Writing Lab Overview

Mission Statement

The Writing Lab, a nine-hundred-square-foot room, is a place for students to take writing questions, problems, and concerns. Qualified peer tutors and faculty help students develop as writers. While the lab staff do not edit, proofread, or provide a formula for a particular assignment, they do help the writer in the writing process and provide a safe, supportive place to explore writing assignments for all courses.

History

The Writing Lab began in 1973, just two years after ATI opened, as an outgrowth of the developmental education program. The first coordinator of the lab was also the coordinator of the developmental education program and a tenured faculty member. When ATI was awarded a grant under the Perkins Vocational Education Act (Olson 88), a nonfaculty tutor manager/coordinator was hired, and the lab was moved to its own space, an old science lab complete with sinks and gas jets. It was with Perkins funds that the original computers were purchased for the Writing Lab. The coordinator believed strongly in the social constructionist theory of helping students to learn the conventions of the academic discourse community, as well as in the empowerment of all students. From the very beginning, even when there were only two tutors, all tutors formed a community of support between themselves. As other tutors were hired, they helped remodel the room by removing the sinks, painting, decorating the walls (since no funds were given for the renovation of the lab), and planning the placement of the computers based on their understanding of "community" which was being fostered in the lab (Harris).

Computing

Computers were set up in groups of two facing another group of two so that collaborative work could take place. It became apparent that the theory matched the design. A large table was set in the center of the lab where students could work on their individual writing with the tutor. When writing across the curriculum was adopted, the requests for writing assistance increased, and the Writing Lab policies and procedures were established. Also, with the loss of Perkins funding, the Writing Lab coordinator was reassigned under Title III as a curriculum specialist, and the Writing Lab coordination was reassigned to the coordinator of the Writing Program (a tenured faculty member) and placed in an academic division. Political ramifications were felt throughout the Institute. The coordinator of the Learning Assistance program, a tenured faculty member, was angry at losing her power, and the staff in the Learning Assistance area worked hard to make sure its territory remained intact. The challenge to the coordinator is to deal with little funding, old equipment, tutors trained by another instructor, and territorial issues.

Since the original purchase of computers with grant funds, any upgrades in computers have come from other areas in the college as there has been no specific money set aside for purchasing Writing Lab equipment. While the Writing Lab is often pointed out to visitors and prospective students as a user-friendly place in which to write, there is a constant requirement on the part of the coordinator, now a tenured faculty member, to assertively seek funds and tutors for the continuation of the lab.

Tutoring Course and Funding

When Perkins funding ended, tutor training became a major concern; a course, the Development of Tutor Effectiveness, was approved as a social science elective. The course is intended for all peer tutors rather than being limited to Writing Lab tutors, so specifics about Writing Lab situations are provided by the Writing Lab coordinator. As a part of the course, students must tutor a minimum of six hours per week, or forty-two hours per quarter before they can be paid. The course has provided quality tutors (there are no English majors at ATI) in all subjects and has helped the financial budget for tutors. Ongoing communication was and continues to be essential between the lab coordinator and the tutoring course instructor and the tutors. Writing Lab tutors also meet every two weeks with the Writing Lab coordinator. For the first half of the meeting, they go over issues that need to be addressed such as specific assignment concerns, techniques for working with the process of writing, student learning styles, and other topics discussed in the course which need further discussion and feedback. The second half of the meeting is devoted to concerns of the tutors as they share issues that have surfaced, problems among themselves, organization of the lab, and lab regulations.

One continued problem is the funding for tutoring. The tutoring budget for the Writing Lab was $6,400 in 1996–97. There has not been a year when the financing was adequate. This past year (1996–97) the coordinator of the Writing Lab and Writing Program received $1,500 annually for the next five years from a Kellogg grant to be used to further student-centered learning, so some of the money was used to fulfill the tutoring budget for spring quarter. Aside from that funding, and the tutoring funds from the Institute, there is no budget for the Writing Lab. Materials to help decorate the lab or for name plates to identify tutors is taken from the $1,000 Communication Skills (Writing Program) budget. Training tutors in a networked lab will be a new challenge for the coordinator.

Current Lab

New computers for the lab are actually used ones that come from other computer labs when they are updated. For example, the Writing Lab now houses fifteen 486 SX Compaqs with 120 MB hard drives and 4 MB of RAM. Many of the computers in the other academic lab are Pentiums, with 75 MHZ, 32 MB RAM, and 2.5 GB hard drives. The Writing Lab computers do not have enough memory to run new software, so students find it impossible to work up graphics and presentations for technical writing courses. On more than one occasion, it is through discussion in the hallway that the Writing Lab coordinator learns of new updates and programs being installed in other labs; then, through last-minute maneuvering, the coordinator may be able to find some funds from a source not designated for the lab in order to upgrade the Writing Lab.

The Writing Lab still functions as a "community," a comfortable place to study, to write, and to seek support. Tutors use the book *Working It Out* by Barbara Clouse to strengthen the writing process; but tutors also stress product (usage and grammar, sentence combing) (Dykstra).

As guidelines were (and still are) established for the lab, many of the priorities and guidelines in "Priorities and Guidelines for the Development of Writing Centers: A Delphi Study" (a chapter by Bené Scanlon Cox in *Writing Centers Theory and Administration*)—those which affect a two-year college program—have been followed—again—practiced before theory supported the program. But new policies need to be developed as the structure of the lab changes.

The Writing Lab is not networked and at this time tutors have chosen not to become a "research site" (Blythe) so that tutors can work with students on writing issues and not have to monitor use of the Internet or e-mail, which could tie up computers and tutoring/studying space in the lab. This will change soon.

Staff and Space

Aside from the Writing Lab/Writing Program coordinator, there are no TAs or adjunct faculty in the lab. When classes are held in the Writing Lab, faculty—many of whom do not have computer expertise and some of whom have little rhetorical/composition background—are present with the students as well as a tutor who is assigned for that class period. The Writing Lab is open Monday through Thursday from 8 A.M. to 9 P.M.; Friday 8 A.M. to 5 P.M.; and Sunday 6 P.M. to 9 P.M. While there are computers, the central table allows students to bring food and drink into the lab for tutoring sessions, and the best test of the lab's popularity is that those who coordinate the other computer labs resent the use and comfort level of the Writing Lab.

Key Charge

Very little is written on the funding of Writing Labs and the politics of them. A search of *The Writing Center Journal* ERIC database found no articles on the subject of funding, and in Olson's *Writing Centers Theory and Administration* (88), Olson in his article and then Jolly in her article "The Bottom Line: Financial Responsibility" give generalities but not certainties for funding. In all situations, one must be clever in order to secure funding and navigate the politics for a program that meets the needs of the students but is not a required part of a technical program. How do you do that as a Writing Lab coordinator?

In 1995, at the Annual Convention of the Conference on College Composition and Communication, Jeanne Simpson spoke about college administrations' perceptions and realities regarding writing centers. Though her talk was not based on empirical data, she found that the most common perceptions the writing center personnel hold regarding central administrators are that administrators have little direct information about writing centers because they do not have time to visit them; they think in terms of staffing and personnel dollars and space allocation and believe, then, that the program is not being marginalized.

How do you improve the training of the Writing Lab tutors, increase part-time faculty involvement, and plan policies for a networked lab with no discernable budget and a climate that acknowledges the need but marginalizes the support? How do you keep up with the technology, pedagogy, and atmosphere with no budget? The problem will compound when the Learning Assistance area, which is adjacent to the Writing Lab, is renovated with no plans to do the same for the adjoining Writing Lab. The major challenge continues to be funding and political positioning in a technical, two-year college that says writing is essential but places its main resources and action in the technical equipment, technical programs, and technical faculty.

AUTHOR'S CASE COMMENTARY

No one at The Ohio State Agricultural Technical Institute will tell you that the Writing Lab is unnecessary. In fact, most of the part-time and full-time faculty in all disciplines gladly send their students to the Writing Lab; it saves them time and energy. However, when it comes time to upgrade the technology or increase the budget for tutors or renovate the existing space, the Writing Lab is not on anyone's priority list except the coordinator's. How has the lab stayed as important as it is when it has been marginalized throughout the Institute? A strong coordinator who listens, responds, and persists has been important.

Listening is essential to finding out what is going on throughout the college. Eating lunch with other faculty and staff, being active in faculty governance, and talking to staff about their issues have played a major role in fighting for the needs of the Writing Lab. While training new faculty, the coordinator asked the computer technician at the Institute to join the meeting so part-time faculty would know who they needed to talk with regarding their e-mail. During that meeting, three weeks before the beginning of the new school year, the computer technician announced that all the other labs were having a new software package installed, but that the computers in the Writing Lab were not equipped to handle the program, so students would not be able to go from one lab to the other. The coordinator spent the remainder of the day talking to people, locating funds, and scheduling meetings with those individuals who would be responsible for the upgrade, if there was to be any. Money was found, but it was not money originally planned for the Writing Lab. If the coordinator was not listening, was not responding to the need, and was not persistent, the Writing Lab would have been technologically behind for the new school year. This time it worked; sometimes it might not. The Writing Center coordinator must listen, respond, and persist, but also must be proactive.

For several years now, the administration has discussed renovating the Learning Assistance Center which adjoins the Writing Lab. Each time it is discussed, the coordinator talks with the Learning Assistance staff and the administration. Each time the response is, "We are not ready yet." What now? Be proactive. Persistence will play a major role with this problem. The coordinator must take a proactive role in requesting that she be on any planning committee with the Learning Assistance staff and administration to ensure that the Writing Lab receives equal funding for its renovation (which may only include painting the walls). It will be imperative that the renovation be done by the contractors and not the tutors, as has been the case in past years.

Ensuring that the Tutor Effectiveness course remains a rigorous one with new pedagogy and psychological research integrated into the course will also take listening, responding, and persisting. It is not part of the curriculum that the individual teaching the course remain in contact with any of the faculty employing tutors. Once again, a proactive stance might be to build such contact into the course itself.

What has not worked is the institutionalization of the Writing Lab so that budget planning, tutor course planning, tutor recruitment, equipment update, and renovation plans include the Writing Lab coordinator during the initial discussion and planning of all those areas which affect the Writing Lab. Here lie the issues of budgeting and politics. Is the Writing Lab important enough to receive separate funding or at least be included in the plan, and can the administration allow the Writing Lab to play a powerful role in the program, thus ending the territorial and power struggle of who controls whom and who has more territory?

10 From Virtual to Reality: Thinking about Technology and the Composition Program

Deborah H. Holdstein
Governors State University

You are new to Grand Lake University, having been hired the previous spring as an untenured assistant professor. You have been asked to direct the existing program and, as you do, to reconfigure it; since the administration is eager to integrate technology within the curricula represented at the university, you also have a great deal to assess and, if you so determine, to implement. As you learn about the university, you recall a warning from your dissertation director at prestigious Golden Spike University: that your being untenured in so responsible an administrative-teaching position might be a liability, as WPAs often must venture fully into a university-wide, politically complex arena.

Institution Overview

Grand Lake University is a fairly small (6,000+), state-supported, open-admissions school with four colleges: Arts and Sciences, Business, Health Professions, and Education. Its PR department markets Grand Lake as a regional university that has, since its founding approximately twenty-five years ago, served primarily adult, returning students; the population, however, is changing slightly, with younger students from "feeder" community colleges swelling the ranks at junior and senior levels. The majority of Grand Lake students at both graduate and undergraduate levels attend part time, serve as heads of their respective families, and hold full- or part-time jobs.

The administration cares a great deal about enrollment and retention. In fact, Grand Lake's enrollments have steadily increased since the arrival of a brilliant, new, energetic president approximately three years before. Earlier and longer registration periods and, some argue to you, lower standards for retention seem to account in part for the rise. You see the position as a tremendous challenge for several reasons: first, the upper-division nature of the institution (a rarity among colleges and universities), where everyone is a transfer student; and second, the knowledge that writing programs have received inconsistent support—if not outright hostility—in the past.

Library

Despite a committed and excellent library staff, the collection is fairly small; similarly, despite the fact that the university's mission statement boasts "technology" among its four components, the computer lab barely seems to keep up. Within the Computing Center, one finds one Macintosh classroom (with older, good, but ill-maintained equipment) and several PC classrooms boosted by desktop computers in a more public area of the center. Other components of the mission statement include "diversity," "service," and "teaching," with "research" conspicuously absent.

Writing Program Overview

Adding to the complexity of your task at Grand Lake is the absence of a coherent writing program despite the university's acknowledgment that such a program is necessary. Since the most recent writing director's resignation in 1994, there has been a series of adjuncts supervising other adjuncts and TAs; the program has been comparatively small (no more than ten sections per semester) and manageable. Recently, a newly arrived faculty member specializing in literature was given responsibility for the writing program within the English program, adding a sheaf of new writing courses to the catalog but teaching none of them. In fact, there is some concern, you hear, that there is little or no involvement in composition by full-time faculty, and you wonder what impact that has on the program generally. For instance, a new course in professional writing (duplicating an older course on the books) was assigned to an adjunct–graduate student. In its inaugural offering, the course received little or no publicity and hence too small an enrollment for it to continue past the "add-drop" time.

Challenges

To add to perceived difficulties with composition courses and requirements, a new university director of WAC, a role separate from yours, has changed the essay-competency exam given to all new students to a machine-scored exam. While the latter pleased the administration for its "objectivity," other concerned faculty complain to you that students are not "getting the help they need" for the sake of larger retention fig-ures and less controversy surrounding the testing process. These fac-ulty tell you that the previous essay exam, while controversial, placed students more accurately into necessary coursework. The writing sample, however, was difficult for administrators to defend; despite interrater reliability and other forms of statistical validation, it was seen as a deterrent to student retention. You wonder what implications this unfortunate assessment policy might have as you initiate and plan tech-nology-enhanced aspects of the writing curriculum. Unlike other insti-tutions, then, Grand Lake seems to have no coherent writing program and, not surprisingly, no coherent approach to using technology in the writing classroom.

Indeed, there is no autonomous program in writing; nor is there a separate budget or formal "director's" position. In the past, attempts to integrate computers within the writing class have been something of a catch-as-catch-can enterprise. Adjuncts or other faculty wishing to use computers as part of the writing/teaching/learning process found that they were competing with every department in the university for computer classroom time. Given that Grand Lake's returning learners generally work during the daytime, computer classroom reservations have been particularly difficult to get during popular class meeting times: once a week, from 5:00 to 7:20 P.M. or from 7:30 to 9:50 P.M. Often (based on hastily sought advice from computer-knowledgeable faculty), frustrated adjuncts, TAs, or other instructors have sent students to the computer center on their own time merely as part of assignments, with no in-class time or ongoing discussion about technology. A coherent philosophy regarding technology, therefore, has seemed impossible to devise or implement; determining whether or not such a philosophy is desirable or even possible in this context will be part of your job.

Because Grand Lake is a commuter institution, it also seems im-possible to schedule any time of training and preparation for technol-ogy and writing during orientation, since there is no formal orientation week as it is known at more traditional, residential schools. Issues of training, then, for both faculty as well as students, also surround the question of how extensively to implement technology within the writ-ing program at Grand Lake.

Graduate Program

The M.A. program in English is strong, but small. Talented graduate students are targeted for work as TAs in composition classes, but tech-nically there is no such "title" for graduate student teaching. Moreover, since the time of the director who departed in 1994, there has been no formal training program, although there is a "Seminar for Writing Teachers" available for those who choose to take it.

As part of the M.A. program, students are required to take a graduate-level course in rhetorical/critical theory, a variable subject seminar taught regularly by a rhetoric and composition specialist. Undergraduate courses in writing stress mostly a necessary, if junior-level, version of first-year composition; this course has become politically charged, given that all Grand Lake students have taken composition elsewhere. One rhetoric course, "Theories and Practices of Rhetoric," is required of all English majors and has become a requirement for students in several majors within the College of Education and elsewhere in the institution. Another rhetoric course, "Studies in Rhetoric," has not been offered for at least five years since faculty energies have focused on core and other courses deemed more crucial and central to student needs.

Students

While Grand Lake has done a great deal to attract and enroll foreign students, there are no formal ESL courses; the student population has always been reasonably diverse, with African American and Hispanic/Latino enrollments increasing. Administrators seem particularly interested in "integrated" studies and ethnic studies, areas that have little trouble securing or having diverted to them university and college funds. (Indeed, over twenty years ago, Grand Lake was the first university in the state to require a course in black authors as part of its English major.)

Computing

Academic Computing has recently absorbed the personnel and purposes of the EducatioNet, the latter being the primary e-mail and Internet resource for the university. Within Academic Computing, it seems difficult to determine who controls which resources—room scheduling, equipment maintenance, equipment purchase, and so on, and requests for assistance, you are told, seem to fall within a labyrinthine set of referrals from one student assistant to another.

Key Charge

Clearly, the opportunity to be WPA at Grand Lake offers the traditional division between good news and bad news. On the one hand, the situation seems wide open and ready for productive strategies and curricular reform, with or without technology. On the other hand, there appear to be few existing lines of support, whether financial or collegial; prospective colleagues are eager to inform you of others' past failures, inappropriate solutions (the machine-scored exam, for instance), and administrative lip service to writing.

Before you complete negotiations for your position, you ask the dean of the College of Arts and Sciences to ensure the following as much as possible: her cooperation in enlisting faculty support to develop a comprehensive, undergraduate writing program appropriate for Grand Lake, and her cooperation in securing assistance and, if necessary, funding, for technology-based composition efforts. You also ask to have delineated as clearly as possible (in writing) your responsibilities and those of the WAC coordinator, with particular attention to those areas of professional overlap—the placement/competency assessment, for instance, since you rightly object to machine-scored assessment of writing. Your status as an untenured faculty member in a decision-making role and your need to be able to make those necessary choices about writing demand the above (and probably other) negotiated strategies. How will you and your WAC colleague be mutually supportive, each of you with autonomous and yet often-linked programs in writing? How can you join together to share technology efforts with mutually beneficial results?

In addition to creating a coherent writing effort that works well within the English program and supports budding efforts at WAC, you know that you need to help evolve some type of philosophical and practical approach to technology and composition.

Your key challenges: access to technology, access to learning resources regarding technology, and the degree to which technology will be a formal part of the curriculum. The following, equally crucial challenges also merit your attention:

- learning resources—becoming familiar with philosophies and pedagogies
- hardware resources—existing computing center or other? What are funding sources?
- developing relationships across the university with administration and staff, both for the writing program and to implement and maintain technology support
- creating a community of technology users while allowing for individual teaching preferences, a group that will also be part of your creating a collaborative, generally supportive community of colleagues in writing and other disciplines to help in-

form and support your curricular and research efforts, whether "plugged" or "unplugged"

Another, even more basic series of concerns you will need to address include the following:

- curricular issues—will a formal, technologically based effort enhance instruction at Great Lakes? *When* should you implement such an effort? How?

- budgeting—will the effort you devise cost anything? What about software? Should you try to share existing lab space? Raise funds for a space devoted to English programs?

- personnel—who should help? How to prepare them? Who will prepare *students*?

- external and internal funding sources

- key figures in faculty and administration to assist with technological issues and support

As the above issues make clear, deciding how and when to implement technology within a writing curriculum crosses the boundaries of every essay in this text: preparing new TAs; issues of process/rhetorical models versus socially constructed theory-pedagogies; portfolio assessment; personnel and administrative issues; and so on. You will need to decide not only what is feasible at Grand Lake, but also what is an effective and appropriate use of technology for your particular writing program. What should happen next? What alliances have you formed among colleagues—those who seem eager to help *and* those who seem to be potential roadblocks? (Remember the old but often-true notion to keep your friends close and your enemies closer.) What pedagogies are at work in the program as it presently exists? How will these have to change (or not) as you offer your staff the option of in-class technology? Can the institution itself even support such an offer— even for just one or two classes at the start? Indeed, what many areas of potential support around the university support must you assess before you even begin? (And don't forget an important issue: What is the technological literacy level of Grand Lake students? How does this situation compete with their literacy levels in other areas—such as writing?)

AUTHOR'S CASE COMMENTARY

Some readers familiar with Governors State might think that my description of Grand Lake University resembles GSU, its faculty, and its institutional complexities. Its upper-division status, for instance, serves well the purposes of a case study for WPAs, since it injects an additional and useful level of complexity that many WPAs will be able to avoid. But Grand Lake is not GSU: I've chosen to highly fictionalize this account of this imaginary university to offer, perhaps, a worst-case scenario for new WPAs. Why? It's relatively easy, in practical terms, to implement technology at institutions where technology prevails and where there is enough in-class computer time to concern oneself solely with issues of theory and effective pedagogy. Then, one might also have the luxury of focusing on other philosophical-practical concerns, say, debates about whether chat rooms and Net surfing should be part of in-class time in writing courses. The scenario at Grand Lake, however, might help new WPAs to best prepare themselves for situations that prove to be particularly complex. It might be particularly instructive for you as a new WPA to envision the Grand Lake scenario as if it does, in fact, represent your administrative destiny.

Without doubt, your first task is to look closely at the institution, the history of writing at the institution, and, perhaps most important, student needs to best organize a writing program at Grand Lake. Yet administrators will probably demand that you nonetheless address ways to implement technology as a formal part of that program—even before one can realistically or truthfully use the term "program" to describe what goes on at Grand Lake. You first must assess whether or not you and your colleagues will even have computers readily available to you with Net and Web access (this should also become a condition-of-hire); if so, you might immediately search for and subscribe to several computer pedagogy-related discussion lists as well as one for WPAs and encourage your colleagues to do so as well. Together, you can brainstorm issues and questions to which you will seek answers, both at Grand Lake and online. You must seek bibliographic sources—on line and off.

You must decide immediately that to implement technology here, as anywhere, will have to be a matter not only of substance, but also of degree. That is, you must not implement technology solely because "everybody has to do it" and because other administrators want you to, but because you can articulate potentially real academic benefits for writers and prohibit any attempt to make instructors follow one another lockstep into any one approach. Similarly, you must not be persuaded to attempt an immediate technological sweep—full, dedicated laboratories for every section of composition in the writing program, for instance—but to carefully weigh the *degree* to which you might set the stage for gradually and flexibly doing so. Given all the unknowns regarding not just technological support but also curricular issues at Grand Lake, this would seem to be the wisest and most sound approach, both administratively and pedagogically.

From the moment you first walk on Grand Lake's expansive campus, you cannot assume that you will have access to a lab at any time in the near future, nor can you or your faculty plan to teach in one during every class period, should you have regular access to it. (And were you to obtain, somehow, a dedicated laboratory for writing classes, you and other administrators should not demand that it be used during every possible class period with full classes simply because it is such a large financial investment. To decree that every computer be used during every period would violate the flexibility so crucial in writing-related pedagogy.) In short, what you have probably known and assumed is true: just as there is no one preferred in-class methodological approach to teaching writing-as-process, so too is there no one way to implement technology within the writing classroom. Even the decision to formally implement some form of plain vanilla word-processing requires careful thought and depends entirely on access within the institution and *students' access to that access*. Among other issues that will occur to you as you get to know Grand Lake and its students, consider this: Is it appropriate, for instance, to require in-lab computer use after class time when a working parent at a commuter institution cannot come back to campus?

And yet you might influence enough change at Grand Lake during your watch to make you decide that program instructors might, if they wish, encourage students to share and critique writing in anonymous, paperless peer groups through e-mail, both on and off campus, and you may have one or two eager faculty who would like to see such efforts develop quickly. However, at the start, there seems little option for most of you but to implement technology from afar: you may decide to suggest to faculty in your program that they advise students generally on their optional use of word-processing outside of class, on their own, with hard-copy drafts brought to class for peer review and discussion-demonstrations of deep revision. Why?

This point bears re-emphasis. Each of your decisions regarding technology and its role in teaching and learning the writing process must stem from the following considerations: Grand Lake's instructional and professional contexts; the ways in which you and your colleagues each most effectively teach the writing process and the atmosphere in which your students in particular find it most conducive to learn; the contexts that you help develop for teaching (the way your new composition program evolves, your and your colleagues' relative freedom within it, and the type of department in which it is housed); the political realities that make technology available to you, to your colleagues, and to your students (or that remove it from your collective or individual use); and the criteria by which you will evaluate colleagues involved in technology and the impact it might have on the evaluation, retention, and promotion process.

Consider, too, this last point—the ways in which technology might change the processes by which you and your colleagues are evaluated *and* the ways in which you evaluate your students. Technology-based classrooms are inherently more collaborative, more noisy, and more physically active than many other types of classrooms. Will you together with interested colleagues generate evaluative procedures to make such nontraditional classrooms acceptable at teacher evaluation time? How will it be possible to distinguish the various manifestations of useful, *productive* classrooms, then, from the ones that are less successful?

Will program-related, in-class technology work go beyond word processing? (Will you and your colleagues together develop advisory guidelines for even the simplest forms of computer use—advisories against slavish attention to spelling and grammar checkers, for instance?) The issues to consider can indeed seem far-ranging: for one, many well-meaning instructors encourage a certain, allegedly liberating "anonymity" online as part of a list dedicated to members of a specific class. You might wish to ask yourself and discuss with your colleagues whether or not anonymity is, indeed, a good idea: does the short-term liberation given to some by identity-masking merely prevent students from being accepted and known as themselves and delay students' accepting aspects of difference?

Perhaps you might question whether or not Web page design, for example, belongs in the writing classroom if it prevents students from working with reasoned, extended argument (if that's a goal of your curriculum), or whether unchecked Web surfing has any place at all in the formal classroom itself. At what forum will those who believe so (or not) be able to discuss and share these practices to persuade you and others of the potential value or pitfalls involved in various types of teaching strategies that might stem from computer use? Perhaps many of these issues will seem moot, since few if any computer terminals in the existing facilities at Grand Lake offer convenient Web and other Internet access; yet these issues will demand your attention if you wish to join with others to make additional facilities available for those instructors and students wishing to use them. And will various forms of formal, class-related computer use fit well with mandated assessment policies that come from elsewhere in the university?

Perhaps the most important thing to keep in mind is this: that the composition instructor who chooses to teach with technology must primarily remain a teacher of *writing*. You'll find outstanding teachers of writing who choose to limit their pedagogical use of technology (or must, due to limited resources) to out-of-class word processed and revised drafts (with hard copy brought to class for peer review, for instance), the word processing itself optional for those who have limited or no access to technology. You might find yourself questioning the pedagogy of another who employs in-class, lab-supported, sophisticated MOOs and MUDs that potentially serve as occasions for writing persuasive argument. Are the goals for the class being met, or are students at all distracted by the technologies themselves? Obviously, then the presence or absence of computer technology does not in and of itself ensure good teaching and learning. Let me paraphrase something I wrote in 1987 that, to my surprise, I find myself still having to repeat to colleagues and at institutions where I serve as consultant: If students can't revise, the computer won't in and of itself help them do so.

With your colleague at Grand Lake in charge of WAC, consider developing interdepartmental colloquia on writing and related issues to forge alliances and discuss technology-related (and other practical and pedagogical) concerns, these in addition to regular and writing-program-specific meetings. Certainly this will offer the opportunity to discuss ways in which faculty might learn about aspects of new technologies, to discuss opportunities for training (collaboratively, with writing specialists and lab-employed computer specialists), and to create goodwill among those who will assist your efforts. And computer-related readings and orientation should be part not only of the "Seminar for Teachers of Writing," but also for the orientation/learning of graduate students and others teaching in your program. Similarly, will you have any role in determining or enhancing computer-related *writing* literacy of students entering Grand Lake with little experience? Would such intervention on your part be useful?

In addition to considering these many questions, your job, in part, is to make alliances across the university. Along with your leadership and your own colleagues' contributions, these will enable your faculty and students to avail themselves of technology in ways that enhance the teaching and learning of writing and to ensure that faculty members are empowered to use (or that they feel empowered to choose *not* to use) computer technology as a formal part of their teaching. Remember that technology can be implemented in a very wide range of equally appropriate, useful ways—and a range of inappropriate ways. Keep in mind that the ways in which you and your colleagues choose to enact aspects of the challenge of technology will serve as microcosm and metaphor for the contextual knowledge, scholarly background, decision-making, wisdom, and organizational abilities you bring overall to your leadership role as WPA.

11 Computers in the Writing Center

Sara E. Kimball
University of Texas at Austin

*This chapter describes technological, staffing, and audience consider-
ations facing the director of a hypothetical writing center who is establishing and maintaining online writing center services. It is presented
not as a single problem that admits of only one solution, but as an
ongoing series of challenges and possibilities that admit a number of
approaches. Directors are urged to find their own solutions by educating
themselves about current computer technology, analyzing their potential
audiences, and planning services that enhance their center's missions.*

Writing Center Overview

Position within Institution, Funding, and Mission

Your writing center has an independent budget. Although your university has a solid reputation as a research institution and has departments
and graduate programs that have achieved national recognition, you
are funded to work only with undergraduates, since your writing center is supported by a student fee of $7 charged each undergraduate each
semester. Most of your budget goes to paying salaries and benefits for
staff, including consultants, an administrative assistant, and you. You
have a half-time faculty appointment in a writing department of which
your writing center is a part; the other half of your appointment is
funded through an administrative line in the writing center's budget.
Neither your writing center nor the writing department is officially
connected to the English department, although your writing center
employs graduate students from the English department as consultants.
In your role as writing center director you report to the writing
department's chair, who reports in turn to the dean of the College of
Liberal Arts, who reports to the president and provost.

This is a young writing center in its second year of operation. The
writing department of which it is a part is also a new entity on campus,
having been split off from the English department two years previously,
and you and your colleagues are concerned about increasing the writing department's visibility on campus. The plans for your writing cen-

ter were drawn up as part of the process of planning the writing department. The first year the writing center was in operation, you concentrated on getting the center up and running and developing a computerized record-keeping system, publicity, and staff training. Mostly, you worked with students enrolled in courses offered by the writing department. This year, one of your major goals is to extend your services to undergraduates from all departments throughout the university, and you are anticipating up to four thousand student visits during the fall and spring semesters. In addition to working directly with undergraduate students, as the center becomes fully operational over the next two or three years, you are expected to advise faculty teaching writing-intensive courses in departments across the university through workshops and individual consultations. At the present time, however, this program is mostly in the planning stage.

Staff Size and Composition

Your writing center has a staff of approximately forty consultants each year. The writing department is committed to hiring graduate student instructors from the English department, an unusual arrangement stemming from your department's historical ties to the English department, and in any given year you expect to employ approximately twenty-five English department graduate students who also teach one section of first-year composition for the writing department. As a general rule, you hire all of the graduate students from English who are in their third year in the graduate program and their first year of teaching composition. You also hire a few more advanced graduate students from English and a few other departments, some of whom have had experience teaching in networked classrooms. Half of each consultant's salary is paid from the writing center's budget, and half is paid from the writing department's budget.

You also have up to ten undergraduate peer consultants on staff who have trained for their positions by taking a for-credit course you offer each spring. You select undergraduate staff on the basis of their performance in this class, and they are paid an hourly wage of $7.25. Because you work with students from across the university, you have found it desirable to recruit some undergraduate staff who are not English majors. You are also able to hire graduate students from outside of the English department, and you have already hired a few in order to acquire expertise in writing in areas such as science, technical writing, engineering, and business.

Clientele/Students

Most of the undergraduates enrolled in the university are of traditional college age (seventeen to twenty-four years old). Most students either live in on-campus housing or they live close to campus in apartment complexes or fraternities and sororities. Approximately 30 percent of the undergraduate population is enrolled in the College of Liberal Arts with the rest enrolled in the Colleges of Natural Sciences (ca. 22 percent), Business (ca. 12 percent), Communication (ca. 10 percent), Fine Arts (ca. 5 percent), Nursing (ca. 2 percent), Pharmacy (under 2 percent), and Architecture (under 2 percent). Since one of the justifications for supporting the writing center through a university-wide student fee is that it serves students from all colleges in the university, it is essential that your writing center attract students from the various colleges in roughly the proportions in which they are enrolled. So far, you've been successful in this.

Although your state is large, has several urban centers, and is economically and racially diverse, the prevailing ethos among students is largely middle class and suburban. Perhaps because of the atmosphere on campus, and perhaps because people remember several racially tense incidents in the recent past, enrollment at your university by people of color is significantly below percentages of people of color living in the state. This is a major concern to the administration, which is actively involved in efforts at recruitment and retention of people of color. Getting these students to use the writing center and recruiting students of color as staff members are two of your priorities as director.

You also realize that an online writing center could contribute productively to the public image of your university. Like other public universities, your school has to satisfy various sectors of the public, including a legislature that has always been skeptical about the university's commitment to undergraduate education, and parents concerned with the cost of education and with getting good value for their money. You are lucky enough to have an administration that recognizes the public relations value of a writing center in displaying the university's concern with undergraduate education, and you think that going online might provide you with opportunities for public outreach.

Computer Technology on Campus

The administration of your school has embraced computer technology enthusiastically, and there is a campuswide initiative coming from above to get the campus community online. The administration, for example, has surveyed faculty members about their access to and use of computers, identified faculty members most in need, and upgraded or replaced inadequate equipment. Students pay a computer technology fee, which has enabled various kinds of computer access. All students may request an e-mail account, and the payment of a nominal additional fee entitles students to an account on one of the university's UNIX computers, allowing them to run various UNIX-based applications and to access the World Wide Web and FTP in addition to e-mail.

A large student-use computer center administered by the Computation Center provides students with twenty-four-hour access to Macintosh and IBM-compatible personal computers which run word processing programs and various other software applications as well as providing Internet access. In addition, several smaller departmental computer labs are scattered about campus. Some of the dorms have already been wired for Internet access, and over the next few years there are plans to wire them all. A few departments have networked computer classrooms run on an experimental basis. Although you have never taught in a networked classroom, your writing department is very proud of its computer-assisted writing classes and is in the process of expanding its networked classroom facilities.

Library and Technology

The university's library system is a key player in the introduction of information technology on campus, providing various computer databases for students and faculty, and providing classes on using the Internet for research. The Computation Center runs the campus server computers, provides user accounts, and makes available some software for purchase at a nominal price. The Computation Center also has a help desk and a user-advice telephone service and is accessible through e-mail for answers to various technical computing questions.

For all of the hardware that is being acquired, the process of computerizing your campus hasn't been entirely smooth. Although your colleagues are delighted to have received new computers, the introduction of this hardware has raised the collective level of anxiety. Many of the faculty have been using computers so antiquated that they have little or no idea of all that they can do with more up-to-date equipment. A significant percentage, for example, have never used e-mail or the World Wide Web. There is also a certain amount of concern among department chairs about educating faculty to use computers as productive tools for research and teaching, not just as glorified typewriters. Although computer technology is theoretically available to all students, you sense that it has been somewhat slow to catch on, especially in Liberal Arts. A show-of-hands poll in one of your classes, for example, indicates that about 60 percent of the students have e-mail accounts, but not all of them regularly read their mail. When you ask your students why they're not using their e-mail accounts, they tell you that they can't figure out how to use the software.

Computing

Your Access to Technology

Electronic services were promised in the proposal for a writing center submitted to the central administration three years ago as part of the process of planning the writing department. The director of the writing department and your dean are very enthusiastic about computer technology, and now that you've got your center up and running, you figure it's a good time to start getting the center on line. Your writing center has seven Macintosh computers, one of which you use for record keeping, and your budget is generous and flexible when it comes to obtaining hardware and software, so obtaining equipment is not the problem.

Your own experience and the various other demands on your time are, however, part of the problem. You are basically computer literate. You routinely use e-mail and you can surf the Web productively, but you are not exactly a computer technician, or techie. Someone else, for example, had to set up your SLIP connection. You also have many other duties in connection with the writing center, such as tutor training, scheduling, record keeping, and consultations with faculty. You also can't ignore the fact that half of your time is supposed to be spent on faculty duties. You teach a 1/2 load and serve on various committees. As a member of this prestigious research institution, you are also supposed to be making regular and significant contributions to scholarship in your field.

Key Challenge

You direct the writing center in a large, public university that enrolls approximately 25,000 undergraduates each semester. You are planning to set up and administer an online writing center in addition to your face-to-face work with students. You expect to provide various electronic services to campus users, including offerings on the World Wide Web and online consultations. You also see that an online writing center can help you to respond to various other audiences, including faculty teaching writing-intensive courses and members of the general public. You are not, however, responsible for maintaining a computer lab or otherwise providing students with direct access to computers, printers, or software through the writing center.

Your mission is to figure out what services you will offer and how you will implement, staff, and maintain them—good luck!

Key Charge

Setting up, building, and maintaining online services is not a single, simple problem that has a single solution, but rather is an ongoing series of challenges and possibilities that admit a number of approaches. Given the scenario outlined above, there are many approaches that might lead to successful services that would enhance the writing center's mission. What you will have to do is get some sense of the services you can offer and those you want to offer. The process of setting up online services includes training staff and attracting a clientele, and you need some sense of the costs in terms of your staff resources and your own time and effort in maintaining services on a day-to-day basis.

An obvious first step is to get an idea of the kinds of online services other writing centers offer. But other considerations are crucial. One is determining possible sources of expertise and support in setting up and maintaining your services; another is figuring out how much computer expertise you must acquire yourself and how much time and energy you are willing and able to put into the task of setting services up and keeping them running. Even if money for equipment is no problem, you need to know what kinds of hardware and software to purchase, and you need to know what to do with the hardware and software you've obtained. Above all, you should do some thinking about your clientele; the process of setting up online services is in large part a matter of finding or developing an audience and meeting its needs.

The most basic question to ask yourself is "What do I want to do?" The phrase *online services* is deliberately vague, but its vagueness may well reflect the reality of your situation. Computer technology is very attractive to academic administrations. It is current (trendy even), and a new computer facility or service can be exhibited to students, parents, trustees, or regents as an example of how up-to-date the school is. Administrators may, however, have little knowledge about or direct experience with computers and computer services. You may very well be under considerable pressure, therefore, to offer "online services" from people who cannot articulate what they want very clearly. On the one hand, this situation can be unnerving; on the other hand, it offers you all kinds of possibilities to set your own priorities.

How will you allocate your own time and energy? How much of the project can you take on yourself, and how much should you delegate to others? How will you fund any technical support that you might need?

Administrations don't always recognize the need for training and technical support services, and even if this need is recognized, funding for such support may be scarce or nonexistent. You're lucky enough to have an independent budget, which means you don't have to depend on a department or university administration to pay for technical support, but any money you spend on support will come out of the money you need to fund adequate staffing, and it may be difficult to supplement your budget. Most schools do have computation centers that offer support services, and some of this support may be free, but customer service is not traditionally a value in such centers, and the help you may obtain may not be exactly user-friendly. Students are entering universities with more computer experience than ever before, however, and you shouldn't neglect your own staff as a source of computer knowledge.

Who are you doing this for? Do you have a ready-made audience? What work will you have to do to develop a clientele? If you feel you have several audiences, what are your priorities among them? The hypothetical university writing center described above has a number of possible audiences for its online services among students, faculty, administrators, and the general public. The services you offer should meet their needs and be accessible, given the level of knowledge about computer technology and its use on your campus. Ideally, you should try to meet needs that are difficult to address without technology. For example, students who live far from campus, or who work during the day and have little time to use face-to-face writing center services might be especially interested in an online writing center. An online writing center could also be used for outreach to the community beyond the university. If one of the administration's priorities is recruiting and retaining students of color, for example, you might want to think about ways of using computer technology for outreach to these students in formulating your plans. You should also try to plan your offerings so that they complement and support both your center's mission and goals, and the missions of other units in the university with which your writing center has special relationships. For example, if the writing department and other departments offer classes in networked classrooms, the students in these classes might prove a technologically sophisticated, enthusiastic audience. If the library also offers online services and education, you might consider how you could work with them.

Suggested Reading List

If you are going to set up an online writing center, you should be aware of a number of sources of information available online. Electronic mailing lists devoted to computers and writing are invaluable because, unlike print sources or the World Wide Web, the information they provide is not static. Joining a mailing list can be like entering a conversation among knowledgeable and sympathetic colleagues, and most questions and requests for advice are answered with useful information. Various print sources on online writing centers and associated technological and administrative concerns are also available, both on the Internet and in traditional print formats.

For writing center people, the most useful discussion list is probably WCenter, a list for writing center professionals run by Lady Falls Brown, director of the writing center at Texas Tech. To subscribe send a message to listproc@unicorn.acs.ttu.edu that reads: subscribe wcenter-l <your name>. Archives of WCenter discussions are available on the World Wide Web at http://www.ttu.edu/lists/wcenter/. ACW (The Alliance for Computers and Writing) also has a discussion list that might be useful to directors of online writing centers. To subscribe send an e-mail message to LISTPROC@UNICORN.ACS.TTU.EDU with subscribe acw-l <your name>. An archive can be found at http://www.ttu.edu/lists/acw-l/.

The homepage of the National Writing Centers Association (NWCA) is an excellent collection of links to useful information about online writing centers as well as other writing center concerns. It is available at http://www2.colgate.edu/diw/NWCA.html and provides links to a number of centers, including Purdue's OWL and the University of Missouri's Online Writery.

An especially helpful source of information is volume 12 (Winter 1995) of the journal *Computers and Composition*, which is devoted to computers and writing centers. The articles by Muriel Harris and Michael Pemberton ("Online Writing Labs (OWLs): A Taxonomy of Options and Issues") and by Dave Healy ("From Place to Space: Perceptual and

Administrative Issues in the Online Writing Center") are especially helpful, since they provide general overviews of options for setting up and running online services and discuss both technology and administrative issues. Other articles in this volume describe specific projects and are helpful too. The Winter 1995–96 issue of the *ACE Newsletter* (Vol. 9.4, NCTE Assembly on Computers in English) describes online projects at a number of writing centers, and *Writing Centers in Context: Twelve Case Studies* (Joyce A. Kinkead and Jeanette G. Harris, eds. Urbana, IL: NCTE, 1993) has sections on how computers are used in each of the writing centers described in the book.

AUTHOR'S CASE COMMENTARY

The first thing you will have to do is to educate yourself. Here is some very basic information about the kinds of online services writing centers offer. You'll learn more, however, by getting on the Net and exploring.

Many writing centers call their computer services an OWL, an acronym for Online Writing Lab. This comes from Purdue University Writing Lab's OWL, one of the first writing centers to offer online resources, at first in the form of handouts provided through a Gopher menu. Purdue's services now encompass written resources, including handouts, offered over the World Wide Web; an e-mail advice service; and e-mail commentary on papers. Purdue's OWL is one of the largest and most technologically sophisticated OWLs—a "full-service OWL"—but in practice OWLs can fall anywhere on a continuum from being simple information servers to complex systems offering a range of interactive resources. An information server simply makes information of various sorts available online for users to access and perhaps download at their convenience, while an interactive site, by contrast, involves some degree of communication between writing center staff and computer users.

The most common way of providing information is through a World Wide Web site. A minimal Web site would offer information about the writing center's location, hours, and services, but other material is easy to provide. Examples might include handouts produced by your staff, a copy of your center's mission statement, and personal pages for center staff. You can take advantage of other people's contributions to the World Wide Web by offering links to other sites—either writing center sites, such as Purdue's OWL or the Online Writery at the University of Missouri, or other online resources for writers and scholars such as

Carnegie Mellon's English Server or the Human Languages Page. You could also include links to pages with information on technical, business, and science writing, or links to your own library's pages. An FTP (File Transfer Protocol) server could be used to make handouts and other materials available for downloading.

One advantage to the information server approach is that it's fairly low maintenance. In contrast to interactive services, you don't have to allocate much staff time and attention to it on a regular basis once you've gathered the material and placed it on a server. HTML, the coding for World Wide Web documents, is easy to learn, especially if you're not interested in fancy bells and whistles such as elaborate multimedia presentations, and a university interested in promoting use of computers is likely to offer both classes on Web publishing and space on university servers for Web authors. Web pages do need some maintenance, however, since information can go out of date and links can be broken if a site you have linked to moves to another server or disappears. You need at least one person on your staff who knows HTML or is willing to learn it and who will take responsibility for maintaining your World Wide Web offerings.

There are various options if you choose to set up interactive services. Broadly speaking, there are two kinds of interactive communication over computer networks: asynchronous communication and synchronous, or real-time, communication. In asynchronous communication users post messages to an e-mail address or server computer, and other users may access these messages at their convenience. Personal e-mail, bulletin boards, newsgroups, and e-mail discussion lists are examples of asynchronous communication systems. Real-time communication involves two or more users connected over a computer network. Messages are typed into the computer, sent over the network via communications software, and, although the arrival of messages can be somewhat delayed by problems with the network (netlag), for all practical purposes messages are received and sent with little delay. To use an analogy from the noncomputer world, asynchronous communication is like exchanging letters through the U.S. Postal Service, while synchronous communication is like having a telephone conversation.

The simplest interactive service is answering questions about grammar or writing issues over e-mail. All you need is an e-mail account and a mail program such as Pine, which can be used with dialup access and is available on many UNIX systems, or Eudora, which requires a SLIP or PPP account. The e-mail address to which users should send their questions can be publicized on your Web site (and you can use a special HTML tag, mailto, to provide users with a way to send a mail message from your site).

Some writing centers offer advice about drafts over e-mail. Students e-mail drafts of papers to which writing center tutors respond in e-mail. The Purdue OWL and the OWL at the University of Michigan provide this online service, while the Writing Center at Dakota State University in South Dakota exists only online.

Newsgroups and e-mail discussion lists are other asynchronous options. A newsgroup is in effect a computerized bulletin board. Subscribers to a newsgroup post messages (also called articles) to a server computer, which stores them in a named file. Other users can access this file by accessing the server computer and calling up the file with special newsreader software. In most cases, an account on a UNIX system gives users access to simple newsreaders, but there is also more sophisticated, user-friendly software available. Subscribers to an e-mail list, by contrast, send mail to an address on a computer that runs special software that redistributes messages to the addresses of a list of subscribers. Mail goes directly to users' accounts rather than being stored on a server computer. Newsgroups can have national or worldwide distribution, meaning they can be accessed by anyone, or they can be local, and restricted to users from a particular campus. The University of Missouri's Online Writery, for example, sponsors such a local newsgroup. E-mail discussion lists can also be open to anyone who wants to subscribe or restricted to subscribers approved by the list's manager, or "owner."

A few writing centers offer real-time conferences over the Internet. A number have experimented with MUDs. The word *MUD* is an acronym for Multiple-User Dungeon, Dimension, or Domain. MUDs and their descendants, including *MOOs, MUSHes,* and *MUCKs,* are text-based virtual realities run as programs on a large server computer. A *virtual reality* is a location or experience created using computer technology and human imagination. In a MUD, characters created through programming code and textual description authored by users interact in real-time with other characters and with objects and places also created through textual description and programming code. Some sophisticated forms of virtual reality use audio, 3-D video, and devices such as datagloves to convey a sense of acting within a real environment and interacting with and manipulating objects within that environment, but inhabiting the reality of a text-based virtual reality like a MUD is more like living within an interactive novel. The sense of being in a place is created by descriptions which appear on a user's screen.

Purdue operates a MUD, as do the University of Missouri's Online Writery, the Virginia Tech OWL, and the University of Texas at Austin's Undergraduate Writing Center. Jennifer Jordan-Henley and Barry Maid use a MUD for conference in a project that links Jordan-Henley's students at Roane State Community College in Tennessee with Maid's graduate rhetoric students at the University of Arkansas at Little Rock. IRC (Internet Relay Chat) and other types of chat programs also allow for real-time communication, but normally the user is not presented with textual description. Web-based chat programs or "chat rooms" are increasingly common on the Internet, the software for them may be relatively inexpensive or even free, and they are easy to use provided users have access to frames-capable browsers. The California State University at Chico runs a virtual writing center using such software (http://www.csuchico.edu/engl/owl/interact.html).

The interactive approach provides direct connections between a writing center, its clientele, and the rest of the world, and it can be a good way of publicizing your services, but it requires more work than the information server approach. It's very important to be sure that users can access your services productively. Although you can normally count on campus users having e-mail accounts, and most schools also provide access to the World Wide Web, accessing a MUD is easiest with special software called *MUD clients* that even experienced Internet users may not be aware of. This software can be made available for downloading from a Web or FTP site or through a university computation center, but you need to let your clientele know it's out there, and you need to educate them in how to use the MUD.

Some schools and Internet service providers restrict or prohibit MUD access. MUDs can consume a lot of bandwidth, and in some quarters they still have an unsavory reputation growing out of their origins in dungeons and dragons adventure games and out of unfavorable coverage in the popular media. You will need to find out whether your users will be subject to such restrictions or prohibitions.

Interactive services also require time and writing center resources for staffing, staff training, and routine maintenance. Since a MUD, for example, is a program run on a server computer, you will need access to a server and someone who has the expertise to program it and perform regular maintenance chores. You will also need to develop systems for getting clients' drafts to writing center staff for review, for scheduling appointments for synchronous conferences, and for allocating staff time to responding to drafts either on a MUD or over e-mail. Even a simple e-mail question-and-answer service requires planning. Someone has to check the writing center account regularly, answering questions or forwarding messages to the appropriate respondents. Finally, you need to formulate policies on who you help and how much help you provide. Being on the Internet opens you up to the whole world, and while it is a good way to let others know about your center's accomplishments, there may be limitations on how much time and effort you can devote to assisting users not affiliated with your university.

12 Productive Change in a Turbulent Atmosphere: Pipe Dream or Possibility?

Rita Malenczyk
Eastern Connecticut State University

The administration micromanages, the faculty is distressed over issues of professional authority, governance, and (last but not least) staffing and financial resources. The English department is asked by the administration to take over the university's developmental writing program; citing governance and authority issues, the department refuses. How do you, the WPA, handle this situation?

Institution Overview

Administrative Authority and Faculty Governance

You are an assistant professor in the English department at Northfield State University, in the third year of a tenure-track appointment as director of the university writing program. Northfield, a comprehensive institution, is part of a four-campus state university system which enrolls approximately 35,000 students each year. Northfield markets itself as the liberal arts college of the state university system and, in its catalog, emphasizes—in addition to student and faculty diversity, educational access for academically qualified students, and opportunities for experiential learning—a student-centered environment and a faculty committed to excellence in teaching. The catalog is, however, somewhat misleading on the subjects of diversity and teaching excellence: a close reading shows that, despite aggressive recruiting efforts, both the undergraduate student body and the faculty remain predominantly (approximately 77 percent) white. Furthermore, the faculty teach four courses per semester. Though they try their best (and often succeed), they sometimes find it difficult to teach well and stay sane while meeting their departments' expectations for scholarship and service.

However, Northfield still has much to recommend it to both students and faculty. With approximately 4,600 full- and part-time students, only 300 of whom are graduate students, the emphasis at Northfield is on undergraduate education. (Northfield has no Ph.D. programs, and its only master's programs are in education, organizational relations, and professional and teacher certification.) No class has more than forty students, and a number of classes—science labs, for example—are limited to twelve students. Writing classes are typically capped at twenty or fewer students; some are as small as twelve or fifteen. Though Northfield is located ten miles from the state's flagship Research I institution, and though Northfield students often go to that university's library to complete extended research projects, students have also been known to leave the Research I institution for Northfield's more intimate atmosphere. This intimacy extends to faculty relations: most faculty are pleasant to work with, cooperative, and collegial. It is in part this collegiality—as well as, no doubt, the tight academic job market—that keeps most of the Northfield faculty from looking for work elsewhere, despite the heavy teaching load.

Transition

The period of your appointment has seen three major changes at Northfield: a new state university system president, who took office the same year you did; a new dean of Arts and Sciences, who also took office the same year you did; and a budget cut from the state legislature, which drove Northfield and the other SU schools to draw on their cash reserves for spending. The system president responded to the budget cut by raising tuition, a move that angered the state's Board of Governors for Higher Education, since enrollment at all four campuses has been stagnant for the last five years and is not likely to rise with tuition increases. Northfield's president has charged the director of admissions with increasing enrollment by aggressively recruiting both in-state and out-of-state students, and has directed his staff to increase retention efforts: like many comparable institutions, Northfield is presently losing first- and second-year students at the rate of 30 percent a year. Northfield also has a number of international students, and the president is hoping to see the international program grow, having established reciprocal agreements with several universities in the Middle East and Asia.

Concerns

Unfortunately, the president's attempts to increase enrollment, coupled with the truncated university budget, is one of several sources of tension between the Northfield faculty and higher administration. Since the president took office seven years ago, enrollment has remained stable, yet the number of full-time faculty has fallen from 135 to 117. Eighteen positions vacated by retirement have not been filled, though the departments doggedly request searches every year. Despite their heavy teaching load, most full-time faculty are opposed to excessive reliance on, and exploitation of, part-time faculty. The perception of many faculty is that the administration's priorities are to hire more administrators: anger still exists about the president's having hired an associate vice president for finance four years ago—the position having been vacant for a number of years—when more full-time faculty members are needed to staff courses and maintain class size at its current level. Attempts to recruit international and out-of-state students are seen as exacerbating a problem that the administration has chosen to ignore.

Also of concern to the faculty is the top-down, micromanaging style of the higher administration, exemplified by the interference of the executive vice president—possibly upon orders from the president, though no one is quite sure—in departmental matters. Faculty search requests, for example, often come back to departments rewritten without consultation, and without regard for professional standards: last year, one department's request for four positions came back with the directive that all four positions be rolled into one. (The department, maintaining that such a position was inappropriate for a four-year institution, refused to conduct such a search and has gradually been getting what it originally asked for.) Furthermore, candidates who come to Northfield for on-campus interviews typically spend less time talking with their future faculty colleagues than they do meeting administrators. The higher administration decides who will be hired for faculty positions; though faculty search committees actually conduct the searches and generate the lists of finalists, they are not allowed to rank the finalists. Deans are charged with delivering the news of higher administration decisions to the departments. Though the executive VP has been told on a number of occasions, by both faculty and mid-level administrators, that many people have difficulty with his management style, he has not changed it. Not surprisingly, many faculty are unhappy with the administration—threats of no-confidence votes have been in the air for some time, though they have never come to anything—and it has been hard for the university to keep deans, who do not enjoy a supportive, collegial network of the kind that faculty provide for each other. The new dean of Arts and Sciences, with whom you have a cordial relationship, has told you on several occasions that he feels that the higher administration considers deans to be clerks and that he is already looking for positions elsewhere.

The primary advocate for hiring more full-time faculty, and the channel for handling complaints about governance and authority issues, is the faculty union, the state university chapter of the American Association of University Professors. All the SU campuses are union shops, with a collective bargaining agreement negotiated every three years by union and management representatives from each of the four campuses. In recent contract negotiations, the union won a part-time faculty percentage of 20 percent, though the exact formula for working this out department by department is fairly complicated. Because it is higher than what the national office of the AAUP recommends, the union is working to bring this percentage down even further in the present negotiations, thereby forcing the administration to hire more full-time faculty to replace those who have retired and staff the courses needed to accommodate the influx of new students. As regards governance issues, the union wants written into the contract a formula for search procedures that would guarantee academic departments at all SU institutions more power over hiring. The administration, for its part, contends that union demands for salary increases and more full-time faculty are contributing to the financial woes of the university system, and wishes to keep search procedures the way they are.

Writing Program Overview

History and Your Job

The University Writing Program in its present incarnation dates from the 1989–90 academic year, when your predecessor—charged by the previous administration with "encouraging" writing across the curriculum—successfully got the University Senate to pass a bill establishing a WAC program. Requirements established by this bill include a placement essay; completion of one first-year writing course, sometimes preceded by a basic writing course, depending on placement; a sophomore-year competency test; and a 300- or 400-level writing-intensive course in the major. An interdisciplinary University Composition Board was also established by this bill: the UCB is composed of faculty from the humanities, sciences, social sciences, and professional studies, with the

WPA an ex officio member. The UCB is an at-large committee of the University Senate; members are elected to rotating three-year terms and tend to be faculty who have taught in, or are otherwise committed to, the WAC program and therefore enjoy serving on the committee. All writing-intensive courses must be approved as such by the UCB; changes in program requirements must be granted by the UCB and the full University Senate.

During the 1990–91 academic year, the first UCB was charged with articulating program goals and figuring out how to implement them. The UCB discussed with the administration ways of compensating faculty for teaching writing-intensive courses: both the UCB and the administration felt that reduced class size was the best option, though for large departments unable to reduce class size, a big-class-with-workshop-added option was granted provisionally. Working, then, with academic departments, your predecessor and the members of the UCB helped departments develop writing-intensive courses in their disciplines and held a series of faculty workshops, some given by outside experts, to "certify" faculty to teach them. Though some of these workshops have gone down in faculty lore as "workshops from hell"—due to the forced attendance of faculty who resented the passage of the Senate bill—others helped to establish a community of WAC instructors across the disciplines. These instructors helped the WPA develop an in-house timed impromptu placement test for entering students, and they are still among those faculty who are recruited and compensated for reading placement essays each year. Though far from perfect (students only have thirty minutes to write the essay), the placement procedure nevertheless provides a yearly place for instructors across the disciplines to get together to talk about student writing and to see the work of entering students.

WPA Position

Until fall 1994, the WPA position rotated among the tenured literature faculty in the English department. However, in 1993 your predecessor announced her intention to return to full-time teaching. After intense lobbying by the English department, the WAC faculty, and an outside evaluator from the Research I institution, the administration was persuaded to add an additional tenure-track line for an assistant professor specializing in rhetoric and composition (there were at the time no rhet/comp faculty in the English department or anywhere else in the university, though one professor in the elementary education department did teach a graduate-level course in writing process and language development).

You are offered the position in May 1994 after a national search during which—you learn later—the executive vice president never makes it clear whether the position will actually be funded or not. However, you apparently make a good impression on him, according to the interim dean who interviews you on campus. Your responsibilities, as the new hire, are to direct first-year composition, to facilitate writing across the curriculum, and to oversee the first-year placement and sophomore competency tests. As WPA, you report to the executive vice president, though as a member of the English department and of the faculty union, you are evaluated for renewal, promotion, and tenure by your home department and by a university-wide faculty promotion and tenure committee, who send their recommendations to the administration.

Key Challenges

During your first year as WPA, you operate under the assumption—having not been told otherwise, and having received positive feedback in your interview—that it is up to you, working with the faculty in general but with the University Composition Board and the English department in particular, to develop the writing program as you see fit. And you do, in fact, feel that certain aspects of the program need to be further developed. Placement and sophomore-year competency testing procedures need to be reworked and revised; more publicity for the program has to be provided; a coherent first-year writing curriculum should be developed and articulated; continued, and more extensive, faculty development should be provided for. You would also like to develop a course-based peer tutor program, since tutorial services on campus—provided by untrained tutors at the Academic Resource Center, an administrative unit—are minimal and inadequate; furthermore, discussions about writing have been confined to the faculty and do not seem to have influenced the student academic culture at Northfield. By the middle of your first year, you have begun recruiting students for a pilot peer tutor program and have received a verbal promise of funding for it from the executive VP, who tells you that you are "doing great things" with the Writing Program.

However, as time goes on you have found "doing great things" more and more difficult, due to the additional challenges of money and time. You have, for example, no real budget under your discretion and control. Like your predecessor, you have applied for and received grant money for funding faculty workshops and other WAC projects, but that is soft money and therefore impossible to count on as a continued resource. The larger writing program budget is folded into the budget of the executive vice president. While he has been supportive of many of your requests for funding, you nevertheless find this arrangement unsatisfying. You also feel that it bespeaks a lack of real commitment to the writing program on the part of the higher administration.

Compounding the difficulties presented by your budget situation is your lack of secretarial support. Your predecessor did not have any secretarial staff, despite repeated requests for it, but only an occasional work-study student to help with filing and large mailings. When the executive VP offers you the position, you say you will need secretarial help, and the VP tells you that you will share a secretary with the director of the Center for Excellence in Teaching, whose office is down the hall from yours. However, you fail to get this in writing, and when you arrive on campus in the summer—having already signed your contract—you are told by the executive VP that the secretary is not yet in place and, when she is, will not work for you. Instead, you will have two work-studies who will report to that secretary, who in turn reports to the head of the CET. You still do not have secretarial support to answer phones, field student requests, schedule workshops and meetings, and do the other administrative tasks that multiply as a writing program grows. You have begun to request additional help from the dean on a regular basis, but so far have had no success. You are beginning to wonder if teaching two courses a semester and having responsibility (but no financial authority) for all facets of the writing program is perhaps more of a challenge than you want.

However, you have done rather well with respect to some other challenges you have faced, particularly with issues of curriculum and pedagogy. Contractually, you have no authority to "make" faculty teach writing and read essays the way you want them to: classroom teaching is the responsibility of the individual instructor, and at Northfield— particularly in the English department—faculty traditionally reach agreement on curriculum by consensus. You are initially somewhat put out by this situation because you are, after all, the only rhet/comp specialist on the faculty. However, you find that you are good at helping faculty to reach consensus in discussions, and have earned the respect and trust of the English department and much of the WAC faculty, including the UCB.

Working with an English department committee, you have articulated a set of goals for the first-year composition course and produced a handbook for the course. Enlisting the secretarial and financial help of the Center for Excellence in Teaching, you have run a successful series of faculty workshops in writing across the disciplines, attended willingly by some faculty from departments that initially resisted WAC, as well as by some new junior faculty who are simply interested in having students do more writing in their classes. Furthermore, with the help of the University Composition Board, you have begun the slow process of talking with academic departments about finding alternatives to the sophomore competency test. You have also recruited students into your peer tutor program and designed a training course in composition theory and pedagogy, which has been granted permanent status by the University Curriculum Committee. Because there has been no undergraduate pedagogy course in the university, the course attracts many students—not just peer tutors—who are planning to go into teaching. Its existence also alerts a number of your colleagues in the English department to the status of composition as an interesting, evolving, developing field, and you institute a series of brown-bag lunch reading groups to accommodate their expressed interest in learning more about it. Where curricular change is concerned, then, you have learned to take the long view, and are trying to take the long view of your secretarial and budgetary problems as well. Having the support of your department and the UCB helps.

Key Challenge

In May of your first year at Northfield, the English department's specialist in British Romanticism suddenly decides to retire. In addition to teaching Romantic lit, this professor also teaches an extremely popular general education course in critical thinking, along with another popular general ed. course in mythology. The English department considers it crucial to its curriculum that this position be filled, not only because not having a Romanticist would weaken its literature curriculum, but also because the other two courses this professor taught are in great demand. The department recognizes that, because of his late announcement, it will be impossible to get administrative authorization to search for a tenure-track replacement. However, at its end-of-year retreat, the department agrees to ask for authorization to search immediately for a one-year, non-tenure-track replacement, and to request authorization to search for a permanent, tenure-track replacement in the fall. Both searches would ideally be for a specialist in Romantic lit who could also teach courses in critical thinking and mythology.

A month later, you are at home on unofficial maternity leave (you are on ten-month contract and your baby is due in July). As you lie at home one day waiting to go into labor and watching your ankles swell, you receive a call from your chair informing you of an interesting situation: the executive vice president has indeed authorized a position for the English department, but not the one the department wanted. What he has authorized, instead, is a search for a specialist in developmental writing. At present, all developmental writing and math courses are taught through the Academic Resource Center, which also oversees a summer program for underprepared students. The executive VP has told your chair that he feels the ARC (which has done this job for at least ten years) does not really know what it is doing; he wants to hire someone who does. In a conciliatory gesture to the department, he states that this person may have a subspecialty in any area the department sees fit—but that those subspecialties should include testing and evaluation, and use of technology in the teaching of writing. No provision is made in his description for the general ed. courses.

In many respects, you can see advantages to a new arrangement for developmental writing; in fact, you have always found its present situation, in two words, archaic and difficult. The developmental writing and math courses are taught by the ARC as general studies courses, and students can only use up to six hours of general studies credit toward their degrees. Furthermore, those who teach developmental writing, all part-time faculty, are supervised by the assistant director of the ARC, a specialist in math education. While you have tried to meet with them occasionally, it is difficult for you—given your already overloaded plate—to keep up with what they do in the class, and furthermore, you don't want to step on the ARC director's toes. However, the isolation of the developmental writing course not only from the WPA's authority but also from the rest of the writing courses in the university emphasizes the course's "remedial" status. Recent work on mainstreaming, as well as Mike Rose's and David Bartholomae's critiques of "basic" and "developmental" writing courses as such, makes you feel that it is high time for a change.

Concerns

Unfortunately, there are also a good many problems with the executive VP's proposal. For one thing, he has hijacked an existing tenure line that means a good deal to the English department. You wish to keep the good will of your department; furthermore, you see department members' point. The union/Board of Trustees contract, on which life at Northfield runs, states that academic departments shall have primary responsibility for the development of programs within their discipline. It might be said that the higher administration, by telling the English department not to hire a Romanticist but rather someone with a specialty in developmental writing, is in effect telling the department what to teach. (The department does not feel it is possible to do as the executive VP suggests and search for someone with a "minor" in Romanticism: a candidate with competency in both fields—with a primary specialty in developmental writing—would be difficult to find.)

Another problem with the proposed position is the reason for it. No one outside the higher administration, including the dean of Arts and Sciences—who by this time has gotten another job and plans to leave in six months—knows why the executive VP wants the English department to take over developmental writing. Though he has told the department that the existing setup of developmental writing "isn't working," he has not told them what he bases this judgment on, though he has repeatedly been asked. You would like to think that he has read Mike Rose and David Bartholomae as well as the recent material on mainstreaming, but you feel that this is unlikely, since he has not read material you have given him in the past.

There is a good deal of scuttlebutt floating around campus: some rumors have it that pressure is coming from the new system president to eliminate the ARC; others, equally plausible, have it that the VP's push for a new developmental program is an attempt to increase retention. However, the department is unwilling to take the program over based on mere rumors. Yet another problem with having the English department take over developmental writing, in your mind and in the minds of most people in your department, is the setup of the proposed faculty position. The executive VP has told your chair that he envisions the developmental writing specialist doing nothing except teaching four developmental writing courses each semester. You and your colleagues, however, envision not only burnout for a faculty member brought into such a situation, but also isolation from the rest of the department faculty—all of whom have more varied workloads—and difficulties at promotion and tenure time. Nothing has been said about released time or opportunities for working with the WPA on program/curriculum development—opportunities that would make a developmental writing position attractive to good candidates, would provide them with a fair shot at promotion and tenure, and would utilize their expertise in the best way.

Unfortunately, the English department is also reluctant to have a new faculty member take on released-time work right now, due to the difficulties you yourself are presently having with the higher administration. The difficulties date back to March of the first year of your appointment, two months before the executive VP approached your chair about hiring a developmental writing specialist. At that time, you and a tenured full professor on the University Composition Board attended a meeting, called by one of the executive VP's staff, at which replacing the current in-house placement test with standardized testing was suggested. The UCB—the body authorized to change placement procedures—has always been opposed to standardized testing; at this meeting, you and the tenured UCB member reiterated your opposition to such a move. The following day the executive VP summoned you to his office to discuss placement testing and outcomes assessment (though you were not told in advance what the meeting was going to be about). Saying that "this university cannot afford negative people," the executive VP told you that the WAC program needed to justify its existence and suggested that you implement pre- and post-testing procedures; it was clear to you from the discussion that the executive VP wanted you to think about alternatives to the present placement test, and to do so without consulting the UCB.

In your mind, the executive VP's suggestions constituted, if not a lack of knowledge of, then at least a lack of respect for, faculty governance procedures. Out of respect for those procedures, you reported the meeting to your department chair and the chair of the University Composition Board. Both chairs reminded the executive VP in writing that the English department and the UCB had oversight of placement testing and that the testing procedure could not be changed simply by his pressuring the WPA. They also reminded the executive VP that program assessment was the province of the Academic Program Review Committee, another committee of the University Senate, and of the academic departments. The matter seemed to have been laid to rest. However, that fall you clashed again with the executive VP: an upper-division writing-intensive course that had been capped at twenty students was suddenly found to have an enrollment of forty, and at the department's request you negotiated with the dean of Arts and Sciences for an additional load credit for the instructor. Then, in yet another meeting—this one called by the dean—you and the executive VP disagreed on whether or not class size was a pedagogical issue in a writing course (you claimed that it was). You reported the substance of this meeting—with a reference to your disagreement with the executive VP—in a memo to your department chair and the UCB, with copies to the executive VP and the dean.

Two months later, in your yearly retention review, you received enthusiastic recommendations for renewal from both your department and the dean; the executive VP, however, sent a negative recommendation to the president—giving no reasons—and on his recommendation the president refused to renew your appointment. You spoke with the faculty union, and under threat of an academic freedom and contract grievance, the administration backed down. However, since that time, the administration has made—in your opinion—a number of attempts to control you, the latest of which resulted in the issuing of a job description for you (one, albeit informal, already exists). The English department, which has been unanimously supportive of you and your position regarding placement testing and class size, now has a grievance pending over the job description, claiming that the administration has violated its contractual rights to determine the criteria by which all its members are evaluated.

The department contends that writing program administration is a discipline within English studies, and that what constitutes good performance for a WPA with released time is therefore most appropriately judged by the English department. The administration, on the other hand, claims that your released time is for administrative work, and that it therefore had the right to issue a job description for you. However this question is decided—and it is believed that it will go to arbitration—any new faculty member would, under the terms of the contract, have to be untenured when hired. The English department, given the executive VP's history of micromanagement and retaliation, does not want to hire any more untenured faculty with released time unless you win the grievance. Your next retention review is coming up in six months. You are apprehensive about it; though your willingness to stand up to the administration, particularly as an untenured assistant professor, has reinforced your good standing with the faculty, you feel that the administration has become more, not less, eager to get rid of you. Whether they can legally do it is still an open question. Even if they cannot, the executive VP has refused to support your initiatives: he has, for instance, told the dean that he never approved your peer tutor program and that there is no funding for it.

Key Charge

After the initial summer meeting with the executive VP, your department chair solicits opinions from the other English department faculty about whether to take him up on his offer. Does the department want to hire someone with a specialty in developmental writing and a "minor" in Romanticism? The unofficial consensus is no. Some faculty—though they are in a minority—feel the responsibility for remediation lies with the high schools and the community colleges, not with the English departments of the four-year universities. Others are reluctant to give up the English department's authority to staff its courses as it sees fit and to determine what courses it will offer. Still others feel that, given resources, it might be appropriate and possible for the department to take over developmental writing, but that to hire one professor without released time is not the way to approach the matter. The department, then, agrees to accept a one-year appointment on the administration's terms, simply to fill the following year's courses, but reiterates its original request for a Romanticist.

While this request is being processed, the dean of Arts and Sciences—having gotten wind of faculty discontent about the way this matter was handled—calls an ad hoc committee composed of members of the math, English, and education departments to discuss alternatives to the present developmental program and make recommendations to the executive VP. You are a member of this committee and remain frustrated with the administration's refusal to explain exactly why, and in what ways, it wants the developmental program changed. Your frustration notwithstanding, the committee makes a recommendation for an intensive developmental education component during the fall semester, closely coordinated by the English, math, and education departments and the ARC, and sends its recommendation to the executive VP (who has also attended a meeting of this committee). The executive VP does not respond. Another academic year passes, and in the fall of 1996, the executive VP—with no mention of the recommendations of the dean's committee—requests again that the English department search for a position in developmental writing. Following this request, he meets with the English department to state that the department "must take over developmental writing" but, again, gives no reasons why. The department agrees to discuss the matter. The following day, your chair asks you to lead such a discussion with members of the department. You agree to do so. Your chair schedules it for the following week.

In thinking about the upcoming discussion, however, you are not quite sure how to approach it. You realize all too clearly how difficult circumstances such as those at Northfield are for a WPA: the challenge in such circumstances is to isolate the issues, consider them in terms of the institutional culture, and figure out how one might make not just temporary but lasting change. This realization, however, is not much help to you in preparing for the discussion. You feel confused and frustrated by the multiplicity of issues, the VP's refusal to volunteer information, and the feeling that any developmental writing specialist coming into Northfield would be at a disadvantage: they would be either resented by the English department or at the mercy of the administration. Neither situation would be conducive to the promotion, tenure, or—perhaps more important—the happiness of a colleague in rhetoric and composition. And, while you feel it would be nice to have another composition specialist in the university, let alone the English department, you are reluctant to set that person up to fail. So, on the one hand, you are tempted to tell your chair to forget the discussion—the English department should not hire a developmental writing specialist, period. On the other hand, the existing situation of developmental writing is not good for the students—if you could get the English department to take it over willingly, the students would benefit. Is there, then, a way out of this conundrum? More immediately, what approach should you take to the departmental discussion?

AUTHOR'S CASE COMMENTARY

As I look back on my description of events at Northfield State University—which resemble, though not completely, recent events in my life—all I can say is, with Charlie Brown, "Good grief." In many ways, these circumstances are impossible; one wonders whether the best advice one WPA could give to another in a similar situation is simply, "Hit the job market." And, in fact, faced with a situation not unlike the one described, I thought seriously (surprise!) about doing exactly that. I chose not to, at least as of this writing, largely because of family circumstances: my husband is also an academic, and since we have very small children and will both come up for tenure at around the same time, we thought it prudent to wait a couple of years before deciding whether, and where, to move.

Even if I had been single and unattached, however, I think I would have had second thoughts about leaving "Northfield" immediately. This sounds odd, given the difficulty of the situation described. Unfortunately, some of the circumstances described are no longer particularly rare, at least at state colleges and universities. It is true that better WPA jobs are available—positions with more staff support, more generous budgets, more financial and philosophical support from high-level administrators. However, some problems will remain everywhere, for the foreseeable future. Higher education is coming under greater and greater demands for accountability; state appropriations for higher education are often, shall we say, less generous than they were in the past; tensions between faculty and administrators over issues of governance are intensifying. So, in some sense, I felt my desire to leave to be akin to Huck Finn's urge to "light out for the territory": understandable, but ultimately unrealistic. Furthermore, I was reluctant to find myself in a similar, or worse, situation without tenure, since another thing I would be unlikely to escape would be the WPA's unique situation of having the frequent opportunity to tell administrators what he or she thinks about their ideas. If I have to be outspoken at yet another institution, I would like to be able to do it with tenure.

And in fact, inescapability notwithstanding, the situation at "Northfield" does have its good points. The WAC faculty, for instance, are for the most part supportive of the WPA; the faculty is unionized, and the union supports the WPA's battles; the WPA's home department is also supportive. Furthermore, the writing program is relatively young. Its youth has drawbacks, notably the fact that there is only one rhet/comp specialist on the faculty, untenured, who has to fight for a lot of things that rhet/comp specialists in more established programs might take (sort of) for granted: course offerings in composition and rhetoric, monetary and secretarial support, a tutoring program. However, the writing program's youth also brings with it opportunities for the WPA to make her mark. If, for example, she manages to develop and teach a significant number of courses in composition theory and/or rhetoric, it might be difficult for the higher administration to continue to claim that developing and running a writing program is purely administrative, and not academic, work. If she manages to sustain her peer tutor program, she will create a "writing culture" among the Northfield students that was not there before. Furthermore, if she manages to solve the problem presented by the "key challenge"—what to do about developmental writing?—she can benefit the students in yet another way.

The challenge, then, for a WPA trying to find her way out of a conundrum like the one presented by developmental writing at Northfield is—as I said in the case study—to isolate the issues, consider them in terms of the institutional culture, and figure out how one is most likely to make not just temporary but lasting change. Doing these three things requires, in my opinion, thinking both locally (in terms of the particular institution) as well as globally (in terms of the profession of composition, the intellectual work of the WPA, and the politics of faculty/administrative work). It also requires reducing the plethora of issues to some kind of manageable number, or at least prioritizing those issues so they don't seem to be coming at the WPA all at once.

First, then, to isolate the issues. It seems to me that there are five areas of difficulty at Northfield:

1. The personality and management style of the executive vice president: rigid, controlling, top-down, patriarchal.

2. Placement testing and outcomes assessment. The executive VP wants to decide how these things will be done; the WPA, as well as the English department, feels that decisions about assessing writing are best made by someone in the field of composition.

3. The WPA's released time grievance. The executive VP wants to gain control of the WPA's decisions by claiming that writing program administration—and therefore placement testing and outcomes assessment—is not academic, but administrative, work.

4. Developmental writing (existing program). The current developmental writing program is based on a "remediation" model: outmoded and ineffective.

5. The executive VP's request that the English department hire a developmental writing specialist and take over the developmental writing program. The department, as well as the WPA, are concerned that the executive VP will not provide budgetary and secretarial support to a new developmental writing specialist and that the VP will try to control the developmental writing specialist (as he is trying to control the WPA). The department also feels that the VP is trying to dictate the content of its programs.

After one isolates the issues, one might reduce them to a manageable number by taking the local issues (as described) and setting them beside their global equivalents:

LOCAL ISSUE	GLOBAL ISSUE
micromanaging, authoritarian executive VP	faculty vs. administrative governance
placement testing and outcomes assessment	professional authority (who decides how to do these things?)
WPA's reassigned time grievance	professional authority (intellectual work of the WPA)

| developmental writing—existing program | "remediation"—outmoded and probably ineffective |
| hiring a new developmental writing specialist and taking over the developmental writing program | faculty vs.administrative governance |

Considered in global terms, the local problems seem somewhat more manageable. Five local issues fall into three global categories: governance, professional authority, and remediation. The question, then: Considering the institutional culture as well as her own knowledge of writing program administration, how should the WPA prioritize these issues?

My own way of approaching a similar question was, first, to consider my own strengths and successes as WPA and decide to what degree those successes had been determined by the strengths and concerns of the institution, as well as how much they meshed with the corresponding global issues. It will be noted, for instance, that the Northfield WPA was hired partly to direct a writing-across-the-curriculum program, and that her successes were based in Barbara Walvoord's first principle of WAC: "Start with faculty dialogue" (14). In "Getting Started," the first chapter in Susan McLeod and Margot Soven's book on developing WAC programs, Walvoord cautions against beginning a WAC program with the assumption that faculty in disciplines other than writing are "heathen to be converted to the Right Way" and advises, instead, a respectful approach to the concerns of faculty across the disciplines and an acknowledgment of their expertise (15). Walvoord's approach to faculty and curricular change implies that a WAC director, or coordinator, should be patient in trying to implement a new WAC program or further develop an existing one: faculty, particularly permanent, tenured faculty, cannot be expected to change immediately. However, they are necessary to the success of WAC: as Toby Fulwiler and Art Young point out, "Most WAC programs are teacher-centered, premised on the belief that permanent faculty are the route to stable institutional change" (3).

As it happens, the belief that permanent faculty are the backbone of institutions and the route to institutional change is shared by the AAUP, the collective bargaining agent for the faculty at Northfield. Issues of governance and professional authority thereby mesh with the concerns of WAC, at least at Northfield. They also mesh with the stance of the Council of Writing Program Administrators, as expressed in the

Portland Resolution as well as the recent draft statement on the intellectual work of the WPA, that WPAs be regarded as professionals in a discipline. The coming together of these issues, as well as the WPA's willingness to (as I put it in the case study) "take the long view" of curricular and programmatic change, is probably the primary reason for the Northfield WPA's success with the faculty.

What I decided to do, then, in approaching a developmental writing conundrum similar to the one described at Northfield was (1) to decide, once and for all, that the faculty, and not the administration, was the key to what successes I had had as WPA and (2) to build on what had worked for me in the past. I approached the department meeting scheduled by my chair, then, as an open-ended faculty dialogue. However, not willing to ignore the third global issue I've raised in this commentary—remediation—I also built on the trust I had built with the faculty to make clear my own biases about developmental writing. At the departmental meeting my chair asked me to lead, I began by distributing materials about recent mainstreaming activities at CCNY and the University of South Carolina (Soliday; Grego and Thompson) and talking a little bit about the way developmental writing was presently regarded by compositionists. I also made it clear, however, that I felt there were serious problems with our taking over the developmental writing program at the behest of the administration, for all the reasons I enumerated in the case study (and which we had already discussed as a department on another occasion). This took less than five minutes. I then turned the meeting over to the other department members with the expressed intention of trying to ascertain where each of them stood on the issue. One young and well-respected faculty member, who had been hired on a one-year contract to fill the position the department had refused to fill permanently (and who has a master's in rhet/comp), suggested thinking creatively about developmental writing by, perhaps, proposing to the administration that we hire a number of people in varied literary specialties who were also preferably trained in composition and who would be willing to work in a reconfigured developmental writing program. This suggestion was not pursued at the time: the department decided at the end of the meeting to reiterate its original request for a Romanticist and to consider taking over developmental writing only after that position was filled. I assumed then that the matter was dead, at least for a while, and turned my attention to other matters.

However, several months later at our department retreat, my chair raised the issue again, saying—unexpectedly, at least to me—that she felt the English department had an obligation not only to its majors but to all students, "underprepared" though they might be, who had been admitted to the university. She asked that the department come up, collectively, with a set of circumstances under which it would be willing to take over developmental writing. Having had by then a good deal of time to let ideas about this matter come to me—and having familiarized myself with the "stretch" program at Arizona State University (Glau)—I suggested reconfiguring first-year composition as a two-semester sequence, taught within the department; a new line could be developed for someone to work with me on reconfiguring first-year composition and training peer tutors, as well as developing a writing center. This suggestion, along with the suggestions of other faculty members (fueled, perhaps, by my colleague's suggestion at the previous meeting that we hire other faculty with literary specialties who would also be willing to teach in a reconfigured writing program), was well-received. Yet another colleague suggested—assuming the administration approved the writing center idea—reconfiguring the first-year composition course in a slightly different way, as a one-semester course with tutorial attached (a mainstreaming approach similar to one that has been tried, apparently successfully, at other universities). These ideas have been submitted to the administration in the form of a proposal.

So far, there has been no word from the administration, so we may be back at square one. And, at least to my mind, problems still remain: the grievance over whether my released-time duties are "academic" or "administrative" has not been settled, and if a new person were to be hired with released time, evaluation procedures would have to be meticulously worked out beforehand in consultation with the union. Furthermore, the management style of the higher administration has not changed, and I do not expect it to do so; this is the one aspect of the Northfield problem (and I think it's a pretty big aspect) that I feel to be unsolvable. I still keep a letter of resignation in my back pocket in anticipation of either a negative tenure decision or my circumstances becoming more unbearable than they already are. However, my feeling is that the faculty dialogue approach has so far worked to a limited extent: the members of the English department have, at least to some degree, reached consensus among themselves.

III Professional Issues of Departmental Authority and Professional Development

13 A New Millennium for the Writing Program: Introducing Authority and Change to Traditional Folks Who Employ Time-Worn Practices

Ben W. McClelland
The University of Mississippi

This chapter presents a situation in which you, a newly arrived writing program administrator, are attempting to implement a theory-based program in an institution that has been employing early writing process pedagogy (laced with lore). The central issue involves gaining the trust and confidence of graduate instructors who are being asked to risk changing their ways of teaching. Having been apprised of the situation shortly after your arrival on campus in late July, you work, first, to arrange the various issues in a priority and, second, to develop strategies for addressing them.

Institution Overview

Central University* is a medium-sized, public institution, the flagship of a six-campus state system. Hailed throughout its century-and-a-quarter history as a good party school, Central has, however, attracted fine teachers and excellent researchers in recent decades. Through solid political connections to the federal government, Central has landed huge federal contracts to direct national research centers in such areas as school food service administration, physical acoustics, and pharmaceutical products from natural plants. The spillover effects of the research phenomenon have been good and bad: additional research ventures

---

*The institution and individuals portrayed in this essay are fictional and bear no resemblance to any real institutions or individuals.

have been spawned with success, but the teaching enterprise has taken a distant second place as institutional rewards tilt toward research, research, and more research.

The Schools of Law and Medicine supply the state with the bulk of its professionals in those areas. English, journalism, and pharmacy are strong programs, attracting bright students. Majors in accounting, business, and education are highly popular with average students. A well-funded Honors College was recently established, giving promise to further upgrade the school's academic reputation and spurring on its bid to gain Phi Beta Kappa status by 2002.

Funding

In the mid-1980s Central netted $50 million in a capital fund drive that established endowments for several academic programs. Some new ventures were initiated, and several existing academic programs (deemed "excellent") were given additional funds to stay at the top of their games. Central's president plans to launch a second capital fund drive next spring on the 125th anniversary of the school's founding. He is seeking succinct proposals from the faculty for items for which they want additional funding. The campus is abuzz with proposal-making and with rumors about which areas the administration will select as top priorities. The president has already tipped his hand, stating that he believes that Central needs renewed efforts in student recruiting and retention in all appropriate program areas, not just the admissions office.

Students

Most of Central's 13,000 students matriculate from well-to-do suburbs of the cities across the region, forming a nearly monochromatic social fabric that is neatly woven by members of student government and academic, social, and service organizations. Membership in national fraternities and sororities hovers around 45 percent of the student body, prompting one alum to refer to the school as a club, not a university. What diversity there is comes from the African American students (who compose 10 percent of the total student body) and the other 3 percent, primarily Asian Americans and Hispanics/Latinos. Because of the state's large community college system, most of the senior institutions have very little need for remedial courses. In fact, the state legislature has prohibited funding for remedial courses at the senior universities. While Central has little need for remedial services, the fifty-some first-year composition instructors find in their classes a wider range of student academic abilities than they prefer. Approximately 1,000 students take first-year composition in classes of twenty-seven students each.

Central's athletic teams are very competitive in its league conference, drawing large fan participation from students, alums, and the general public from the region. Fall pre-game tailgating parties at home football games are highly celebrated social events where thousands of fans gather to maintain friendships and cheer their team on to victory. While alcohol is banned from campus, it flows freely, if discreetly, at tailgate parties. The jovial fan spirit is captured in an alum's quip, "We may not win every game, but we ain't never lost a party."

Writing Program and Writing Center Overviews

The English department is fondly referred to as the jewel in the crown of the Arts and Humanities school. In the capital fund drive a decade ago, it was the sole program within Arts and Humanities to receive an endowment that yields $100,000 annually in "excellence funds." The twenty-five-member English faculty has chosen to allocate the money to itself for these items: four summer faculty research grants, a pool of travel money, and one graduate fellowship of $10,000. Funding is already available from the graduate school for some summer faculty research grants, and funding for travel grants is available from the dean of Arts and Humanities. However, the faculty has chosen to augment with its "excellence" money the amounts available in both categories.

Faculty

The English faculty has carried on effectively the study of the rich literature of its region. In doing so, individual faculty have built national reputations as well as situating Central in a privileged position in the minds of colleagues in the Modern Language Association. The undergraduate English major is almost exclusively a study of literature. While many faculty teach a junior-year advanced composition course, the course content ranges widely from the study of belles lettres to autobiography and even writing poetry and drama. At the graduate level, the department offers M.A. and Ph.D. degrees in literature. While it offers creative writing courses at the undergraduate level, it is prohibited by state mandate from offering a graduate degree in that area. No such prohibition exists in the area of composition and rhetoric, yet the department has no graduate program in this area. Save for a teaching practicum course, there are still no graduate courses in rhetoric or writing. Three recent hires in literature are the department's first faculty to be conversant with current literary theory. A linguist has interests in writing, but they seem quaint when compared to disciplinary topics in contemporary graduate programs in composition and rhetoric. While English departments in universities in neighboring states have active sites of the National Writing Project and offer graduate courses relevant to public school teachers' work, those teachers who seek advanced study at Central's English department—other than traditional literary study—are directed by department personnel to inquire at the school of education.

Graduate and undergraduate students collaborate on the production of a departmental literary magazine, published annually. Writing contests are held in poetry and in fiction (with two categories: long and short); $500 prizes are awarded each spring at Central's honors day program. These ventures are sponsored by the department's student literary society.

Courses

The English department offers a two-semester sequence of courses in first-year composition as well as a two-semester sequence of courses in sophomore literature. All four courses are required of all entering students. Administration of the composition and the literature programs has traditionally been handled by various up-and-coming young faculty members who rotate into the positions for a couple of years, irrespective of their areas of expertise. Forty-eight graduate instructors carry the workload for the composition program. Slightly less than half of them are master's degree candidates, with just over half studying for the Ph.D. Forty percent of the doctoral candidates are either studying for comprehensive exams or writing dissertations. The pedagogy, so far as it can be named, is characterized as early-1970s process writing. Senior graduate instructors also teach the required sophomore literature course. Since Central's English faculty actively recruit only graduate students who are studying literature, graduate instructors prefer to teach literature courses, seeing composition teaching as an assignment to be endured until one has enough seniority to move on to literature teaching. There is no local community of compositionists and little sense of the wider composition community in the academy.

Writing Center

Still, Central has had a writing center for some years, owing to a computer zealot among faculty, the linguist, who wanted students to learn how to word-process. Twice upgraded within a six-year period, the equipment offers powerful software programs and Internet connections so that students may conduct online research for term papers. The director of the center, who holds a staff position, supervises a group of undergraduate peer tutors who provide assistance to students in using the computers. Though they have little formal training in peer tutoring, the staff members also confer with students about their writing when called to do so.

Writing Across the Curriculum

While no writing-across-the-curriculum program, per se, exists at Central, writing is supported in a few disciplines. The writing center director has given workshops at the request of faculty in biology and geology. Faculty in those departments now regularly assign "papers" and refer their students to the writing center for assistance. The business school recently replaced its upper-level literature requirement for majors with one in advanced composition; the new requirement will go into effect next fall. Anticipating the consequent shift of hundreds of students from literature to advanced writing courses, the dean of Arts and Humanities has asked the English department chair to present plans for a new teaching schedule. On two occasions over the summer the chair has postponed meeting with the dean on this subject.

Last spring the accountancy program asked the English department chair for assistance in developing a writing course for its master's degree; he referred them to the writing center director, who has been meeting with the curriculum committee over the summer.

The law school added a legal writing program five years ago through an ironic twist of fate. A former lawyer, an alumna of Central's law school, returned seeking a Ph.D. in English. After two years of study, she became simultaneously disgruntled with her literary studies and enthusiastic about teaching composition. She proposed a legal writing program to the law school dean who jumped at the idea, hiring her to administer it. Through the program of continuing education she also offered highly popular writing seminars for judges. Following still another vocation, she entered divinity school, leaving the legal writing program as her legacy to Central. A new legal writing expert was hired and is scheduled to arrive on campus this fall to direct the program.

The undergraduate student pre-professional adviser, who works out of the office of the arts and humanities' dean, has long been concerned over historically low scores by Central's students on the writing portions of medical and law school entrance exams. "Curiously," she observed in a memo sent to several department chairs a year ago, "the students' verbal scores are high. So are their grade point averages. How can this be? Why are our students' writing scores low so consistently?" For two years the adviser has hired freelance teachers to conduct noncredit writing seminars for students prior to their taking the entrance exams. Yet, she has urged that the dean seek more systematic and routine means for improving students' writing in the undergraduate curriculum.

Scheduled Meetings

Historically, graduate instructor staff meetings are not regularly scheduled, except for ritual gatherings at the beginning of each semester. Even then, attendance is spotty. The agenda consists primarily of announcements and various "housekeeping" items. The department faculty are an autonomous sort; they have never held a professional development seminar, nor have they thought of doing so for the graduate instructors.

Budget

Budgeting at Central has been a tightly guarded process involving only a council of central administrators, including vice presidents and the president. Department chairs and program directors are directed to discuss budget issues with their respective deans. All deans report to the vice president for academic affairs, who presents the budget for the academic side of the council. However, the academic affairs vice president holds the least seniority among the current council membership. The square-jawed vice president for financial affairs, enjoying his thirty-sixth year in that position, outranks everyone else by far and feels emboldened to quash any deviations from his personally authorized budgeting practices. He even calls into question some of the president's initiatives, feeling it his duty to cite precedence for the status quo.

Funding

Over the years the vice president for financial affairs has squirreled funds into various channels that only he knows exist. Besides, he has made Central the largest landowner in the area through several questionable real estate purchases, and has insisted—over each of the last ten years—that program budget increments be made at 7 percent across the board, except in the very few cases when he was outvoted. (Faculty salaries, of course, have experienced variable increments over this time, ranging from zero growth to an 8 percent increase. The average annual increase over the decade has been 3 percent.) Rare has been the moment when all of the other vice presidents have formed an alliance against him. Usually he plays one against the other, keeping them all off balance and mistrustful of each other.

In 1991 the legislature made the universities reduce their budgets in the midst of the 1990–91 fiscal year. While there were other political resolutions available to avoid a state budget crisis, the legislators chose this path, not wanting to face the fallout from other more powerful constituencies. The effect on Central was chastening, to say the least. The English department was forced to eliminate $33,500 from its budget, which it chose to take from the annual allocation to the writing center. A graduate administrative staff position, a secretarial position, and three-fourths of the student wages were eliminated, decimating the service available to students. Now that budget times are much better for Central, there still is no way of redressing such funding imbalances, nor to make a case for new program development, other than importuning the dean, who is still very far from the power center.

Considerations

Last semester a consultant who examined administrative affairs for the president made a number of recommendations. Among them were these: (1) redesign the vice president for academic affairs position as a provost's position, putting him at the head of the administrative council, and (2) adopt a zero-based budgeting procedure with budget hearings open to all department chairs and program directors. A commission of administrators, faculty, and students is due to report this fall on implementation of the consultant's recommendations. The vice president for financial affairs does not sit on the commission.

TA Population

About the only progressive thing that the teaching assistants have insisted on is being referred to as graduate instructors. Two years ago a graduate student newcomer from another state introduced the idea and it took hold like a hybrid seed in freshly tilled soil. But there is no sense of community among the English department's forty-eight graduate instructors. Departmental governance at Central reflects the hierarchical structure of the rest of the university, and the English department is no different in this regard. Graduate student loyalty is reserved for major professors. Small clusters of students follow their professors around campus like so many groupies at a summer rock festival.

The large majority of the English graduate students matriculate to Central to study with its prestigious literature faculty. While it would be possible, technically speaking, to write a thesis or even complete doctoral studies with an emphasis in composition and rhetoric, it is not practical, owing to the dearth of composition faculty (two—you and the linguist) and the absence of graduate courses in that area of study.

Another power center to which graduate instructors gravitate is the faculty office of the immediate past writing program director, who was removed after one-too-many conflicts with the department chair. A creative writer who has a national following for his gritty fiction, he is also popular in the department and is the darling of the local social scene, despite his frequent inebriety. He regularly carries several graduate instructors along on his evening soirées as well as entertaining them at dinner parties in his art-deco apartment. This man, who did not favor hiring a new writing program administrator, holds on to the fealty of as many graduate instructors as he can. Over a dozen graduate instructors, mostly senior students who have completed their course work, are set to resist the new writing program administrator's innovations, as a recent memo (see page 176) indicates.

Space

The graduate instructors have offices, so to speak. There is no central location for them; groups are scattered in four buildings. None of them are located in the same building with the English department faculty or the writing center. Most offices are shared by two graduate instructors, even though usually only one desk is available. In one location, however, seven graduate instructors share a large second-story room in an old gymnasium that overlooks a baseball practice field. The graduate instructors refer to it as "the bullpen." They have telephone access in only two locations; in each of these a common phone is placed on a chair in the center of the hallway.

The dean has promised office space for everyone, in a building that was formerly a dormitory. While there are no funds for renovation at this time, he offers immediate occupancy on two floors for the exclusive use of the first-year composition graduate instructors. There's even space for a lounge. Upon hearing about the dean's offer, the writing center director volunteers to assist in carrying out the move before classes begin. She knows of a warehouse in the old railroad depot where usable surplus desks, chairs, and bookcases can be obtained.

Charges

You meet with the dean the day after you arrive at Central. He acknowledges that you have a monumental task and that you are being placed in a difficult situation. Nevertheless, he has high expectations of you.

He lists these goals:

- Establish a theory-based philosophy of teaching for the graduate instructors and design a two-semester course syllabus for them to model. Because the dean believes that collaborative writing activities in first-year courses can have a positive effect on student retention, he favors this approach.

- Build a professional development program for the graduate instructors, introducing other contemporary theories of instruction in order to enable them to develop personal philosophies based on current theories.

- Design strategies to counter the resistance to program reform on the part of graduate instructors and English faculty.

- Upgrade the practicum course and develop sufficient other graduate courses in composition and rhetoric to offer a program track within the existing English Ph.D. degree.

- Assess the actual budget needs of the first-year composition program to present to the administration, if "zero-based" budgeting becomes a reality at Central.

- Build a base of support for the composition program across the campus and look for ways to increase writing in upper-level courses.

Key Charge

Establish within the first-year composition staff and the English faculty a culture of composition studies. This challenge depends heavily, of course, on straightening out the untoward budgetary and authority issues in the English department.

Your Challenges as New Writing Program Administrator

At the insistence of the new dean of Arts and Humanities, the English department has gone outside of the department to hire for this position for the first time since the position was created over fifteen years ago. The dean gave the department a new faculty tenure-track line for this purpose. At the beginning of the search process, the department committee forwarded to the dean a position announcement listing a specialty in literature plus the administrative assignment on a one-quarter-time basis. He revised the description, sending back to the committee a position announcement that sought a specialist in composition and rhetoric.

As the new writing program administrator, you have been hired to develop the composition program, bringing academic standards fit for a sound program in the twenty-first century. On first surveying the needs of the program upon your arrival in late July, here's what you find:

- The English faculty see little need to reform the composition program. To them, it's primarily a place for their graduate students to gain classroom teaching experience.

- The first-year composition program has no budget. The English department chair allocates funds from the English department budget on an "as needed" basis. Thus, you must make a separate request to him for each item that you want.

- The first-year composition program shares a secretary with the English department. She has been with the department for twenty-one years and is very loyal to the chair, whom she is fond of referring to as "the first among unequals." On more than one occasion in your first weeks on the job, you have observed her either grilling or dressing down graduate instructors on such matters as dress, duties, or the content of their course syllabuses. She also resists some of your work directions. For example, she has delayed sending your memos, failed to deliver phone messages for you, and "forgot" to notify you of a meeting called by the writing center director.

- A memo from a group of senior graduate instructors arrives a week after you take up your post. They have heard that you are planning a week-long workshop on teaching just before the opening of school. They list a number of concerns, among which are these:

  Will they be paid for participating in the workshop? They have heard from the department chair that no funds are available for paying them to come to campus early.

  They have heard that you come from a teaching program where students develop writing portfolios and where the teachers take a whole-staff approach to grading. They present rationales (1) for the need to grade essays separately as they are turned in and (2) for what they term "teacher autonomy and academic freedom in an age of the socialization of education."

  They want better access to copying services. As is, they must turn in material to the department/program secretary for copying. Often they wait for over a week before their requests are filled.

  They want better access to computers. While each department faculty member has an office computer with Internet access, no graduate instructors do. They are able to use writing center computers, but often have to wait over an hour to get to a computer to send e-mail and use Internet services.

Even though you need to unpack boxes and arrange your new living space, you work late into the nights of your first weeks on the job to arrange the various issues in a priority and to develop strategies for addressing them. You first categorize the various issues under the following headings: administration, budget, curriculum, personnel, program philosophy and policies, and other. Then you begin brainstorming lists of potential strategies for each item.

AUTHOR'S CASE COMMENTARY

While listing the various matters under categories is helpful in separating issues in order to think them through, an administrator finds that working them out in real life doesn't follow any neat categories. Whether an introvert or an extrovert, a good administrator gets to know the people in an organization, working from those within the closest circle of associates outward. This affords opportunities for building a base of political support as well as determining the mettle of potential opponents. Working to develop camaraderie with TAs is especially important. Usually, it will soon become apparent on which side of the fence TAs stand and which ones are straddling it. In the early days take the time to talk face-to-face with colleagues and staff members, whenever practicable; use the telephone as the next-preferred means of communication; resort only last to written notes or memos. And keep your written communications short and to the point.

Discussing the practical realities of a program philosophy with TAs, especially pointing out benefits for them personally and professionally, can win converts to a new system. Also, whenever possible, make connections between writing theory and literary theory, with which they are likely more familiar. Moreover, rolling up your sleeves and helping TAs paint and move furnishings into their offices also builds esprit de corps and may give you a measure of trust hard to win otherwise. No matter how much you try, a number of TAs will likely remain loyal to old ways. This will change over time as some TAs with a wait-and-see attitude eventually join your cause and as senior TAs leave and are replaced by newcomers.

Compromising on the matter of conducting a week-long professional conference is probably the best order of the day, given the situation in your first semester on campus. Shorten the time to two or three days. Involve TAs in the planning of the program. Find willing faculty or administrators to host social gatherings in the evenings of the workshop days. Public relations is a tool that you should employ as effectively as your rhetorically sharp mind will permit. Put the focus on the work of the program and the individuals on your staff, rather than on just you. Develop a good write-up of the conference and get the campus and local press to write stories and take pictures.

Resolving budget matters is a long-term proposition. Small gains may be achieved in a short time, depending on the will of the dean and the department chair. However, for working out a new budget center for your program, you will have to get into the university budgeting cycle. Usually, that means preparing budget proposals in the spring for the next fiscal year that will begin in July. Find out what administrative colleagues or staff personnel are astute in university fiscal matters and seek their mentoring. Practice discipline, detailed notetaking, and precise data collection. One way of increasing the allocation of resources to your program may be to conduct a cost-expense study. This will probably require the approval of a fiscal officer and the assistance of one of his or her accountants. Here's what to do: for one academic year, determine how much money the university took in through tuition dollars for all registrants in your program; similarly, find out how much the university spent on instruction in those courses (including tuition remission to TAs, if it is provided). Subtracting the latter from the former will tell you how much profit the university is making from your program. Of course, it is accepted procedure that low-cost programs will help defray the expenses of high-cost ones. However, the difference may be so great in your case that you can argue for the return of at least a small percentage to your budget. Developing a zero-based budget for your program will enable you to put forth a strong argument on how the additional funds will be spent. You may also find a mentor's help invaluable in developing a zero-based budget.

Seek support from others in building a culture of composition and in raising consciousness across campus for writing instruction. Nationally prominent outside speakers in rhetoric and composition can lend prestige to your effort in raising faculty awareness of areas of expertise. Seek alliances with faculty from English and other departments to invite renowned colleagues to your campus. Perhaps the Renaissance faculty would work with you in bringing a rhetorician to campus to speak on humanist rhetoric. Perhaps members of the philosophy department would join in inviting a speaker on rhetoric and philosophy.

Moreover, outside consultants can bring clout to your program-building interests. Normally, with the cooperation of the department chair and/or the dean, funds can be allocated to invite a team of Council of Writing Program Administrators' consultant-evaluators to campus. Using a self-study that you and your colleagues would prepare, this team can interview you and people across campus; within a few weeks they can mail a report with recommendations for next steps in program-building.

Throughout all of your work, keep your spirits up and sustain your administrative acumen by staying in touch with the regional and national composition and rhetoric community. Join the Council of Writing Program Administrators. Attend the annual convention of the Conference on College Composition and Communication and especially the Thursday-morning WPA breakfast. Attend the WPA Summer Workshop and Conference each July. The workshop is an essential post-graduate activity for every new WPA. Ask anyone who has attended it.

14 Running a Large Writing Program

Linda Myers-Breslin
Texas Tech University

How can WPAs handle a large writing program of over seventy teaching assistants and three thousand first-year students? With a large and continual turnover of TAs and students each year, you face the challenge of ensuring educational quality for students and TAs. This chapter's scenario outlines three problematic areas involved in maintaining a large writing program: (1) running a large composition program in a department dominated by literature faculty, (2) high instructor turnover and inexperienced instructors, and (3) distribution of authority.

Institution Overview

Congratulations on your promotion to Writing Program Administrator of Texas Tech University's first-year writing program. This promotion did not come as a surprise; last year, you were hired as the Associate Writing Program Administrator. You were fortunate to have a year to get to know the program, the department, and the school. Texas Tech is a large, state-supported university, with about 24,000 students (20,800 undergraduates, 1,850 M.A.'s, and 1,050 Ph.D.'s) and 1,600 faculty. The university has forty-one master's programs and twenty-one Ph.D. programs. Students primarily come to Texas Tech from the region, which includes many small towns surrounded by farmland and cotton fields, as well as the Dallas and Houston areas. Twenty-two thousand students come from Texas, 2,000 from out-of-state, and 1,000 from other countries.

Students

Undergraduate

Our student body, totaling 20,806, is fairly homogeneous: 82 percent White, 10 percent Hispanic/Latino, 4 percent Native American, 3 percent African American, and 2 percent Asian American, with 3 percent Nonresident Alien. Most undergraduate students come to Tech directly after high school. Most first-year students live in dormitories. Students represent a variety of interests. Composite ACT scores average 26, SATs

1,160. Applicants who do not have these scores can be provisionally admitted; these students must pass six semester hours of college work with a grade point average of 2.0 or higher prior to their initial fall enrollment. Retention of students is important, as it is at many schools. Incoming first-year students participate in an orientation program during the two weeks prior to the fall-term start date. Admission information can be found at http://www.texastech.edu/admission.htm.

Graduate

Our university currently has 3,580 graduate students: 1,869 master's, 1,075 doctoral, and 636 law. Ninety-eight master's and fifty-four doctoral degrees were awarded last year. Full-time enrollment is 2,131 students, and 1,449 students attend part time. Of these students, 1,641 are female and 1,939 are male. The majority of graduate students, 2,347, are from Texas; only 569 are from out of state; and Tech has 569 international students. Once students are accepted into the university, they apply separately to their own department for funding. More information can be found at http://www.ttu.edu/~gradsch/gradadmit.htm.

University Writing Center

The University Writing Center lends much assistance to students, especially in our English writing courses. In 1982, Jeanette Harris was hired to establish an English department writing center. The mission of the writing center was to provide one-on-one instruction for students enrolled in developmental and first-year composition courses, although students from any course in the English department and in the university were welcome. At the time, the staff consisted of the director and four graduate teaching assistants who served as writing consultants. The center was open from 10 A.M. to noon and 1 to 3 P.M. Monday through Friday.

Statistics over the years have indicated an increase in the number of students seeking assistance in the writing center; statistics also show that the writing center was serving students from across the university and from all levels. In 1995, the English Department Writing Center became the University Writing Center, reporting to the Office of the Provost rather than to the chair of the English department, and having a separate budget.

As a university-wide facility, the University Writing Center has been able to expand its services to include not only the onsite writing center where students make appointments or drop in for consultations but also an online writing lab (OWL) and a satellite writing center located in the Advanced Technology Learning Center in the library. The staff presently consists of eight onsite writing consultants, four online consultants, three student assistants (one of whom is also a peer tutor), and the director, Lady Falls Brown. Located in the English department, the University Writing Center is open from 9 A.M. to 5 P.M. Monday through Friday. The satellite in the library is open from 7 to 9 P.M. Monday through Thursday. The OWL has no set hours of operation, although papers submitted on Friday afternoon are not distributed to the consultants until Monday morning. More information can be found at http://english.ttu.edu/uwc.

Writing Center Goes Online

In fall of 1995, the department's writing center, directed by the past president of the National Writing Centers Association, Lady Falls Brown, was designated the Texas Tech University Writing Center and provided a separate budget, allowing the UWC to purchase three Power Macintosh computers with dual Mac/Windows capability and seventeen-inch, high-resolution color monitors. These computers greatly expanded the UWC's ability to provide online and shared-screen tutoring, and they promise to make the UWC a national leader in electronic writing center services.

Computers

The English department at Texas Tech University has had an interest in microlabs and computer-based writing instruction since the mid-1980s. Thomas Barker began the efforts in 1985; Fred Kemp joined the efforts in 1988. In 1990, the English building was Ethernetted, and the writing program began to run Daedalus Integrated Writing Environment software and engage an increasing number of students in file exchange and ENFI (Electronic Networks for Interaction) activity. We could also access the Internet, and Kemp started MBU-L (Megabyte University), an electronic discussion list concerning computers and writing.

At that time, Kemp gave the collective effort of the classrooms and instructors the name of English Department Computer-Based Writing Instruction Research Project. Among the project goals were the following: (1) discovering better methods for using computers in the teaching of writing and literature, (2) training graduate students in the use of computers in writing and literature instruction, and (3) providing graduate students with methods and procedures for entering and participating in the computers and writing community. The project was and is primarily a support facility for research and training in computer-based writing and literature instruction. In 1994, the department hired a technician to help with the myriad of work that it took to run the classrooms. Since 1990, we have averaged over forty sections of computer-based writing instruction, twenty-seven instructors, and seven hundred undergraduate students per semester.

Distance Learning

The Texas Tech English department's distance education initiatives are the natural evolution of the department's Computer-Based Writing Instruction Research Project. The networked computer has demonstrated its ability to move instruction spatially and temporally beyond the walls of the classroom. The next logical step in computers and writing research is to stretch the boundaries of time and space further by merging with distance education research. Currently, Tech teaches several composition and technical writing courses through distance learning arrangements. The work is interesting and rewarding, requiring much personal time and commitment on the part of our instructor/researchers.

Texas Tech Online-Print Integrated Curriculum

TOPIC is a project of the Texas Tech English department with the goal of developing a fully complementary online-print integrated composition curriculum. The TOPIC development team hopes to link publisher print materials with online Web interactive capabilities in a technology-based instructional environment that does not depend upon the computer-based classroom. The goal, envisioned by Fred Kemp, is an "integrated print-online composition curriculum." "Print-online integration" places online and print resources in truly complementary and mutually supporting roles. This concept differs from "online support" because it hypertextually provides a great deal more of what is already in the printed book. History places print as primary; the future may not. In any case, a truly complementary print-online curriculum draws on the co-active strengths of both. (Kemp's further description and important distinctions can be found at http://english.ttu.edu/topic/).

Budget

Your writing program does not have a budget line; all salaries come from the English department. The program does get some funding from the sales of the common syllabus. The syllabus is printed in three manual formats (M-W, T-TH, and MWF) according to when the classes meet. Each student whose teacher uses the common syllabus (which is most of them) must purchase this manual. In 1995, handbook publishers agreed to place this information into the front of the spiral-bound test at a cost of $1.00 per student. We received $3,200 that year from the inserts. This money went toward meeting orientation costs.

While you control no budgets as WPA, your chair has a couple hundred dollars of discretionary money that she may grant to a good cause. You can also approach your dean who has been supportive of innovation in the writing program. But, as everywhere these days, budgets are tight, so make your plans frugally—preferably without any costs.

English Department

Our English department serves thousands of students; of these, approximately 350 are undergraduate majors, forty-five are M.A.'s, and eighty are Ph.D.'s. Twenty-five percent of these students are female; and 75 percent are male. We have 41 faculty members: 12 full professors, 11 associate professors, and 18 assistant professors. The department has six programs: literature, creative writing, technical communication, linguistics, composition and rhetoric, and film studies. Each of these areas offers bachelor's, master's, and doctoral degrees. Sixty-nine of the seventy-four graduate students are teaching assistants for the composition program. The program also has ten lecturers. Running this program will be a big job. There are 140 sections of first-year composition, fifty in computer classrooms [numbers approximate].

In 1982, the composition program came into existence with the hiring of a writing program administrator. The battle for recognition and respect in a traditionally literature-based department was long-fought and bitter, and caused a number of WPAs to leave before the discipline could gain ground. Although Literature still dominates the department according to the numbers, the other disciplines (such as Creative Writing, Composition and Rhetoric, and Technical Writing) are strong, active, and expanding.

Courses

The first-year composition program is a two-semester requirement: ENGL 101 and 102. The first semester focus is the personal essay; the second semester focus is the research paper. High SAT scores or a Pass on the CLEP Test give students credit for the courses. A student who is admitted provisionally must pass ENGL 001, our Basic English course. Our enrollments have been changing over the past decade:

Course Year	001 # of Sections	Students per section	101 # of Sections	Students per section	102 # of Sections	Students per section	Total # of students
1987	21	22	85	24	37	22	3162
1997	2	17	99	23	38	24	3223

Our overall withdrawal statistics have gone from 6 percent in 1987 to 2 percent in 1997. The number of teaching assistants has increased from forty-five in 1987 to seventy-four in 1997. Our number of lecturers has decreased from fifteen in 1987 to ten in 1997; this decrease in lecturers was intentional. In the past (as happens at many schools) the lecturers formed an underclass that displayed passive-aggressive behavior such as ignoring directives from the WPA. The number of these instructors were allowed to decrease through attrition.

Texas Tech also has a sophomore writing requirement which most students must take. Students select from a Creative Writing, Technical Writing, or Literature focus for this writing intensive course. Often, our students take these courses as juniors or seniors; however, first-year students who have tested out of the first-year courses also can take these courses.

ENGL 101 and 102 are taught by graduate teaching assistants from the English department and by composition and rhetoric faculty. The department offers an undergraduate major in literature and a minor in technical writing. The graduate program consists of master's and doctoral degrees in most of our department programs. There are approximately 345 undergraduate English majors and 125 graduate students in the programs. The seventy-four graduate teaching assistants are responsible for teaching two courses per semester. Six of these TAs teach for technical writing; you are not responsible for them or their students.

Teaching Assistants

They are between twenty-two and fifty years of age, and range from those who just received their undergraduate degree at this school or elsewhere to those who wish to begin or change careers. Their reasons for study vary, as do their goals. Some want to become creative or technical writers, while others want a doctoral degree so they can teach in four-year or two-year schools. Most come to us from the surrounding community and elsewhere in Texas, although we do get three or four graduate students from out of state each year.

Some have taken creative writing, enjoyed it, and have selected that discipline to study in graduate school. Most of these students are apt in writing and have therefore tested out of undergraduate composition courses. Thus, they have not taken (much less taught) a composition course. Those who have taken a composition course might have taken it a decade or more previously. Some of these graduate students have taught in high schools or other graduate programs. Others have never taught anywhere. All must learn the needs of this particular school, its English department, and its students.

Faculty

As stated, the department's faculty consists of 41 tenure-track faculty members: 12 full professors, 11 associate professors, and 18 assistant professors. Similar to many schools across the country, the department is dominated by Literature faculty. Twenty-five faculty members, the majority, teach literature; four, creative writing; four, technical communication; four, composition and rhetoric; two, linguistics; and one, film studies. These professors all have Ph.D.'s and teach from two to four courses per semester, depending on their administrative duties. The department has several senior faculty who believe that teaching writing should be grounded in the study of literature. Most do not focus on what is happening in the composition program, except to note that we "do not teach enough grammar" because the students in their classes make too many errors.

Your predecessor as WPA began the computers and writing interest here at Texas Tech. He is supportive, but now that you are here to take over the administrative duties, he is taking a well-deserved, semester-long sabbatical; he also knows that you need to establish your own authority. There is another Associate WPA who was hired from graduate school. Although her area is writing centers and although she is unfamiliar with Texas Tech, she knows administration and she might be helpful in establishing administrative policies. The other assistant professor in your program is trying to get tenure and is glad that you were hired so that she does not have to take on administrative duties in this dauntingly large program.

The TAs and lecturers who teach first-year composition are ineligible for administrative posts. They were hired to teach the basic writing courses and composition sections for which we did not have the funding to hire more TAs. Nearly all of these people are comfortable with the prior administrator and are wary of what you have planned. Most of the TAs "live" on the fourth floor of your English building, although a few have an office in the building across the street. They have their factions, of course, but primarily they stick together. They can be divided into the following groups: (a) those teaching in the computer project; (b) those who could not care less about composition; and (c) those who want to keep everyone happy and stay on a good note with all faculty. The first group tends to be the one which is most involved in the department, the departmental graduate student organization, and their teaching duties. You wish that you could keep all of them, but the director of technical communication handpicks her TAs as does the director of the writing center. You have the remaining TAs in this group, most of whom are interested in their students and are good teachers.

History

The history behind the two-course, first-year writing program you have inherited is, like most writing programs, rocky. For most of the department's history, the WPA position was passed among literature faculty members who used the 101 and 102 courses as introduction to literature courses. In 1982, Christine Hult was hired as the first composition WPA and Jeanette Harris was hired as the first Writing Center Director. Both professors recall the tension between faculty members in other programs and those in Literature. The Composition Committee consisted of seven literature faculty with a couple of composition faculty members and graduate students as ex oficio members; thus, only the literature members had a vote on the Composition Committee. The battle to rid the program of an "exit exam" was long and emotional. In faculty meetings, tenured literature faculty members openly belittled and discounted work completed by untenured composition faculty, making several cutting comments about the work in composition being wholly unworthy of tenure and promotion.

Fortunately, things have improved. Over several years and after many battles, the program has changed considerably. There are now five compositionists (four professors and a graduate student) and two literature professors on the Composition Committee. The composition graduate program has expanded to become quite visible in the department. Training for the TAs has improved and has become a required, credit-bearing course. First-year composition course content has moved from expressivist writing in 101 and an introduction to literature in 102 to the personal essay and argument in 101 and argument and research in 102. Your direct predecessor is a social constructivist who has incorporated much collaborative learning theory into the pedagogy of both courses.

In 1993, Texas Tech's composition program began to use a common syllabus as a way to train its TAs and to maintain program standards. A publisher took the syllabus that we created and published it for us. When the composition faculty replaced the literature faculty on the Composition Committee in 1994, the program director began to consider a single text adoption as a way to solidify further the ever-growing number of composition instructors and students. The program moved to a single text adoption in 1995, when a faculty member published a rhetoric that could be used for both 101 and 102. This selection saved our students money and helped further solidify the program.

All TAs and lecturers were asked to use the text for at least one semester of each course. If they did not like the text after using it, they were free to submit a proposal for teaching the course with a different text. Those who use the common text are free to use the common syllabus, which gives a daily description of assignments for class work and homework. All TAs new to the program are asked to use this common syllabus for their first year; other TAs have the option. Orientation for new TAs also began in 1994. The program, which began with a two-day agenda, is now a week-long learning seminar with one day of orientation for all TAs new to the College of Arts and Sciences. During this day, our new TAs have the opportunity to meet graduate students from other departments and to hear about university policies and procedures. The last day of the week, all TAs come in for a day of orientation during which the department chair and the composition director and staff reiterate our pedagogical goals, policies, and procedures for 101 and 102.

The program that you are maintaining in its overall structure is accepted among most of the TAs and lecturers teaching the majority of the 101 and 102 courses. Some of the senior faculty who like(d) the introduction to literature and formalist approaches stop you in the hallways to complain about the lack of student preparedness in their undergraduate literature courses, but so far their grumblings have not caused you much difficulty. Student complaints and grade appeals have decreased over the past few years, so the dean is happy as well. Overall, the program runs smoothly, so most faculty and the administration feel that the program is now running well, requiring only occasional input from you.

Key Charge

Most faculty outside of the program do not realize the intensity of running a program as large as this one. You are responsible for the training and performance of approximately seventy teachers and for providing quality education for over three thousand first-year students. Your department has a history of using TAs in its first-year courses, but there has not been much uniformity prior to the single text adoption. During your year as Assistant WPA, you heard rumors of TAs using comic books as texts in their classes; teaching their first-year classes as introduction to literature or creative writing classes; canceling classes once a week; declaring courses finished midway through the semester; not showing up for classes; running only thirty-minute classes; etc. With so many sections and so many teachers, what can you do? You are untenured. Your department likes the status quo and, unfortunately, perpetuates the feeling that writing is a simple discipline that can be taught by anyone and should be taught via literature in order to give it "real" substance and validity.

Your charge actually breaks down into three areas:

1. Lack of experienced teachers—most of your TAs tested out of first-year writing and have not previously taught;

2. High instructional turnover—with a large number of TAs, naturally, many of whom graduate and leave each year;

3. Distribution of authority—most of your TAs are in other disciplines of study such as creative writing and literature. They look to those professors for guidance in the classes they take and the classes they teach; they do not look to you or your staff.

Other Challenges

You are in charge of maintaining the first-year writing courses; supervising TA performance; dealing with student complaints; chairing the department Composition Committee; overseeing composition staff (a secretary, two associate directors, and an assistant director); teaching graduate courses in writing pedagogy, undergraduate courses in advanced writing, and first-year courses in composition; and training new, incoming TAs for the 101 classroom. Additionally, you must remember to keep producing publications if you expect to get tenure. Because the senior faculty view your program as self-running, your publication standards are equivalent to those who teach three courses. After all, you get a course off to complete all of the work listed above.

Scenario: Working the Graduate Program

Now that you are in charge of the program, you have to prove yourself. You have seventy-four graduate teaching assistants, twenty-four of whom are new and, like most students in English, have had an undergraduate curriculum of literature. You also have a variety of attitudes among the TAs. Some are cocky, thinking that if a person can write, that person can teach writing; that all writing is taught the same way; and that they know best, never mind what your program demands. Others are terrified, wondering how they will ever be able to control a class or know enough to teach anything to anyone; some of these have been brought to tears in front of their classrooms during the first few weeks of teaching. It is your charge to bring all of these TAs into an effective, coherent program.

You have a new chair who has just joined the department. She has met with you to find out the status of the program. You both acknowledge the challenges of your new position (listed above). The meeting is quite cordial and goes well. You realize full well, however, that although many colleagues appear supportive, many are also watching. This is your year to prove yourself. You are still considered "new" faculty and many want to see what you are made of, especially the graduate students and the ten lecturers who teach in your department. You need to earn the respect of TAs as well as faculty.

Scenarios: Problematic Situations

Each fall, an unfortunate annual event occurs when the dean of a department such as engineering or chemistry calls your department chair to say that he has more first-year students coming in and needs more sections opened. The notion of more sections is not bad in and of itself, but there are ensuing problems. Because the school is remotely located, there is not a pool of English majors for part-time hire to teach any of the extra positions. Your department grants teaching assistantships to graduate students with problematic GRE scores and no teaching experience. You are expected to make these people (who often do not know what a comma splice is) into effective composition teachers. Fortunately, your new chair seems sympathetic to the problems this practice causes for you and for the writing program. *What steps can you take toward restricting the number of new sections added to your program at the last minute? How can you make others realize the domino effect of problems that this situation causes? To whom should you be speaking about this situation?*

You do not have a say in who are hired as TAs. The Director of Graduate Studies fills these positions. His decision is based primarily on GRE scores, which are minimal. You have no idea how much (or little) training these graduate students have had, what their majors are, nor what their personalities are like until they show up at your orientation.

Do you need a say in TA hiring? Do administrators at other schools have a say? Is the GRE an adequate standard by which to evaluate someone's potential teaching ability? What steps can you take toward convincing others in your department that just because someone can write, that does not necessarily mean that he or she can teach writing? To whom should you be speaking about this situation and for what purpose?

Your administration prohibits you from dismissing TAs who are not doing their jobs satisfactorily. Because the teaching pool is limited, you would have to teach the classes yourself, or you would have to find a TA who is ABD to take the classes. Finding an ABD student is frowned upon because the school does not want to hinder progress toward graduation, especially now that you have "the ninety-nine hour rule" to contend with: in Texas, students may no longer be funded after ninety-nine attempted hours of study. So, you have much pressure to keep TAs in the classrooms. When a TA is troublesome, your administration has recommended that you "work with" that student, rather than let him or her go. *The TAs know who among them is not doing an adequate job. What does your inability to fire TAs do to your ethos as administrator? What might be steps toward changing this "hands-off" policy? To whom should you be talking?*

You also have to run the writing program with an idea of what is happening in the TA classrooms. There is only one of you and sixty-eight of them in your charge, each teaching two sections. In effect, you are responsible for their 136 sections plus the two that you teach. *How can you get past the rumor mill to find out what is really going on? What are ways that you can make sure that all students are on the same pedagogical page? From whom can you solicit assistance? How can you best help TAs who excel at teaching? How can you best help TAs who are floundering in their classrooms?*

You soon discover that the hours you spend advising and comforting TAs, visiting TAs' classes, and listening to students complaining that their TA is doing a poor job count as "service." *As you are yet untenured, the need to publish is constant. How will you maintain your own scholarship and still maintain an efficient writing program?*

Considerations

- You are new and "untested" by the TAs. You are untenured. This has many implications, including the need to get your own work done, a limited power base, and the need to prove yourself.

- You have held the previous Assistant WPA over from the previous year. A TA who has taught here for several years, she knows the ropes, is quite competent, and has ideas for helping keep track of TA actions.

- You have an Associate WPA who is new to the position and the school. She is well versed in theory and practice, but is unfamiliar with how Texas Tech and its English department function.

- You have a large number of TAs who have never had their teaching observed, so you have no idea how they are doing in the classroom, and you have twenty-five new TAs to train. You have a week before school starts when all faculty, including TAs, must be "on duty." During this time, TA orientation is scheduled.

Questions to Consider

1. Your goal is to run a program that efficiently provides quality education to first-year writing students. What do the terms *efficiently run* and *quality education* mean to you? What do other large (or small) programs do to maintain quality education? How can you apply some of their ideas to your program?

2. Who are important contacts in furthering the existing program toward your goal? How can you get in touch with these people? When should you contact them? What do you want from them: Belief and support in your goals? Help? Funding? Motivation (for you and for the TAs)?

3. What are your management strengths? What do you need to work on? How will you present yourself to the TAs and others? Are you a supportive friend, a tough boss, a supportive boss, or a tough friend? How will you evaluate TA competence (besides rumors)?

4. With sixty-eight TAs and three thousand students in your charge, how and when will you get your own work done toward tenure? How important is tenure toward your position? Aside from publication, of all the areas that may need addressing in order to run a more efficient program, what will be your signature initiative (your main goal)? What are one or two other areas that you would like to address during the next year? Next three years? Next five?

AUTHOR'S CASE COMMENTARY

We are addressing the three most problematic areas of your program in the following ways:

High Instructor Turnover

High turnover of instructors is expected in any first-year writing program. After all, our goal as an institution is to help graduate students through their degree programs. An unfortunate (but essential) side effect is that high TA turnover keeps training constantly necessary. In order to maintain TA training, we developed a few strategies, policies, and procedures.

Orientation

We used money from syllabi sales to increase our orientation from a few days to a full week. All faculty, including TAs, are officially "on duty" the week preceding the first day of classes, so our only expense is coffee, pastries, and lunches. A full week allows time to look at and discuss the syllabus, to practice a few techniques, and to get an idea of what it is like to be in front of a classroom.

Orientation training moved from filling out benefit forms and looking at the book and syllabus to a series of mini-workshops, in which we place the new TAs in mock teaching situations—evaluating and commenting on student papers, creating a support network among themselves, and so forth. The director and associate directors of the Composition Program make sure that the TAs understand the syllabus—not just how it works, but why.

The day devoted to Arts and Sciences orientation and the day with all TAs reviewing the fine points of our program are still in place. This program-review day includes talks by the department chair, the secretaries, the Writing Center director, the director of ESL, the head of security, and a representative from the student affairs office. TAs get a sense of the whole university, then the department, and then the writing program. We have added break-out sessions that require TAs to create and "teach" lessons, using each other and us as audience, along with grading sessions. Some of the more experienced TAs volunteer their help with these sessions so that we can keep the groups small. The feedback that we have received from TAs is that they are not happy when they find out that we have their week planned for them, but by the end of the week they are quite happy that they received all of the information we provide.

Courses and the "18-Hour Rule"

Understanding the pedagogy behind the syllabus is taken care of primarily in the course "Teaching College English." All who have not taken the equivalent of this course at another school must take the course. We started offering the course in the second summer session so that students could learn the theoretical and historical information before teaching in the fall semester. Our program had to answer to the "18-hour rule," which states that graduate students must have 18 hours of graduate work completed before they can instruct a course. With our large program, this placed us in quite a situation. We decided to further TA training by requiring two semesters of course work in teaching college writing.

The first semester is the "Teaching College Writing" course, which now focuses on the theory and history of writing pedagogy. Graduate students gain insight into teaching college writing as well as the instructional methods and classroom management issues that pertain to such teaching. This course is now offered during the second summer session, before teaching assistants enter a classroom. In the fall semester, the TAs from this class do enter a classroom, but as apprentice teachers.

Each new TA is paired with an experienced TA (who gets a small stipend). The new TA observes the senior person, helps plan classes, grades a set of papers, and teaches a section of the course. The new TA can do more, but these are the required activities. The TAs must also meet periodically with the apprentice director, for whom the new TAs complete some reading and writing assignments.

Workshops

The workshop program has been enhanced. In 1993, workshops began as part of an attempt to keep TA pedagogy current. TAs were asked to attend four workshops per year. These workshops were given by faculty with only 20 percent attendance. Obviously, this low rate of attendance would not do, so we made a few changes. We asked some of the experienced TAs to participate in presentation of the workshops, to share their special talents and ideas with their fellow TAs. We also made the workshops mandatory. Each TA had to attend three workshops per semester in order to meet our requirements. Later, the number of required workshops was reduced due to the addition of other duties (explained below). This last semester we offered 28 workshops; only four were given by professors. Students learn much from each other, presenters get material for their vitae, and faculty get data they can use in letters of recommendation for their TAs.

Probation

We also make it clear that TAs do *not* have tenure in our program. We will let them go, finding others to fill their classes for extra pay. A probationary policy was created, stating clear guidelines for all TAs. If a TA does not meet these criteria, that TA has a meeting with me. I place him or her on probation. This means that during the subsequent semester, the TA has a series of meetings with me to assure compliance with the criteria focusing on quality in teaching. Should the TA not improve over the next semester, that TA will be let go. Of course, actually letting a student go is still a challenge in our department due to the reasons listed in the chapter, but our new chair is supportive. I still search for ways to explain to the faculty and administrators from other disciplines within the department just how problematic these TAs are.

Inexperienced Instructors

Common Texts and Tasks

The orientation and workshops greatly help our inexperienced TAs. Further support comes from several sources: our single text adoption, common syllabus, and special topics proposals. The fact that all TAs new to our program use the same text gives them all a common foundation from which to talk about their teaching. The common syllabus gives not only common content, but common class activities that TAs can use or adjust to suit their teaching styles.

More experienced TAs share the adjustments that work well for them in workshops. Other experienced TAs select a text and/or a technology to use in teaching their classes. This gives the TAs a chance to plan their own classes, working together to create a meaningful learning environment for their students. And we know what they are doing in their classrooms because of the proposal that must be submitted to and approved by the Composition Committee. TAs do not have to work in groups; however, the common pedagogy promotes social constructivism (we hope that the TAs want to work together). Just as it is difficult to learn in a vacuum, it is difficult to teach in a vacuum. It is also difficult to administrate in a vacuum, working alone.

Distribution of Authority

Faculty Observation

The more contact points that the director and associate directors have with TAs, the easier it is to encourage strong teaching among TAs and to administer a large program. We have contact with TAs during orientation, during the theory and history course, during the apprenticeship program, and at workshops. These contact points assure us that TAs are getting information. But then the question arises—are they using it? Two forms of observation let the TAs, and us, know how they are performing in the classroom. Each TA and lecturer has a tenure-track professor in his or her classroom at least once during the semester. These are not surprise visits; the class period for the visit is agreed upon by the professor and the TA. The visit lets faculty sense the rapport that the TA has with his or her students, and lets the TA know his or her strengths and weaknesses. It also gives faculty a foundation from which to write an accurate and explicit recommendation letter toward the end of the TA's career as a student.

When we had faculty from other disciplines visit the TA classrooms, pedagogical barriers caused some of our more outstanding TAs to receive unfavorable comments. Thus, all visits are made by Composition and Rhetoric or Technical Writing faculty. Peer observations have become a large part of our program.

Peer Observation

In an attempt to give TAs feedback regarding their teaching, we ask each TA to visit and comment on fellow TAs during each semester. This takes much planning, for which we are extremely grateful each semester to our Assistant Director. This position is filled each year by a TA who serves as a liaison between the TAs and the faculty. This position is interesting because while the TA is often considered to have "crossed over" to the side of administration, he or she is still privy to TA perspectives.

Assistant Director Liaison

TAs are often more willing to enter the office of the Assistant Director and convey information to him or her, another TA (even if he or she has "crossed over") than they are willing to enter our offices. The Assistant Director also knows the appropriate time and place (i.e., at a weekly composition staff meeting) to convey information to us so that we can prevent or diminish problems or problematic perspectives. The liaison position allows us to realize the TA perspective and in return allows us to convey our perspective. For example, when we introduced professor and peer observations, TAs felt that they were going to be "spied upon." Our Assistant Director helped us convey the message that the whole idea here was to help TAs get a fresh perspective on their teaching, and to help TAs who had only been in their own classrooms see how other teachers interact with a class and teach certain concepts.

Teaching Teams

We also instigated teaching teams to promote effective teaching by encouraging pedagogical sharing. TAs were placed in groups of three or four; they can self-select their group or ask us to place them into a group. Within these groups, TAs arrange a visitation schedule so that each member is visited by two others before midterm. Close, pedagogical interaction opens discussion of classroom theory and practice between team members. At each visit, a form is completed. These forms are brought to a meeting of all group members just after midterm. All members read and discuss the responses; each member keeps forms regarding his or her teaching and writes a response; the forms along with the response are given to us by the end of the semester.

Peer Collaboration Teams

Thanks to recent hires, we expanded our composition faculty, thus enabling us to expand our teaching teams/peer-observation program. Rebecca Rickly combined peer observation and collaboration in the form of "peer collaboration teams." These teams consisted of four to five graduate composition instructors, a mix of experienced and new instructors. During orientation, TAs volunteered for the program and were grouped by members of the Writing Program Administration. Opportunities for growth and reflection developed through a three-tiered system of professional development:

> Tier I: Peer Collaboration Teams Revisited
> To promote critical thinking, collaboration, and community building among teachers, peer collaboration teams were designed. These instructors visited each other's classes, made note of teaching practices, and met to discuss each other's progress throughout the semester. This not only gave instructors valuable perspective, but also helped them enter the profession, where faculty are often observed by a peer at least once per year. See http://english.ttu.edu/rickly/peercollaborationf98.html

> Tier II: Creating a Collaborative Course Portfolio
> A course portfolio allowed instructors to examine their course from a variety of angles, reflecting on what they did and how well it worked. As part of a collaborative course portfolio group, instructors created a course portfolio and shared it with others in their group. They also wrote a one-page reaction that was included in each other's portfolios. This activity was good for new instructors and those teaching a new course. See http://english.ttu.edu/rickly/courseportfolio.html

Tier III: Constructing a Teaching Portfolio
A teaching portfolio allowed instructors to document their successes as teachers, as well as to reflect on their methods, their underlying epistemology, and their practice. As part of a collaborative teaching portfolio group, instructors constructed a teaching portfolio and shared it with others in their group. Each group member wrote a one-page reaction that was included in each other's portfolio. This activity was good for experienced instructors, and was particularly helpful for those going on the job market. See http://english.ttu.edu/rickly/teachingportfolio.html

For further information on these programs, please see Web pages created by Rebecca Rickly: http://english.ttu.edu/rickly/Peercollaboration.html

15 How WPAs Can Learn to Use Power to Their Own Advantage

Barry M. Maid
University of Arkansas at Little Rock

It is important for WPAs, especially untenured WPAs, to understand that they can effect change within their units while still keeping themselves tenurable in the eyes of their colleagues. I think the key is first to understand your own organizational maze and then control that which appears to be out of joint rather than that which appears to be highly structured.

Institutional Overview

The University of Arkansas at Little Rock is a metropolitan university (what was formerly called an urban university) with an enrollment which has vacillated between just under 10,000 students to just over 12,000 students in the years I have been there (1981 to the present). Like most metropolitan universities, UALR is almost exclusively a commuter campus. The average age of students is twenty-six or twenty-seven. While some point out that students over forty and fifty raise the average age, I have argued that a good number of the students here, though of traditional college age, are themselves nontraditional. They are either married or divorced or single parents. Many have been in or are currently in the military. For a large percentage of UALR students, this is not their first attempt at college.

Local

Little Rock is the center of the state geographically, politically, economically, and demographically. All of this should bode well for UALR, but we have never exploited it. It is an institution whose faculty can't seem to make up their minds whether they want to turn it into a Research I university or a liberal arts college even though, in defined mission and reality, it is neither. UALR's mission clearly defines it to be engaged in applied research, something many faculty trained in the traditional liberal arts have trouble understanding. The "flagship campus" of the system is isolated from the mainstream business of the state in the mountains of the northwest corner. UALR is a relatively new institution. It began in 1929 as Little Rock Junior College, under the auspices of the Little Rock Board of Education. In 1957 it became Little Rock University, a privately supported four-year institution. Finally, in 1969, it became the University of Arkansas at Little Rock, a part of the newly formed University of Arkansas system.

History

I think understanding the history of an institution is important. So much of the culture of an institution and the departments within that institution are a function of that history. Of the twenty-three full-time members of the English department when I arrived in 1981, only six had been on staff in the LRU days. Most had been hired in the '70s. They came fresh from their good graduate schools full of energy and ambition, with a vision of the profession that in no way matched the institution in which they found themselves. Their idea was to change the institution—to remake their graduate schools in Little Rock.

Many of the faculty had worked hard. Despite teaching a 4/4 load, including two sections of composition, they had begun to establish professional careers, publishing regularly. When I arrived in 1981, they were still talking about how the State Board of Higher Education had denied their request for an M.A. program in English in the mid-'70s. The Board had approved a proposal from the University of Central Arkansas (UCA) in Conway (thirty miles up I-40) instead. The English faculty at UALR were convinced that the program went to UCA for political reasons. The UALR attitude was that no other program in the state (including the one at the "flagship campus") could compete with UALR for quality and standards.

So the department had a "chip on its shoulder" attitude that continues to the present. All its focus seems to be in convincing the world that it is the best English department in Arkansas. This title, they feel, is owed to them because of their literary scholarship. The composition program is an afterthought. While they are all teaching half their load in the composition program, it is merely something they do as a condition of employment. What happens in the program is of little concern so long as it does not in any way endanger the image of the department. As a result, they are most concerned that the program make as few waves as possible and never be seen as compromising standards.

Since the scenario I'm going to present took place in the past, I think it makes sense to give institutional information from the past as well as to present current conditions. What's most interesting about the comparison is that while it's clear there is a significant difference in writing programs at UALR in that time, the institution itself has changed very little.

Computing

In terms of institutional resources, we are still wanting. The library is always used as an example of a unit that never has enough. While they've attempted to keep up on books, they've had to cut back on journals. On the other hand, technology is much better now than it was in 1981. In 1981 technology consisted of slide projectors and video-feed of movies. In 1984 the Apple IIe's we put in our writing center were, I believe, the first computers generally accessible to all students on campus. In 1981 no faculty had computers. By 1988 all English faculty who wanted them (one adamantly refused to take one) had a computer on their desk. Today, all rhetoric and writing faculty have a computer on their desktop with an Ethernet connection. Unfortunately, we still don't have a dedicated computer classroom. The writing center, now networked with PowerMacs, is our only computerized teaching space.

Challenges

History

What follows is a real situation which looks at required exit exams. Indeed, it is one I faced in 1982 in my first year as WPA in the English department at the University of Arkansas at Little Rock (UALR). It may be difficult for many, especially those enrolled in graduate programs in composition and rhetoric, to comprehend that the situation I will present was real. Yet, recent visits to several campuses across the country have shown me that similar programs and attitudes still remain in the late '90s. Indeed, with the present necessary emphasis on issues of assessment, of both students and programs, there currently exists an even stronger demand for testing and accountability than we saw in the early '80s. Just as in the early '80s, today many of the external forces on WPAs expect us to develop or use quantitative testing methods. Such methods often give the appearance of being quick, easily understood by outsiders, and relatively cheap. Unfortunately, those methods fail to test a student's writing ability.

No matter how daunting the exit exam scenario may seem, I was able to survive the challenge it presented and was able to move on to face other problems. I would never argue that how I handled the situation of the exit exams was the first step in a natural process of institutional change. However, I do think that my sense of institutional power and how it is handled by people within the departmental and university context was an important piece of that ultimate end. How I dealt with the issue of the exit exams as an untenured WPA, the sole writing specialist in what was essentially a literature department, is an example of how one who ostensibly has no power within an institution can exact more power within the system than those who see themselves as empowered by right.

Writing Program Overview

The Courses

The composition program in 1981, as it is now, was comprised of a three-course sequence: Composition Fundamentals, Composition I, and Composition II. Comp Fundamentals is a basic writing course, and entering students place into either Fundamentals or Comp I. In the early '80s we tested all students on the first day of class with an in-house instrument that was half writing sample and half multiple choice. It was a cumbersome process and most often the multiple choice score was the determining factor because it was easier to deal with under time constraints. We moved to placement by ACT scores in the late '80s. Both Comp I and II are required for graduation. All three courses are graded A, B, C, or No Credit so that students with inadequate skills to pass won't put their GPA in jeopardy.

The Director

The composition director always did the scheduling of courses and the hiring of part-time faculty. We offered around ninety to ninety-five sections a semester in the early '80s. By the early '90s we were offering almost 125 sections a semester. More recently, we've been limited to offering just under eighty sections per semester. Our class size limits have been twenty-five students per section in Comp I and Comp II and twenty-two students in Comp Fundamentals.

Program Resources and Staffing

The program has never had its own budget, adequate space, or staffing. In the early '80s the courses were taught by a combination of full-time and part-time faculty. Everyone in the department taught composition. I suspect the fact that all the tenure-track literature faculty taught composition helped to work against such issues as common syllabi and regular curricular meetings. The literature faculty simply didn't want to be bothered by something as trivial as comp, though for most of them it comprised one half of their assigned duties.

Writing Center Overview

The English department established a writing lab in the late '70s. It was staffed by a part-time faculty member. By 1981 the staffing was done jointly by one part-time faculty member and a full-time faculty with one course release. During the 1983–84 academic year, the directorship of the Writing Center became a full-time position. Back then all the tutoring was done by the director. We had some audiotapes which were outdated even then, but we were limited to tutoring only those students we could work with ourselves. Later, after the full-time Writing Center Director was in place for several years, we were able to use peer tutors.

The Courses

In 1981 Comp Fundamentals was essentially a sentence course, Comp I a five-paragraph-essay course, and Comp II a research paper course. We had exit exams for Comp I and II. However, when looking more closely at both exams, it should become evident that the Comp I exam reflected sentence-level issues—skills which supposedly were being taught in Comp Fundamentals—while the Comp II exam tested the five-paragraph essay—which was being taught in Comp I.

The Comp I Exam

In the first-semester course, the exam was essentially an editing exam. It was designed as a multiple-choice exam so that it could be machine-scored. Part of the job of the Composition Director was to make up this exam. There was a file box full of 3" x 5" cards to help the director accomplish this task. Each card had one question which had been approved by the Composition Committee. All that was needed was to pick the requisite number of questions for each semester's exam. For a new question to be added, it first had to be approved by the departmentally elected Comp Committee. The department and the rest of the university called it "The Grammar Test." Each question was an isolated item something like this:

a. The student claimed that each of his *books' was* eaten by his sister's dog.
b. The student claimed that each of his *books were* eaten by his sister's dog.

c. The student claimed that each of his *books was* eaten by his sister's dog.

d. The student claimed that each of his *books' were* eaten by his sister's dog.

Students needed to receive a grade of 70 percent or they couldn't pass the course, regardless of how well they wrote.

The Comp II Exam

The second-semester exam was a "skeleton essay." Students were given three words. The grouping of words looked something like this: cars, trees, vacations. From this group of words, students were expected to write an opening paragraph, topic sentences for three body paragraphs, and a closing paragraph. They were also expected to identify their thesis sentence. These exams were scored on a pass/fail basis by two different faculty who were currently teaching the second-semester course. There was no training for this reading and no group grading sessions. The faculty read them at their leisure. If the two readers disagreed, the exams went to a third reader. Once again, a student who did not pass the exam did not pass the course.

At that time in order to effect any change in the exams, or any curricular matter, the process would have looked like this:

1. Bring a proposal to the Composition Committee
2. Have the Composition Committee approve the proposal
3. Bring the Composition Committee's recommendation to the whole department
4. Have the whole department adopt the proposal.

Key Challenge

You find yourself, back in 1982, in the second year of your first tenure-track appointment, just having been elected to be WPA. As the sole writing specialist in your department, you are responsible for a first-year writing program in a mid-sized metropolitan university. Your staff is composed of your twenty-two full-time colleagues in the English department, most of whom have tenure and will sit in judgment on your tenure, and a group of around twenty dedicated, though undertrained, underpaid, and underappreciated part-time faculty. You find that almost no one in either group has any real training in rhetoric and composition beyond some kind of hands-on training they received years ago in graduate school.

Within this context you find yourself faced with supervising the first-year writing program's system of exams.

Your Charge

As Comp Director you are responsible for the program's curriculum. However, since testing always drives curriculum, what you've discovered is that most of your teachers, full- and part-timers, teach to the tests. Comp I instructors teach how to take multiple-choice exams. Comp II instructors teach how to take three words, turn them into a thesis sentence, and write an "almost" essay. The only writing taking place in the program is for the required research paper in Comp II. In order to change the curriculum, you must somehow revise or eliminate the exit exams. Simply writing a new curriculum is not enough. You must somehow exercise your power as Comp Director while not offending those who have the power over your future tenure.

How do you do so? The following questions may help as you develop your solutions. Focus specifically on the power relationships noted in the parentheses as well as any others you may think of:

- Does the fact that your colleagues will vote on your tenure affect your response? (Tenured faculty sit in judgment over untenured faculty.)

- Do you think having to force literature Ph.D.'s to teach first-year comp has a significant impact on the situation? (Institutions force faculty to teach courses they don't want to teach and are not trained to teach.)

- What impact does having as many part-time as full-time faculty have on the exit tests? (Are part-time faculty inherently inferior teachers, or is this an instance of full-timers exerting control over part-timers?)

- Should you attempt an immediate elimination of the exit exams or consider elimination by stages? (Who is more powerful in your institution: the one who is seen as decisive or the one seen as reasonable?)

- Does the fact that you work with an elected Composition Committee help or hurt? (Does an individual or a group have more power?)

- Given the current climate with regard to assessment, how do you take on the issue of exit tests? (Can you retain your power/authority if you buck trends?)

There are, of course, many possible responses to this scenario. Since so many administrative decisions are based on local contexts, what follows are more specific details about this situation.

AUTHOR'S CASE COMMENTARY
How I Approached the Problem

My ultimate solution for freeing the department from the exit exams is less important than the process. I am sure there would have been many potential ways to effect that same solution. In order to be successful, however, I am also sure that the key to all of the potential solutions is the effective use of institutional power. One of the first things I realized in taking over as WPA was that the ostensible power within the department was held in balance between the department chair and faculty committees. I also learned (by reading the *Faculty Handbook* from cover to cover) that the department chair did—and some of this was by University Board Policy—have authority in some matters. The chair, partly because the unit treated the chair's position as an elected one (a clear violation of University of Arkansas policy), chose not to exercise its authority. This situation was reinforced by a dean who wished simply to maintain the status quo. In reality, power in the department was vacillating between two groups of faculty. One group was comprised of senior faculty, the other group was almost exclusively junior faculty. The junior faculty had been hired in the late '70s and early '80s. While there remained perhaps no more than ten years difference in ages between these two groups of faculty, the difference was clearly generational. Interestingly enough, both groups of faculty represented traditional academic interests and none of this original group had any training in rhetoric and composition.

Understanding the nature of the department and how decisions were made helped me as I maneuvered through the quagmire of trying to rewrite the composition curriculum and eliminate the exit exams. Two things became clear very early about effecting a departmental decision. The first was that a departmental vote (a majority was all that was needed) could change any curricular issue. The second was that even if I, or any junior faculty, managed to get enough votes to change departmental policy on any particular issue, we had to lobby those votes in such a way that we did not offend or threaten senior faculty who might later oppose granting us tenure. What we see here is a most delicate political situation. The normal procedures to make the curricular change would have looked like this: Steps one through three of the curricular process cited earlier (moving a curricular issue from Comp Committee to department) would prove most easy on almost any matter. The nature of the department was such that only junior faculty or senior faculty who needed to do service were elected to the Composition Committee. As a result, the nature of the committee was generally to back the WPA. The real secret was how to accomplish step four (departmental approval) without evoking unwanted backlash.

My intuition told me not to propose elimination of the exams immediately. Instead, I decided to try some less significant curricular changes to see how the process worked. Initially, my changes came in the area of textbooks. Without eliminating all of the "current traditional" textbooks we were using in the program, I was able to include some of the new "process" books. I didn't think I'd have too much trouble simply changing textbooks. I did, however, encounter resistance from full-time faculty who didn't want to change. My natural inclination toward negotiation rather than confrontation helped me here. I thanked people for their input instead of condemning their choices of textbooks. I began to learn which curricular issues they felt they had a real investment in as well as those issues in which they would be more flexible.

While not aware of it at the time, I was really testing the limits of the organization. I was using the system to find those areas where the system was lacking. What I finally discovered was that the faculty felt little investment in either the system of exams or the entire composition curriculum. What seemed to matter most to them was that their own professional comfort needed to be satisfied. On one level the exams fulfilled that level of comfort. The key was to find an alternative that would not diminish the level of comfort or else (and these are not necessarily mutually exclusive) up the ante on the exams so there would be less comfort in continuing their use.

Without any formal administrative training, I spent a good deal of my time that first year doing what I had been trained to do in graduate school—research. So, I gathered information. In retrospect some of the time I spent doing what I thought would be most helpful turned out to be insignificant within my own context, though it might have been more important in other circumstances. For example, I read a good deal of information about multiple-choice tests. It was clear to me from the outset that our tests were neither valid nor reliable, but these were concepts that were meaningless to my colleagues. I also did an item analysis of the grammar tests for the past three years and discovered that students could get a 70 percent on the test and pass if they were able to give the right answer on simple subject-verb agreement questions, sentence boundary questions (especially those involving semicolons), and apostrophes. In some ways I was surprised by these findings because whenever the Comp Committee discussed new questions about issues that were of concern to the faculty, they were of significantly more esoteric items. Based on my findings, I remember suggesting at one Comp Committee meeting that if we drilled our students on those three issues, more of them would pass. It wasn't a popular suggestion.

Had I been preparing to write a scholarly piece about departmentally constructed grammar tests, all of this information would have been valuable. (In truth, I seriously considered doing so but decided it would be politically unwise.) The other thing I did was begin to talk to my colleagues. I visited them in their offices to talk about program issues that concerned them. Most of all, I encouraged them to talk, to give me their views of the entire comp program and how, in their view, it fit into the department's mission.

I talked to my colleagues and listened to them, filing valuable information in my brain. Ultimately, it became clear to me that no one had a vested interest in the exit exams themselves. Their concerns had to do with department image. If they thought their teaching would be easier, that was all that really mattered. Therefore, any change which would make their teaching easier would be embraced. A change which would force them to work harder would be fought. Finally, perception was more important than reality. As a result, I was able to formulate questions which proved helpful in creating solutions:

- How would any change affect the personal lives of the faculty?
- What were the underlying values in the present system?
- What recommended change can actually be approved?
- If we did away with the exams, would the rest of the university think we were compromising standards?

What Happened

I ended up taking a two-part approach to solving the problem. The first was to reconceive the nature of the exams. That turned out to be relatively easy. One of the things my discussions with the faculty turned up was that almost no one truly believed we were testing writing. We were simply upholding standards, and to some, having a control on the part-timers. The departmental assumption was that all part-timers were inherently inferior teachers. My first proposals were that the Comp I exam be changed to a multiple-choice test which, rather than use isolated items, was an actual essay into which errors had been intruded; and that the Comp II exam move from a "skeleton essay" to a whole essay.

I was personally still uncomfortable with the exams, but I felt this was a change that could get approved. I also told myself that if we had to have an editing exam (which is all the Comp I exam was), it would make more sense for students to edit in context. In addition, the new Comp II exam would at least be a whole essay—even if it wouldn't allow for revision. The other thing that happened was that by proposing changes which seemed to strengthen rather than threaten the established order, I was demonstrating good stewardship of my program to my colleagues. They felt good about giving me the responsibility for the program, and more important, they began to feel they needed to spend less of their own time concerned about the composition program.

It didn't take long after the institution of the new exams for two things to become evident. First of all, the Comp Committee spent hours arguing over the "wrong answers" to the new-format Comp I exam. While apostrophe questions were easy (no one argued over giving students the choice of *its, it's,* and *its'*), we found that given other kinds of questions, once the context was established, that some of the wrong answers we were used to using in the isolated item exam made no sense. "Even my students don't make those mistakes" was a common sentiment.

Second, faculty had mixed feelings about the new Comp II test. Almost all of them agreed that they really preferred reading a whole essay. However, they were discovering that reading whole essays, even just to give them a pass/fail, took considerably more time. They weren't willing to give up the extra time.

As a result of moving away from the status quo, we were able to do away with both exit exams and substitute for them a more clearly articulated curriculum combined with supervision and training for part-time faculty. It didn't happen overnight. The whole process took around four years and two more rhet/comp hires. I'm convinced that had I begun in my first year as Comp Director with a proposal to do away with the exams and revamp the curriculum I not only would not have been successful, I suspect I would have sealed a negative tenure vote for myself. While so much of what we do takes place in an instantaneous environment, I think we need to remember to be patient when initiating institutional changes. Sometimes the most effective changes take the most time to effect.

Maid's Theory of Organizational Chaos

There are many ways to analyze this or other similar scenarios; however, understanding the constraints of the system within which you operate is crucial to implementing the kind of solution you wish. It is also crucial to understand that power exists always as an abstraction waiting to be concretized. It is not something which is, by definition, finite and tangible. Therefore, it cannot be easily systematized, hierarchized, and distributed. Most important, power is not something which can be given or assigned. It must be taken and used. Over time I've developed two rules which I smilingly refer to as my Theory of Organizational Chaos. I don't for one minute assume these rules are monumental; however, I do think they help people analyze problems within organizations in order to create viable, and sometimes creative, solutions.

Rule 1

The best way to understand a problem within an organization is to use what I call my labyrinth analogy. My question to people who seem hopelessly lost in bureaucracy and organizational structure is "What is the best way to find your way out of a labyrinth?" My answer to the question: "Hovering overhead in a helicopter." The best way to understand a problem is to move outside the self-contained system that defines the problem. This is one of the reasons that outside consultants can be immensely valuable. Being outside or above the system allows one to see it more clearly.

Rule 2

All organizations, no matter how structured and no matter how hierarchical, are simply artificial impositions over chaos. People who find themselves in conflict or not "in" the power structure serve their own needs best when they find the chinks in the organization—those places where the natural state of chaos still reigns. By asserting order over a heretofore uncontrollable part of the organization (even if no one has noticed the problem), an individual automatically gains a small degree of power and usually attains a concomitant prestige that is accorded to those who control the uncontrollable.

Analysis of the Solution Based on Maid's Theory

My initial response to the problem (to attack it by means of scholarly research) would have kept me trapped in the labyrinth. That makes sense. One of the unspoken rules of systems is to self-perpetuate themselves and not provide any means of instituting change. So, the system-approved method was doomed from the outset. My other "research," gleaning information from my colleagues, ultimately was my "helicopter" which allowed me to identify the "chaos" in the composition program. The "chaos" I discovered was that the composition program was not only not valued but was perceived as a drain on the faculty's time.

My two-part approach (showing control over "chaos" by making the exams "better" and then "rescuing" the faculty from being overburdened) is consistent with my theory. In fact, once the faculty felt comfortable enough to entrust me with decisions in the program and did not feel the need to spend their time checking up on me, I had a relatively easy time administering the program. The Composition Committee became much more agreeable, and the department and the chair merely wanted to be informed.

What is finally important here is not how I solved my problem. The details of my solution in all likelihood would not work on other campuses. What is important, however, is for WPAs, especially untenured WPAs, to understand that they can effect change within their units while still keeping themselves tenurable in the eyes of their colleagues. I think the key is first to understand your own organizational maze and then control that which appears to be out of joint rather than that which appears to be highly structured.

16 How Can Physical Space and Administrative Structure Shape Writing Programs, Writing Centers, and WAC Projects?

Carol Peterson Haviland
California State University, San Bernardino

Edward M. White
California State University, San Bernardino

While location is not "everything," it wields considerable power over the futures of writing centers and writing programs, first-year composition texts, and university faculty members. This chapter, thus, poses the question, "Where physically and administratively should this campus's composition courses, writing center, and writing-across-the-curriculum program be located?" You are asked to consider the physical, economic, political, and pedagogical choices of the locations they pose.

Institution Overview

California State University, San Bernardino, established in 1965, is one of the twenty-two campuses of the CSU system. Located sixty miles east of Los Angeles, its 12,000 students and four hundred faculty members are an ethnic, gender, linguistic, academic, and economic mix that mirrors much of Southern California. Because the CSU is part of the three-tier public postsecondary system, many students satisfy their general education requirements at community colleges and transfer to CSUSB as they begin their junior years, although a substantial number begin their academic careers as first-year students on the four-year campus; average student age is twenty-seven. The university offers a full range of forty-two bachelor's degree programs, fifteen teaching credential fields, and twenty master's programs.

The campus is a fairly typical regional state university, with large business and education schools and a strong liberal arts faculty. Located in one of the fastest-growing regions of the country, the campus has become a modest cultural center, with frequent speakers, plays, films, concerts, and workshops of all sorts. In the past, the university had an air of exclusivity, with special attention to high standards in the liberal arts. In recent years, that sense has diminished under population and program pressures, though attention to academic quality still remains a hallmark of the campus. This concern for standards is reflected in some aspects of the university writing program.

Courses and Placement

The campus writing program begins with pre-enrollment placement testing, using a system-developed English Placement Test, with both multiple-choice and essay portions. Students place into one of two basic writing tracks or into first-year composition, a required one-quarter expository writing class. A second quarter of writing is required at the upper division. Students who are junior level and who have completed first-year composition must complete an upper-division writing course, to be chosen from the six offered (in multiple sections): English 306, Humanities 306, Social Sciences 306, Natural Sciences 306, Management 306, and Education 306. An unusual asset for the writing program is the Master's Degree Program in English Composition, a high-quality program with over one hundred graduate students, who may elect to be TAs in the first-year composition program or tutors in the Writing Center. Each year, approximately twelve graduate students are TAs and twenty-five are tutors.

Writing Center

The Writing Center, established during the early years of the university, plays an important role in all of the writing programs, as well as supporting writing throughout the university. Under composition faculty leadership, its tutors, who are chiefly M.A. in composition students, conduct one-on-one writing conferences with students writing in courses across all disciplines. As the hub for the writing-across-the-curriculum program, Writing Center faculty and tutors consult with other faculty members using writing in noncomposition courses, conduct in-class draft workshops, and assist students and faculty members writing professional articles and books, grant and graduate school applications, as well as a variety of other writing projects.

Writing across the curriculum is anchored in three programs: the upper-division writing course, the annual faculty WAC seminar, and the Writing Center-based faculty and student conferencing.

Location as Metaphor and Sign of Power

Cereal manufacturers pay premium prices for eye-level display shelves, textbook publishers jockey for intellectual and economic positions within academic communities, and faculty members vie for offices and titles that situate them near desirable centers of power. Recent listserv threads such as the discussion of SUNY-Albany's refiguring of its composition programs document the critical role both administrative and physical location play in shaping programs, curricula, academic disciplines, budgets, buildings, and humans. While location is not "everything," it wields considerable power over the futures of Mueslix, comp texts, faculty members, and students, as well as of composition courses, writing centers (Writing Center), and writing-across-the-curriculum (WAC) programs.

As you work to locate these three academic units advantageously on this campus, you will need to consider the physical, economic, political, and pedagogical implications of your choices. Because the location of each unit will affect the other two as well as many other university programs, try to think first as an "unattached idealist," asking which configuration will best serve the university. Then, reimagine yourself as the director of each unit, arguing for its most productive placement.

Of particular interest, we believe, are the conflicting needs of administrators, faculty members, and students, conflicts that operate both across and within categories. On one hand, for example, the vice president for academic affairs will enjoy the simplicity and convenience of dealing with a single individual if he collects all three units within a single administrative and physical location close to his office. In addition, he may find that this choice will increase the "writing czar's" kinship with administrators while weakening it with the "rabble-rousing" faculty members. On the other hand, consolidating within a single position will invest considerable power in that single location and individual, power that she may use to claim resources that he could set three separate individuals to compete for—dividing them against each other and thus deflecting their attacks from himself.

Use the following data and questions as you suggest "staging" these programs and actors. As you propose your solutions, consider both the theoretical positions and the practical demands that shape each possibility.

Players, Stages, and Possibilities

The Players

The present players are the vice president for academic affairs; the dean of the School of Humanities; the dean of Undergraduate Studies; the English department chair; two English department faculty who have released time to direct, respectively, the lower-division composition courses and the Writing Center/WAC programs; a management professor who coordinates the upper-division writing courses; the English and other-school composition, literature, and creative writing faculty; twenty-five writing tutors, and the students and faculty members who use the Writing Center and WAC programs. In addition, the coordinator of the M.A. in Composition program, who also is an English department faculty member, as well as the graduate students in composition have a stake in any configuration. The required general education composition courses, as we noted above, are two: a one-quarter first-year composition course taught in the English department, and a one-quarter upper-division writing course housed in each of the six schools.

Presently, the Composition Coordinator reports to the English chair, who funds first-year composition; the Writing Center/WAC Director reports her concerns as an English faculty member to the English chair and her Writing Center concerns to the dean of undergraduate studies, who funds the Writing Center; the upper-division writing program director and faculty report jointly to their respective department chairs, who fund the courses, and to the dean of undergraduate studies, who coordinates these courses. Computer facilities are entirely separate from any of these departments; a few composition classes are taught in a computer-equipped classroom that is woefully underequipped and funded. Together the Writing Center and the English department are negotiating the purchase of equipment for online writing tutoring and an up-to-date computer-equipped classroom.

The Stages

The vice president's office is in a central administration building; all other players' offices are on the same floor of a classroom/office building across campus, except for the upper-division writing course instructors, who are assigned to schools other than Humanities and are located within those schools. The Writing Center is located within the Learning Center. Computer facilities, however, are located on the ground floor of the same classroom/office building that houses the English department, the School of Humanities, Undergraduate Studies, and the Writing Center. The WAC program has no physical location other than the offices of the Upper-Division Writing coordinator, the Writing Center/WAC director, and the dean of Undergraduate Studies.

Since the university's founding, lower-division composition courses have been housed in the English department. The upper-division composition courses, begun in the late 1970s, are housed in the six schools, budgeted through the Division of Undergraduate Studies, and taught by a combination of the various schools' faculty and by lecturers with M.A.'s in composition. For a number of years, the program has been coordinated by an English faculty member, but this coordinator may be drawn from any of the schools, subject to confirmation by the participating departments; indeed, when the long-time coordinator retired just last year, a management professor and frequent course instructor was appointed coordinator for the coming year. The Writing Center has been variously located within the English department, the School of Humanities, Undergraduate Studies, Student Affairs, Academic Services, the Learning Center, and the Educational Opportunities Program, but for the past eight years it has been directed by an English faculty member and budgeted through the Undergraduate Studies dean. WAC activities have been sporadically funded by the vice president for academic affairs and the dean of Undergraduate Studies and coordinated by an English faculty member.

The Players' Priorities and Goals

Vice President for Academic Affairs: effective, efficient writing programs and requirements that equip students to write both at the university and in the workplace and that consume as little of his attention and as few of his resources as possible. His understanding of composition theory is modest, but he recognizes its importance and does defer to faculty knowledgeable in the field. Having a single comp czar is appealing because of its apparent simplicity and cost-effectiveness, but it may place formidable power in a single person.

School of Humanities Dean: Theoretically sound writing programs that accomplish four goals: equip students to write well and to learn through writing, provide practicum and TA sites for graduate students in comp, engage both students and faculty in writing as an intellectual activity (including research opportunities), and create general good will for the School of Humanities.

Undergraduate Studies Dean: Provide a visible academic program on Undergraduate Studies' turf as well as generally expand its sphere of influence, contribute to retention goals for at-risk students, and generally improve student and faculty work with writing.

English Department: Most of the department is genuinely concerned that the composition program be theoretically sound both for the students enrolled in composition courses and for the graduate students who will intern in those courses. Many of the faculty see the importance of the Writing Center and WAC programs in the missions of both the department and the university, although some regret the faculty time and the money that goes into them because "students don't arrive on campus already prepared to write as university students." The composition/rhetoric faculty are particularly concerned that the comp courses be informed by current theory so that they provide a stimulating research-practice link for graduate students. They very clearly value the Writing Center as a site both for scholarship and for TA experiences, and to a lesser degree they see the import of WAC projects as study sites for students and faculty. The first-year composition coordinator and the Writing Center/WAC director are individually and collectively invested in their specific sites, both as they provide direct writing interaction with students and faculty and as they contribute to the larger university's investment in writing as a mode of learning. Along with the other composition/rhetoric faculty, they work particularly productively with each other, and they see the theory-practice intersections as vital to all writing activities.

Other Faculty

Other faculty: Relatively few faculty members outside of the English department teach the upper-division writing courses by choice. Although all deans and chairs comment on the importance of writing, these faculty members know that their work in writing does not count toward scholarship in the same ways that more disciplinary-linked investigative areas do. However, a number of these faculty members persist in their commitment to writing, particularly those who have participated in the faculty WAC seminars, and one of them, a management professor, is the newly appointed Upper-Division Writing Program Coordinator. The lecturers hired to teach writing courses part time or even full time are invested both academically and economically in these courses, for most are trained first in composition and second in one of the school areas. In addition, a number of non-English faculty take a very serious interest in writing—their own and their students'. While they tend not to teach the upper-division writing courses in their schools, they do integrate significant writing into the courses they teach and they work regularly with Writing Center and WAC programs.

Tutors

Writing Tutors: During the past seven years that the Writing Center has been directed by an English faculty member and staffed chiefly by graduate students in composition, it has become central to many students' graduate experiences. It not only provides them economic support, but it also creates an important site for studying pedagogy, as well as an academic "home" and even a social center of sorts.

Key Challenges and Possibilities

Several locational possibilities have been proposed:

1. Most conventionally, the configuration can remain in its present cantilevered form. This plan leaves composition most influenced by the English department, chiefly by the composition/ rhetoric faculty as well as by the linguistics, creative writing, and literature faculty. However, this influence may vary as coordinators are drawn from other schools as well. These influences are, for the most part, collegial though scattered and unpredictable. Composition is influenced also by the various schools housing the upper-division writing course, the dean of Undergraduate Studies, who controls the budget for the upper-division course, the Writing Center, and WAC. This configuration is highly dependent on the occupants of the several influential positions. If, for example, the English department's commitment to composition should fade, the program might lose faculty and governance to competing interests. If the Humanities or Undergraduate Studies deans should turn on the English department or the writing programs, again resources could be reshuffled to the writing programs' disadvantage. Presently, the School of Humanities dean is a solid supporter, and the Undergraduate Studies dean speaks volubly about the importance of writing but must be consistently pressed to provide economic support and to delegate theoretical decisions to faculty members.

2. All writing enterprises could be housed under the English department's umbrella. The major argument for this plan is that it could place the program entirely in the hands of composition/rhetoric faculty members. Programs then more certainly would be guided by current theory and by faculty members for whom writing is a central professional concern. However, we see at least two significant objections to this choice. First, the English umbrella may not always tilt its shade or resources

in composition's direction. Second, and perhaps of greater import, when English departments take full charge of writing programs, other academic units are even less likely to see themselves as part of students' writing and learning lives. As Mike Rose argues, when both physical location and funding for writing programs reside within English departments, other faculty members and budget officers feel very comfortable seeing the "writing problem" as a discrete set of skills taught best in faraway places so that their students come already "knowing how to write."

3. Undergraduate Studies' governance could be increased so that all writing programs reported to that dean, including the first-year and upper-division composition courses, WAC, and the Writing Center. While this plan would consolidate all writing enterprises, it would isolate them from their academic links with literature and reading (see WPA listserv thread) and it would gamble on the training and goodwill of that dean, who is not likely to know much about writing programs other than that they can enlarge his turf and budget, and represent an academic "Good Thing."

4. A separate Writing Programs Division might be established, which could report to the dean of Undergraduate Studies or of Humanities or to the vice president for academic affairs. Again, this construction would gather the writing locations in one spot, which offers administrative convenience, but it too risks uninformed or manipulative top-down governance as well as isolates writing from reading and from its academic roots.

Key Charge

Residing within each of these options is the sub-question of writing program governance: should all programs be coordinated by a single comp czar or should each be separately but cooperatively coordinated by teaching faculty who have released time to direct one enterprise. Again, the arguments compete. Full-time administrators tend toward consolidation, arguing that it is both cheaper and more efficient to group administrative work. Faculty members, on the other hand, tend to favor splitting the responsibilities, arguing that those coordinating writing programs ought also to be teaching and that separating the functions allows more faculty members to be invested directly in writing programs. This argument is particularly dear to composition faculty members who are committed to collaborative theory.

As you work on your solutions, consider the following questions:

- Which location would best support the fullest investment of resources—philosophical, personnel, fiscal—in writing?

- Which locations might different composition theories support?
- Which location would be most likely to attract faculty outside of composition to the programs?
- Which location would support the interests of composition graduate students? Faculty members?
- How will your location shape each unit as well as other affected programs?
- Which locations might individual participants favor, and how might they negotiate mutually advantageous alliances?
- How would your proposal affect future building, space allocations, and hiring?
- How might the personalities of key players influence your ideal solution?
- How might your solution affect any of the university system's other campuses?

AUTHOR'S CASE COMMENTARY

Our Solution

The chief conflicts our solution works to resolve are those generated by the differing theories administrators and faculty members embrace. While administrators lean toward the efficiency and simplicity that consolidating projects in central locations with full-time administrators brings, composition theorists argue that writing programs should not be the sole responsibility of a single person or department, for such an arrangement supports the popular belief that writing is a discrete skills that can be taught "in one spot and once and for all." Taking seriously James Berlin's assertion that "English studies has a special role in the democratic educational mission" (54), we consciously use composition theory to shape educational matters both directly within as well as outside of the English department. Our solution, then, is grounded in composition theory, but it considers and incorporates the contending theoretical positions.

Feet firmly in postmodern and collaborative composition theory, we propose a carefully cantilevered location: a core physical location anchored by several composition faculty members but coupled with several university-wide physical and administrative locations. The lower-division composition courses, Writing Center, and WAC, along with supporting computer facilities, should be located together centrally on the campus and adjacent to the English department, preferably in the present classroom/office building. The upper-division writing courses, however, should be housed in satellite offices within the five other schools. The writing programs, which should be coordinated by several faculty members, should report through a coordinators' committee to the vice president for academic affairs. All participants should be linked electronically so that they can confer regularly and support cross-disciplinary teaching and research.

Although administrators may find consolidating writing program administration in one person's hands more convenient, this choice contradicts a more important location axiom: if university faculty and staff are to believe that writing is central to learning and thus to coursework in all disciplines, it cannot be isolated within either a single department or program. Such isolation affirms people's preference to "let someone else worry about it." The positioning we propose emphasizes composition's theoretical stake in composition programs, allowing composition faculty members and graduate students to occupy central roles in program planning and implementation. However, physically locating satellite offices in each school and administratively splitting the several composition programs among composition faculty enacts our belief that writing is a critical element in the full curriculum and is an activity in which all faculty members and students are invested. The core primary location, in addition, demonstrates the centrality of writing center and writing-across-the-curriculum programs and also enacts our belief that no segment of any writing program should be viewed as remedial; rather, each is a site for a full range of collaborative teaching and research activities. However, distributing the coordination of lower- and upper-division composition courses, the writing center, the writing-across-the-curriculum program, the teaching assistant program, and the graduate program among several composition faculty members allows coordinators to remain active teachers and researchers, another essential element for faculty members who model the integration of teaching, research, and service. Our choice to report to the vice president for academic affairs rather than the dean of Undergraduate Studies was made because both undergraduate and graduate programs are involved and because Undergraduate Studies is allied more with student services than with academic programs. In addition, our relationships with the vice president are collegial, while those with the Undergraduate Studies dean are difficult. Clearly undergirding each of these choices is our belief that writing programs have more to gain and less to risk if they see their kinship with the English department as primary and their other kinships more precariously constructed. Although we acknowledge that this is not the case in many institutions, we argue that theoretical common ground makes this the easiest kinship to sustain.

For these location choices to work, English and composition faculty must provide the communication administrators need to be confident of solid programs. The coordinators must be willing to work together, presenting joint funding requests and program direction. Thus, we propose that program coordinators meet monthly and that each year they elect a single liaison with administration. Administrators, then, settle for a more participative and complex structure, while faculty members settle for more communication among themselves and with central administration than they customarily elect. This "loose coupling" (Gamoran) is consistent with composition's collaboration theory, which recognizes multiple contributions and argues that sharing authority needn't mean reducing authority. In sum, each can have more if each is willing to see the other as having different yet reasonable and compatible needs—a novel posture for both!

17 Managing the Writing Center/Classroom Relationship

Dave Healy
University of Minnesota

The relationship between writing centers and classrooms is complex. On one hand, centers operate "at a remove from the normal delivery system of curriculum and instruction" (Kail and Trimbur 9). On the other hand, a writing center's clients are students who are taking particular courses from particular instructors and who usually come to the writing center for assistance with a particular assignment. Thus, writing centers have typically found themselves in a derivative role with respect to the classroom. Writing centers do not always accept that role, however, and theorists differ about just what the relationship between the center and the classroom should look like.

Institution Overview

General College is the open admissions unit of the University of Minnesota in Minneapolis. GC enrolls approximately 1,500 students and maintains a staff of thirty-five faculty and about the same number of academic professionals, including teaching specialists and professional advisers. GC accepts students who would not otherwise be admissible to the U of M. Our goal is, with one to two years of course work and academic assistance, to prepare our students for transfer to degree-granting colleges within the university. GC offers a fairly complete introductory curriculum in the sciences, social sciences, and humanities.

Like other University of Minnesota students, General College students have access to library facilities typical of a major research university. They also have access to computers through about a dozen computer labs scattered across campus, which are funded by a computer users fee paid by all students.

General College vs. Community College

In some respects, General College functions like a community college. We are different from most community colleges, however, in several important respects:

- We do not grant an A.A. or other two-year degree. Our mission is exclusively to prepare students for transfer to degree programs elsewhere in the university.
- Except for math, we make no distinction between "developmental" and "regular" courses. All incoming students take a math diagnostic test which is used for placement, and we have an extensive 0-level math curriculum. In other curricular areas, however (including writing), all students are placed in the same introductory courses.
- All GC courses (except 0-level math) are credit bearing and transfer to other colleges at the university.

Students

Most GC students (90 percent) come from Minnesota, the majority (74 percent) from the Twin Cities metro area. Most of our students ranked in the lower half of their graduating class; their average ACT score is 19. Our students are disproportionately first-generation college students, low-income, and students of color.

Writing Program Overview

GC's two-quarter first-year composition sequence is part of the college's first-year curriculum and aims to prepare students for the academic writing demands of the university. About 85 percent of the sections of these two courses are taught by adjuncts and graduate students. The composition staff undergoes a week of training before fall quarter and meets quarterly throughout the year. In addition, each graduate student who teaches in the program is assigned a faculty or adjunct mentor, and mentoring groups meet periodically throughout the year. Faculty and adjuncts have private offices with computers and phones. Graduate students share offices, phones, and computers. All classrooms and offices are housed in the same building.

Research activity is required for faculty, expected for adjuncts, and encouraged for graduate students. Faculty and adjuncts receive $600 a year for travel. Graduate students who are presenting papers are eligible for $200 travel stipends.

Courses

Neither General College nor the University of Minnesota currently has an upper-division writing requirement, and GC offers no other writing courses at all. The Writing Center serves all GC students in all courses, but the majority of our clients in a given quarter are enrolled in one of the two composition courses. Both courses stress the academic essay, emphasizing source-driven, analytic writing. The first course is built around the theme of education; in the second course instructors are free to develop their own themes. The first course meets six hours a week; the second meets four hours a week. All sections of both courses are taught in computer-equipped classrooms. Class size is kept close to twenty.

Writing Center Overview

The General College Writing Center is part of the Academic Resource Center—a clearinghouse for academic support services in the college. The Writing Center is a walk-in facility staffed by ten undergraduate tutors who work an average of fifteen hours a week. They receive three days of training in the fall and participate in ongoing training sessions weekly throughout the year.

General College had one of the first writing centers in the country, dating from the 1950s (Carino). The fortunes of the Writing Center have reflected the changing fortunes of General College, which has shrunk from a peak enrollment of 3,500 in the 1970s. When I took over the GC Writing Center in 1988, I had a staff of twenty-five. The previous director was tenured; I am not.

As director of the Writing Center, I am responsible for hiring, training, scheduling, and supervising the tutorial staff. I work closely with the director of our ESL program; that person and I jointly hire, train, and supervise four tutors (a subset of the staff of ten) who work directly with ESL instructors and students. I have a nonfaculty (administrative professional) ten-month appointment and an annually renewable contract. In addition to directing the Center, I teach three courses a year. My annual budget for tutors' salaries is $35,000, which is part of the unassigned instruction budget for the college. I post openings for the Writing Center through the student employment office. I am required to interview everyone who applies.

Computing

The Writing Center has one Macintosh computer, which we use to conduct e-mail conferences and face-to-face conferences when students bring in a disk. Neither of these services is used much. We could get more computers, but currently there isn't any need.

Center Operation

Our writing center is open thirty-four hours a week (Monday through Friday, no evenings) and is mostly a drop-in facility. Students can make appointments, either one-time or standing, but over 90 percent of our business is walk-in. In recent years, the percentage of ESL clients has been increasing; they now represent 60 to 70 percent of our business. We hold approximately 1,000 conferences per quarter, involving about 200 different students. The average session lasts thirty to thirty-five minutes. We operate primarily according to what Christina Murphy calls a "liberal" perspective that aims to help writers develop "analytical and critical thinking skills through dialogic exchanges with the tutor" and that attempts to facilitate a writer's development through "apprenticeship learning in which the craft of writing is learned by an apprentice writer from a more experienced and knowledgeable writer, the tutor, who is also able to articulate aspects of his or her craft" (278).

The Scenario

One issue facing both WPAs and writing center directors (WCDs) is the nature of the relationship between the writing center and the classroom, especially the composition classroom. Usually an institution's WPA and WCD are two different people (Olson and Ashton-Jones); sometimes one person fills both roles (Healy, "Directors"). In either case, cooperation between the two entities depends on anticipating potential points of conflict. One such potential conflict concerns the relationship between the writing center and the classroom.

Kail and Trimbur cast the issue in dualistic terms: the curriculum-based model vs. the writing center model. In the former, writing consultants become part of the curriculum by being assigned to work with particular courses and particular instructors. In the latter, consultants operate out of the "semi-autonomous space" of the writing center. Hemmeter argues that the writing center has consistently defined itself in relation to the classroom—to the center's detriment. Grimm challenges writing centers to re-envision their "service" role with respect to institutional practices of literacy. Waldo sees the ideal relationship between the writing center and the writing program as complementary and symbiotic. Healy ("Defense") argues for dualism, claiming that the writing center functions best when it is unencumbered by the expectations of classrooms and curriculum. Both Soliday and Gill present evidence for the success of a limited curriculum-based model of tutorial intervention in which writing center consultants are assigned to particular courses and instructors.

History

Several years ago, General College underwent a major administrative reorganization. The college's three academic divisions (Arts, Communication, and Philosophy; Social and Behavioral Sciences; Science, Business, and Math) were eliminated. In place of divisions and division heads (faculty members who assumed administrative duties in addition to teaching, research, and service), the faculty was reconfigured as a single unit under the direction of two full-time administrators (a Director of Academic Affairs and Faculty Welfare, and a Director of Curriculum and Evaluation)—both elected from the faculty. Among the many things these new administrators turned their attention to was the function of academic support in the college. In particular, they were concerned about the role of classroom TAs within the new nondivisional administrative structure.

Under the old divisional structure, classroom TAs were hired by divisions. A perception prevailed that the distribution of TA support throughout the curriculum was based on favoritism and cronyism. The new administrators took steps to standardize and regulate the assignment of TAs by creating a formula based on class size and whether a course was part of the base (first-year) or transitional (second-year) curriculum. Applying the formula let individual instructors know how many hours of TA support they were entitled to for each course. In addition, instructors were required to submit a written description of how they intended to use a TA.

Challenges

Teaching assistants had formerly been hired by divisions. Under the new order, eligible instructors assumed the responsibility for hiring their own TAs. This arrangement created two problems. First, while some instructors who qualified for a TA were able to do targeted hires because they had particular candidates in mind (most often a former student in their class), others balked at the prospect of interviewing a bunch of people they didn't know. Second, once TAs were hired they received only whatever training and orientation a particular faculty member elected to provide, resulting in widely varying degrees of preparation for the jobs they assumed.

Another problem with classroom TAs was the perception on the part of administrators that TA time was not consistently well used. Many GC faculty have their TAs keep office hours, during which time the TA is available to meet with students. The operating assumption is that some students will feel more comfortable approaching the TA (a fellow undergraduate) than the instructor. However, TAs, like faculty, find that not all of their office hours are used. Unlike faculty, though, TAs don't necessarily have other course-related tasks to perform during slack time. Faculty aren't paid by the hour; TAs are. And administrators are understandably leery about paying people to sit in an office and do their own work.

Key Challenge

The college's reorganization, then, affected academic support primarily by generating questions about the use of TAs. The Writing Center was initially unaffected by these changes. I began reporting to the Director of Academic Affairs and Faculty Welfare rather than to the head of the Arts, Communication, and Philosophy division. In other respects, though, the Center and my position were unchanged. I continued to hire, train, and supervise undergraduate tutors. The Writing Center continued to occupy "semi-autonomous space" within General College and to enjoy faculty and administrative support for its efforts. Although I was not a tenured faculty member, I was treated like one, and the work of the Writing Center was both recognized and appreciated.

Possible Resolution

However, in response to perceived problems with the hiring and training of classroom TAs, after a year under the new structure the administration decided to partially merge the hitherto separate roles of classroom TA and Writing Center tutor. By creating a single pool of undergraduate teaching assistants (UGTAs) which would staff both the Writing Center and the TA positions in the humanities department, the top brass hoped to address the TA hiring and training problems created by collegewide reorganization. They imagined that having one person (me) responsible for hiring, training, and placing all UGTAs—both tutors and classroom TAs—would result in greater consistency and better performance. They further assumed that the new arrangement would make more efficient use of UGTAs' time by having TAs keep their office hours in the Writing Center. If classroom TAs were not engaged with students or paperwork from their course during office hours, they would become available to work with walk-in students in the Center. That assumption was used to justify a 25 percent cut in the combined budgets of the Writing Center and humanities TA support. This cut was not perceived as punitive, but rather as a reflection of anticipated efficiencies in the delivery of academic support services in the college.

Under the new arrangement, individual faculty members could still recommend particular individuals for hire as classroom TAs, and an individual TA continued to receive instructions, orientation, and training from the faculty member to whom he or she had been assigned. TAs generally worked with the same teacher all year, though there was some switching from quarter to quarter depending on instructors' teaching loads and eligibility for TA support. What changed was that all TAs, in addition to whatever training they received from their supervising faculty member, also participated in the three days of training I provided for Writing Center staff. Also, all TAs kept their office hours in the Writing Center, where they would presumably be available to work with Writing Center clients as well as students from the course in which they were a TA.

Insofar as the hiring/training issue was concerned, this experiment was successful. Bringing all UGTAs into one pool did in fact create greater consistency. Where previously only Writing Center employees had regular training, while classroom TAs were subject to the vagaries of the individual faulty members they worked for, merging the two groups brought everyone under the supervision of the Writing Center director, who then coordinated the assignment of TAs to instructors. Another benefit of the merger was the increased communality and camaraderie experienced by classroom TAs. Previously isolated from each other, these employees often felt more like solo practitioners than part of a common enterprise. While an individual TA may have developed a productive relationship with the faculty member he or she was working for, TAs were mostly cut off from each other. They had no consistent opportunity to benefit from other's experiences or perspectives, no fellow travelers with whom to share insights or war stories. Under the new arrangement, TAs, by being collected under the Writing Center umbrella, were brought into more regular contact with each other.

In other respects, however, the merger was less successful. For one thing, many TAs (like faculty) use office hours to do paper work when no students come in, so the savings afforded by having idle TAs available for walk-in tutoring were minimal. More important, by having to wear two hats—tutor and TA—UGTAs experienced heightened role conflict. Who were they—extensions of the instructor with a responsibility to espouse her/his party line, or employees of the Center with an obligation to its philosophy and practices? Were they advocates of the curriculum and the instructor, or advocates for their fellow students? Furthermore, locating TAs in the Center complicated the institutional status of the space. Was it primarily an extension of the classroom, or was it an alternative to the classroom?

Scenario: Duality of the Tutor/Teacher Role

Consider a typical situation: Scott works eight hours a week in the Writing Center and six hours a week as a TA in Introduction to Literature. As a TA, one of his responsibilities is to grade weekly one- to two-page assignments based on that week's readings—work that he often does during slack times in the Writing Center. During week two, Melissa, a student in the literature course, comes to the Writing Center and talks with a tutor, Cherie, about that week's assignment. The next week Melissa returns to the Center. As before, there are three tutors on duty: Cherie, Kim, and Scott. This time, though, both Cherie and Kim are busy. Melissa asks Scott to look at her paper.

Which hat is Scott supposed to wear? As a tutor, he could ask questions, make observations, try to draw Melissa out; he might even make some specific suggestions. But this is a paper that's going to be turned in the next day, and when it is, Scott will have to grade it. What can he possibly say to Melissa that won't be colored by that prospect?

When Melissa asks "What grade do you think this will get?", Cherie has several options. She can play dumb: "Well, since we don't have to give grades here in the Writing Center, I've never really tried to figure out how I would grade things." She can turn the question around: "What grade would you give yourself?" or "How do you think this paper compares to other work you've done for this course?" She can personalize the question as a way of prompting further discussion: "I have the same concern about my own writing; I often end up worrying a lot about what grade I'm going to get" (Healy, "Defense"). However, none of these options is available to Scott.

Furthermore, the options Cherie has with the Introduction to Literature student are curtailed when she encounters students from the course in which she is a TA. What happens to the image of the Writing Center when most if not all of its employees are classroom TAs in addition to being Writing Center tutors? The problem we found ourselves facing was that the Center's semi-autonomous space had become less autonomous. Now we were identified with the curriculum in a way that we hadn't been before.

Considerations

The situation the Writing Center found itself in prompted a number of difficult questions:

- Just what kind of place is a writing center? Is it an extension of the classroom or an alternative to the classroom?

- How are undergraduate peer tutors in a writing center perceived? Can they really be peers, or is "peer tutoring" a contradiction in terms (Trimbur)?

- Whom does a writing center serve? The faculty? The curriculum? Students? And if the answer is "all of the above," how does a center go about determining its primary allegiance(s)?

- What is the most effective relationship for writing center employees to have with classroom instructors?

- How can a writing center take advantage of its "semi-autonomous" space without appearing separatist?

AUTHOR'S CASE COMMENTARY

Although I was certain I did not want to continue the dual TA/tutor role, I was reluctant to give up the advantages of greater control over collegewide training and supervision of UGTAs. Furthermore, I recognized that many classroom TAs had felt like solo practitioners who lacked a meaningful support system, and I was pleased with the relationships that developed among UGTAs when they became affiliated with the Writing Center. I was determined, however, not to inflict the "two hats" problem on TA/tutors.

My response to these conflicting feelings was first of all to state my opposition to the combined TA/tutor pool of UGTAs in the Writing Center. I reasserted the Writing Center as a separate entity—unattached to particular courses or instructors. To avoid appearing separatist, I took several other steps to reinforce a collaborative image for the Writing Center:

1. I issued an invitation to all composition instructors to request Writing Center consultants for their classrooms on an ad hoc basis. My staff would be available to come into a classroom and work with students individually there, perhaps circulating around the room with the instructor and responding to students' rough drafts.

2. Working with the director of GC's ESL program (called Commanding English), I designated a subset of my Writing Center staff as ESL specialists. These tutors are jointly hired, trained, and supervised by the Commanding English and Writing Cen-

ter directors. Each CE consultant is assigned to work with a "set"—a group of CE students and instructors. This involvement brings these tutors into the classroom regularly.

3. With the directors of the GC Math Center and the college's Student Services department, I instituted a training program for all General College UGTAs that consisted of a one-day session before classes start in the fall, and several other sessions during the year.

4. The Math Center director and I created a new umbrella entity for our two centers: the Academic Resource Center. The ARC now serves as a clearinghouse for tutorial services in General College.

The purposes of all these alliances—with the composition program, with Commanding English, with the Math Center and the Academic Resource Center—was to enhance the Writing Center's role as collaborative and cooperative, while preserving our autonomy and our ability to serve students in ways that the classroom and the curriculum cannot.

18 The WPA, the Composition Instructor, and Scholarship

Lisa Gerrard
University of California, Los Angeles

The Portland Resolution lists "designing or teaching faculty develop-ment seminars" as one of the possible tasks of the writing program administrator (1992). Faculty development is especially important in writing programs because many instructors are not specifically trained in composition. But how does the WPA get its faculty to attend these seminars? And beyond in-house training, what professional contribu-tions outside the classroom can the WPA require of its faculty? The primary question for you as WPA is "how to keep writing faculty, most of whom are adjuncts and graduate teaching assistants, professionally active outside the classroom?"

Institution Overview

UCLA is a state research university, located in a heavily populated ur-ban area in Southern California. It enrolls over 35,000 students in un-dergraduate and graduate programs and in the eleven professional schools. Most students come from California, but the student body as a whole represents all fifty states and 115 foreign countries. As a research institution, UCLA has a network of thirteen libraries, which house 6.6 million volumes and receive over 94,000 serial titles per day.

Faculty, Staff, and Administration

UCLA Writing Programs is located within the English department, though it has its own administration: a director, assistant director, co-ordinator of placement, coordinator of TA training, coordinator of the transfer program, an executive committee that advises the directors, and committees for hiring, personnel reviews, curriculum development, and administrative review. The faculty consist of twenty-eight lecturers, whose appointments and re-appointments must be approved by the program, the English department, and the dean of Humanities, a divi-sion of the College of Letters and Science. The program was established and, for its first three years, directed by Richard Lanham, a professor of Renaissance literature in the English department. All of the subsequent directors, both tenured professors from UCLA's English department, and more recently, a long-term, untenured lecturer in the program itself, have held their Ph.D.s in literature. The change in directorship from a tenured faculty member from the English department to an untenured lecturer in Writing Programs, and the addition of the assistant director position, also to be held by a Writing Programs lecturer, occurred in 1992, when the program undertook a major self-review.[1] The program's administrative positions rotate among lecturers every few years. A few of them carry course releases, though much of the work of the program is carried out without such compensation. Most lecturers teach a full course load: seven composition courses a year on a quarter system.

Most of the Writing Programs faculty received their formal training in literature, though a few hold degrees in rhetoric/composition; twenty-three of them hold Ph.D.'s, five hold M.A.'s or ABDs. Lecturers are full time but not eligible for tenure. They are hired on renewable one-year contracts; in their sixth year they become eligible for a three-year contract, which can be renewed as long as the lecturer is evaluated as "excellent" and the department has demonstrated "programmatic need" for the candidate's work. Lecturers on three-year contracts undergo a thorough performance review every three years. Twenty-three lecturers hold three-year contracts; two hold one-year contracts. As needed, the program has also hired temporary lecturers to help staff its courses. Approximately fifty teaching assistants, graduate students studying literature in the English department, also teach in the program. UCLA offers no graduate program in rhetoric and composition.

Courses

Though initially conceived, in 1979, as a five-year program staffed by temporary appointments whose job was to resolve a temporary "literacy crisis," the program has grown in complexity and scope. It offers first-year, intermediate, and advanced writing courses, as well as writing courses in specific disciplines (e.g., sociology, life sciences), and specialized courses (e.g., "Colonial and Post-Colonial Woman Writers of South Asia"), many of which are required by majors in other departments. Although certain majors require students to take one or more advanced writing courses, the university itself requires only first-year writing (between one and three courses, depending on the student's score on a placement exam). There is no upper-division writing requirement.

Key Challenge: Lack of Incentive for Scholarly Activity

The university defines Writing Programs' lecturer positions as teaching positions, and does not require that lecturers do research as part of the grounds for reappointment. This arrangement justifies the substantially heavier teaching load that lecturers carry, compared to that of tenured faculty, who are expected to do research and publish. All of our lecturers are accomplished instructors; they were hired to a large extent because of their pedagogical skill, and they have demonstrated this skill at UCLA; they receive unusually high praise from students on course evaluation forms, and six lecturers have won UCLA's Distinguished Teaching Award. At the same time, lecturers vary greatly in their commitment to the profession outside the classroom. Some have published research and textbooks; been active in composition and literature organizations; offered workshops and conference presentations; worked with faculty at other institutions, K–16; and won awards from such foundations as the NEH, Fulbright, Guggenheim, and MacArthur. Others, mindful of the university's mandate that ours is an undergraduate *teaching* program, of the lack of institutional reward for achievements outside the classroom, and of the heavy value placed on student assessments of our teaching by administrators outside Writing Programs— student course evaluations have historically been the principal criterion for reappointment—these lecturers confine their professional activity to their immediate classroom practice.[2]

Despite this difference in the way our faculty have construed their professional identity, during the program's self-review in 1992, Writing Programs voted to adopt a broad definition of "teaching" to include scholarship, agreeing that our faculty should write, publish, and stay current in the field of rhetoric and composition. Such an expectation conforms to NCTE's position statement on teaching composition: "Writing teachers should themselves be writers . . . [and] should be familiar with the current state of our knowledge about composition." Despite professed agreement with this caveat, many lecturers ignored it. In 1995, concerned that several of the faculty were becoming increasingly detached from the profession, a Writing Programs committee on evaluation wrote a document spelling out more narrowly professional work that would qualify as "excellent teaching" and reiterating that scholarly activity would be expected of our lecturers and evaluated at reappointment time. Our definition of "scholarly activity" was fairly broad: in addition to traditional research and publication in fields related to language, literature, and composition, it included such activities as innovative curriculum development and participation in teleconferences and electronic listservs related to the discipline. The faculty unanimously approved this document. But as I write, two years later, nothing has changed: on paper, we define ourselves as scholar-teachers, and those who have always published books and attended conferences such as the annual CCCC convention continue to do so. Those who have never participated widely in the profession still don't; they have no incentive to do so, and probably never will.

Key Challenge: Why Writing Instructors Should Be Scholars

Our desire to have a faculty of scholar-teachers was based on the assumption that rhetoric and composition is a legitimate academic discipline, with both a research and teaching agenda. Research universities often assert that teaching and research are reciprocal activities—each feeds into and benefits the other. Such reciprocity is certainly ideal, but as we all know, in practice, it frequently disappears; often professors' specialized studies have little to do with the general education courses they teach. In composition, however, the connection between teaching and research can be unusually close. At the very least, writing teachers should write—if not for publication, at least for discernible and discerning audiences (as in readers of grant proposals and formal reports). Beyond that, writing teachers should

> know about the nature of the composing process; the relationship between reading and writing; the functions of writing in the world of work; the value of the classical rhetorical tradition; and more. Writing teachers should use this knowledge in their teaching, contribute to it in their scholarly activities, and participate in the professional organizations that are important sources of this knowledge. (Commission on Composition, National Council of Teachers of English).

I see several reasons for this requirement:

1. Like architecture, law, and engineering, composition has both a research and an applied component. Just as no one would expect someone to teach law or nursing if she or he had never worked as an attorney or nurse, so we should not consider ourselves qualified to teach composition unless we are active writers ourselves. Depending on their specialty, instructors could work in an academic field, such as linguistics, literature, or rhetoric, or engage in professional writing activity outside academia—e.g., through journalism, technical writing, medical writing, or fiction writing.

2. Though doing writing that is judged by and has an effect on others is important, writing in the field of composition itself has a special advantage. By writing about what we do, we gain better perspective on our work. We will also learn more, be more inspired, and have more authority as composition professionals if we engage in scholarship that is tied to what we do in the classroom and if we are familiar with the scholarship of others. In this we assume that written discourse is a way of knowing, not merely a package for presenting already known ideas; like our students, we learn by analyzing and producing texts. People who write and reflect on their writing practice are likely to be much more sensitive and informed writing teachers than those who don't.

3. We will have a larger body of teaching resources to choose from. Teachers who reflect on their pedagogy, keep track of others' scholarship, and do their own writing are likely to produce new methods and the textbooks, videotapes, computer programs, and other classroom materials to go with them.

4. We are less likely to burn out if we have time to engage in creative projects apart from teaching. Working closely with students is satisfying, but it is also exhausting, especially for instructors with many students and multiple composition classes. Having the time to attend both to students and to our writing can both enrich us professionally and invigorate us personally.

5. As compositionists we will be a more unified scholarly community. Although teaching and scholarship should be mutually nourishing activities, many of the researchers in composition do not teach writing and few of the teachers do research. The researchers are often ex-compositionists who have been rewarded for their research by being relieved of their composition courses. They teach graduate rhetoric courses or work in education labs. And the teachers are too busy grading papers—and, as often as not, looking for permanent work—to produce scholarship. Thus, the discipline of composition is split between masses of untenured instructors, who do most of the teaching, and a tiny group of tenured faculty members who do the scholarship.

Definition of *Scholarship*

When our faculty discussed what we meant by *scholarship*, we drew on the four categories Ernest Boyer delineated in his report *Scholarship Reconsidered: Priorities of the Professoriate* (1990):

1. The scholarship of discovery. This is what we usually mean by research—the discovery of new knowledge. In composition, this scholarship includes such projects as ethnographic studies, investigations into how cultures define literacy, how people learn to read and write, how technology transforms perceptions of text.

2. The scholarship of integration: work that interprets other research and connects it to other knowledge. This kind of scholarship is natural to composition because our field is already interdisciplinary. As we study texts, learners, writers, readers, rhetorical circumstances, and cultural influences on writing, we integrate knowledge from many fields, e.g., linguistics, rhetoric, literary criticism, ethnic and gender studies, ESL, history, psychology, philosophy, anthropology, and information technology.

3. The scholarship of application: applying theory to concrete social problems and, in the process, generating new knowledge. In composition, community literacy projects and outreach programs in K–12 would constitute the scholarship of application.

4. The scholarship of teaching. Informed, reflective teaching doesn't just transmit knowledge; it can create new knowledge. Jane Peterson argues that teaching is in itself a form of inquiry, a way of knowing. In reflecting on what happens in the classroom, "generating new questions about language and learning, and developing . . . an ever deeper understanding of our discipline," we perform "acts of creation and interpretation, self-discovery, expression, and communication . . . [that] parallel those of the scholar who works with more traditional texts or the researcher with data" (32). Furthermore, good teaching inspires the instructor and the student to seek out more knowledge.

Boyer's four categories allow for tremendous flexibility in defining scholarly activity, so that they include most kinds of professional activity: textbooks, conference papers, published fiction, science writing, communications consulting, workshops, instructional materials, as well as academic books and articles. This flexibility is especially important in composition because the research pattern in composition can be untraditional, a point the *CCCC's Guidelines for Faculty, Deans, and Department Chairs* makes in recommending criteria for evaluating faculty:

1. Any one individual may publish in several disciplines.

2. Composition research is more closely tied to classroom practice than is the research in many other disciplines.

3. Composition scholars disseminate their work in new ways. "Some innovative textbooks, computer software, . . . and cur-

ricular development . . . represent primary means of communicating the results of extensive research." Conducting workshops can also be a way of disseminating research.

4. Much of the work is conducted and reported on collaboratively.

Efforts to Encourage Scholarship

In the early 1980s, the program routinely invited composition researchers to our campus to talk about their work. These compositionists, among them Frank O'Hare, Rosemary Hake, and Nancy Sommers, along with a series of faculty development seminars, ensured that our faculty kept up to date on scholarship in rhetoric and composition. In addition, throughout the program's history, individual faculty members created and ran workshops on their topics of expertise, including classical rhetoric, ESL, basic writing, feminist discourse, computer-based composition, and theories of literacy. These meetings always attracted a substantial number of people, but no one was pressured to attend, and many never did. In 1992, however, when we reimagined our program we decided that all the Writing Programs faculty should be involved with the ways composition was developing as a discipline.

We wrote a proposal to our dean, recommending a new position, visiting scholar in composition—which we hoped would revitalize composition scholarship among our regular faculty—and a new center, a University Center for the Study and Teaching of Writing to be located within our writing program. This center would support a faculty of scholar-teachers by coordinating applications for funding, organizing research projects, and disseminating research findings through new curricula, public workshops, interdepartmental programs, and publications.

The center would support both theoretical (e.g., discourse studies) and applied (e.g., TA mentoring) projects and would function as a laboratory for many kinds of composition issues—political, theoretical, and pedagogical. We considered the writing program to be a natural place for an experimental research center. As Louise Phelps notes (1991), writing programs are well suited for trying out solutions to institutional problems because they are already unconventional in many ways: their use of classroom space, their scheduling of teaching time, their use of computer equipment, the wide range of their interdisciplinary work, the connections they make with schools and community programs, and the radical value systems implicit in many of the classroom practices.

We also hoped that by institutionalizing our scholarship in composition, we might strengthen our connection to the university's mission, which is to provide students with a liberal education *and* to function as the research arm of the state's system of higher education. In the process, we might reduce our vulnerability as a "temporary" program. Throughout its history, our writing program has faced repeated threats to its existence. At different times, the university has considered ways of seriously cutting and even eliminating the program: moving the basic writing courses to community colleges, eliminating the upper division, replacing lecturers with teaching assistants from departments outside English, or reducing the faculty to a maximum of fifteen. While these plans have not yet come to pass, during financial crises, the university routinely looks to our program as a source of funds. As a result, the program is substantially smaller than it was when it began, both in faculty size and number of course offerings, and is highly sensitive to threats to its continuance. In this context, we hoped a research center might give the program greater legitimacy, given the heavy research emphasis of the university and the widespread belief that writing is a "skill" and writing instruction a form of "remediation" that should eventually become unnecessary.

We hoped as well that a research center would make it easier for us to collaborate with faculty in other departments. Our situation is typical of that of many writing programs, especially in large universities. Writing programs housed in English departments are often overshadowed by the parent department, and even where they're not, public relations between institutions and their writing departments often need improving. The CCCC Committee on Professional Standards cites a dean at a large Midwestern university who told them that "status and support for writing instruction are denied at her school, not because the budget is too tight, but because the intellectual power of writing courses is not apparent to her or to anyone else" (338). This attitude toward composition prevails at UCLA as well, and we hoped that by developing relationships with other departments, our research center might help to alter the university's thinking about the nature of composition—both the course and the discipline—and our own value as a writing program.

Additionally, we considered that even faculty who chose not to participate directly in the center might be energized by its intellectual vitality and that we would all influence one another's classroom practice. The center might also expand possibilities for TA training. While TAs are apprentices, not merely recipients of financial aid, our English department, like many others, gives the opposite message. Concerned that their students lose no time in completing the Ph.D., they discourage them from lavishing energy on teaching—especially if it's compo-

sition teaching. This attitude is unfair not onl
dergraduates who take their courses but also
will study with them when they enter the pro
TAs are learning that teaching will be the leas
when they become professors. To help correct th
that graduate students would participate in tl
search assistants, dissertants, or co-devi
gain research experience, and learn mo.
pline than they typically do in their TA tra
ate students in literature more intensive exi
ies, the center would prepare them for the *cholarship*
teaching they would probably do at their i
more likely to teach composition or a survey course than a seminar on
their dissertation topic. The research center would help fulfill a need
James Slevin identifies in their training: to "set the work of English studies in larger professional and theoretical contexts" (13).

Challenges and Obstacles

Our recommendations, based as they were on an ideal and idealistic
vision of what a writing program could be, never came to pass. The
university vetoed the visiting scholar idea immediately on the grounds
that our mission was teaching, not research. The research center we
proposed was ignored. The message seemed to be that we could write
grants and do all the research we wanted, but at reappointment time
we would continue to be evaluated on our teaching. It was clear that
outside Writing Programs, we would always be seen as temporary
employees, marginal to the principal work of the university, concerned
only with undergraduate education (despite our work with graduate
programs in several departments), providing a needed, but lamentable
service—teaching basic skills. Though aware of our curricular goals and
of the scholarly record of many of our faculty, the rest of the university
continues to hold on to stereotypes about composition and its practitioners. At UCLA and elsewhere, it has served the financial interest of
both upper-level university administrators and ladder faculty to nour-
ish these stereotypes; the low status of composition allows administrators to justify the low pay and job insecurity of writing instructors and,
in turn, to fund the sabbaticals, small course loads, computer grants,
and other benefits that accrue to ladder faculty.[3]

This result will not surprise anyone familiar with the status of
college writing programs. Nor will the reactions of our own faculty,

ded daily of their marginality— feel no pressure
In fact, they have no reason to. Our teaching
heavier than those of tenured and tenure-track
se our program is defined as a teaching, not re-
me reason, we are not eligible for research grants
we in any way viewed as equal to ladder faculty
(we are not members of the academic senate, for example). At reappointment time, it is student course evaluations, not publications, that matter to the review committees outside our program.

Within the program, the committee responsible for personnel reviews faces a contradictory task. Our employment contracts, drawn up
by the university and our labor union, the American Federation of Teachers, require proof of teaching "excellence" to renew a three-year contract (and proof of teaching "competence" for one-year appointments).
However, it gives us some latitude in defining these terms. Given the
language of the contracts, then, it is feasible to require scholarship in
composition—however freely defined—along with course evaluations,
syllabi, and other course materials, as evidence of teaching excellence.[4]
Ethically, however, we have never been able to bring ourselves to en-
force a scholarship requirement. Every year our Writing Programs Personnel Committee, the first of several university committees to evaluate each candidate, confronts dossiers of vastly different scope; in addition to course materials and student course evaluations, some dossiers overflow with evidence of scholarly activity; others have none at
all. Every year, the committee faces the same problem: can we recommend as "not excellent" someone who has no scholarship? And every
year, sensitive to how hard our faculty work in the classroom and how
little compensation, job security, and recognition they get in return, we
decide that we can't. Lack of job security is our biggest problem. Our
positions are chronically uncertain; when the university, as it has several times, chooses to contract the writing program, people lose their
jobs. Though enthusiastically praised for its excellence, the program is
seen as expensive and, therefore, expendable. Thus under current working conditions, a scholarship requirement simply isn't fair.

Our program is unusual in that its faculty all have advanced degrees and all see themselves as composition professionals. But the problem of requiring or at least motivating scholarly activity is compounded
in the vast numbers of writing programs that hire only graduate assistants or casual employees. Some of these faculty may have no interest
in attending conferences, rethinking their pedagogy, or doing scholarship. They see their teaching as a job, not a career; they want to teach

their courses and go home. If they are graduate teaching assistants, they may be biding their time until they get a "real job" teaching Chaucer. Even the most committed teaching assistants must be principally concerned with their own studies, and if their primary field of study is literature, as it often is, they have little time to find out about, let alone contribute to, the field of rhetoric and composition.

Another obstacle that can confront WPAs is that some writing faculty are not qualified to do scholarship. WPAs periodically discover that when a permanent position opens up in their programs none of their part-timers survives the interview: they can't name a theorist or journal in composition; they've never heard of CCCC; their classroom practice is fifteen years out of date. This is not surprising, since few instructors—whether hired from the outside or as graduate teaching assistants in English—get any formal training in composition. The view that many writing instructors are not qualified for professional positions contributed to William Robinson's (1991) and Myron Tuman's (1991) critique of The CCCC Statement of Principles and Standards (1989), a document based on the Wyoming Resolution and intended to upgrade the working conditions of compositionists: " . . . while professionalism in our field is indeed improved, we are kidding ourselves if we believe the average composition instructor has professional qualifications in terms of adequate formal training" (Robinson 345).

Many practitioners, however, would welcome additional training and an opportunity to be more involved in the profession, but have neither the time, resources, nor incentive for such involvement. The biggest obstacle to their professional development is the appointment structure of their positions. Writing instructors are rarely rewarded for scholarly work. And if they were, they wouldn't have time to do it. Most of them are part-timers commuting to multiple jobs, teaching too many students in too many classes, under impoverished material conditions for subsistence wages. Many of them have no office, telephone, or photocopying budget, let alone research or travel funds. Rather than cultivate a professional life, they're spending whatever time they have outside the classroom lining up a job for next term. Compared to the average writing instructor, our lecturers are privileged: we work full time and get medical benefits; we have offices and desks, telephones, (shared) computers, and some travel and photocopying money. These resources have helped support many of our research projects, but they can't compensate for the lack of time, and most of all, the awareness that as compositionists, we can never be valued by our institution.

Implications

This state of affairs raises questions for the profession as a whole. How can composition be taken seriously as a discipline when the vast numbers of its practitioners never write or do scholarship? The profession is rightfully proud of its graduate programs in rhetoric and composition, its journals and conferences, and its alliances with other fields. But as a discipline, composition and rhetoric is still made up of a tiny elite that does research, attends conferences, and writes—and a vast proletariat that teaches writing but does not write, reflect on writing, or otherwise engage in the profession. As a discipline, composition has replicated the status structure that dominates academia, at the top of which are what James Sledd calls the "boss compositionists," many of whom have "contempt for the real teachers of composition": "When compositionists brag about 'the new professionalism' in their 'discipline,' they are thinking of themselves and the disciples who have sat at their feet" (275). Many WPAs, some of them "boss compositionists," are highly sensitive to this difference in status, but they are overwhelmed by the institutional structures that support it.

Key Charge

With the majority of composition courses taught by those with little interest in or opportunity to do scholarship, it is no wonder that our institutions regard our work as a service anyone can perform. We need professional activity to put new curricula into the classroom; we need it to support the intellectual strength of the field; and we need it to maintain our professional integrity. How effective is a classroom teacher who is ignorant of the theories of the field? And how can compositionists ever form a unified community when they're divided into several classes: researchers who seldom teach undergraduates; WPAs, too preoccupied with keeping their program afloat to do research; and instructors, too busy grading papers to attend a conference.

What, then, can the WPA do about this state of affairs? Given all the tasks WPAs typically manage, arranging conditions that allow their instructors to function as scholars is a tall order. How can the WPA motivate, train, and provide working conditions that allow writing instructors to be full members of the discipline? Of the conditions that the WPA can control, which would most foster scholarly activity?

Notes

1. This review was motivated by substantial cuts in faculty positions and by the recognition that the campus, the program, and our faculty had changed since the programs' inception in 1979. Since that time, the number of lecturer appointments has, for financial reasons, been cut by 45 percent, our course load has been increased, and we have had to reduce both the number and variety of courses we offer.

2. In addition to making written comments, students rank different components of the course (e.g., "Class presentations were well prepared and organized") on a nine-point scale. Each ranking is calculated to two decimal points (e.g., 8.02). The score that is taken most seriously by reappointment committees, especially those outside our immediate program, is the one attached to "Your overall ranking of the instructor"; this score has been used to justify reappointment decisions. Given the multitude of variables that affect the validity of these numbers as measures of teaching quality, lecturers have for years contested their interpretation, but with little success. The program has recently created and is currently testing a nonquantitative evaluation form, with questions geared specifically to composition teaching (the other form is used university-wide).

3. In a study of York University's use of adjunct faculty, Indhu Rajagopal and William D. Farr concluded "Institutional benefits in the form of higher enrollment and revenues, better full-time faculty salary increments, and smaller class sizes, could not have been realized without large-scale employment of part-time faculty" (1989).

4. The American Federation of Teachers, which represents lecturers in the University of California system, believes such a requirement is legal, but it has never been tested in court.

AUTHOR'S CASE COMMENTARY

It is clear that this problem lacks a smooth solution. By ignoring lecturers' scholarly work and by relying heavily on student course evaluations in assessing lecturers' performance, our university discourages writing faculty from doing scholarship. Lecturers are well aware that low scores on student evaluations can cost them their jobs, and are far more likely to spend time perfecting their in-class performance than undertaking professional work outside the classroom.

Thus, the program has only had success encouraging scholarly activity in those who do it anyway—for their own professional satisfaction. The program has not penalized those who are not professionally active, but does make an effort to support those who are. It offers limited travel funds for faculty giving presentations at professional conferences; when given a "special needs fund," an unexpected award from the university, the program has allocated much of it for scholarly work and travel. Photocopying expenses have been gradually enlarged over the years. Though we share computers (roughly four faculty members per computer), the equipment is upgraded every few years. The program maintains a small library of rhetoric/composition titles, subscribes to the major journals in the field, publicizes conference announcements, and keeps information on funding sources. Some of its efforts have as much symbolic as practical value: it maintains a display case of books published by our faculty, and it recently convinced the library to honor our library cards for three years at a time, so (because, although some of us have been here for seventeen years, we are regarded as temporary employees) we would no longer have to renew them every year. These forms of support may seem trivial, especially when measured against the generous research grants, allocations of state-of-the-art computer equipment, and most of all, research time (through light teaching loads and sabbatical leaves) afforded tenured faculty. The fact is that only a change in institutional circumstances and in the reward structure of our appointments will make any significant difference. The most we have been able to do is chip away at a monumental institutional and disciplinary problem.

19 Initiating a Peer Tutoring Program in a University Writing Center

Robert S. Dornsife
Creighton University

This essay discusses issues you, as WCD, need to negotiate when initiating a peer tutoring program/training into an institution that traditionally prides itself on providing students with "degreed" professional instruction.

Institution Overview

History of Your Position

First, you were hired one year ago with the understanding that you would become director of the Writing Center at Creighton University at the start of your second year. Now, you are starting your second year and you have just been named director, as promised.

The Writing Center offers one hundred appointments per week, each lasting twenty-five minutes. The staff consists of five tutors, all of whom hold master's degrees. The hours of the Writing Center are roughly "banker's hours," from 9:00 A.M. to 4:30 P.M., five days a week. There is always a waiting list. During busy times of the semester, the waiting lists contain dozens of students.

Creighton itself is ranked number one among universities in the Midwest region by *U.S. News and World Report.* Creighton is a Jesuit university with medical, dental, and law schools. Including these schools, the campus is comprised of about 6,000 students.

Writing Center Overview

Creighton University's Writing Center was, at the time you became its director, two years old. The Writing Center mostly enjoys a good reputation, and certainly enjoys the support of the English department within which it operated. The Writing Center is staffed by a cross-section of part-time faculty, all of whom have earned at least a master's degree in English.

You assumed the role of Writing Center director largely because the director of composition had "too much on her plate." Your transition to the directorship was by all accounts smooth and uneventful, largely as a result of your chair's, and the director of composition's, good will and support. Prior to your new appointment as director of the Writing Center, you felt that undergraduate English major studies had precious little resemblance to the profession of English. For example, it is possible—even commonplace—to find English majors who, on graduation day, had not taught, done any writing resembling actual scholarship, or done any sort of service other than the typical editorial responsibilities on undergraduate literary publications. In short, there are too many English majors who have no experience in what may very well be the three centers of their future professional lives: teaching, research, and service. Therefore, you concluded that part of the obligation as a new member of the faculty was to utilize whatever resources you now had at your disposal to begin bridging this gap between undergraduate preparation and professional expectations. The Writing Center was the first such opportunity for you. Thus, with your own professional experience motivating you, and your concern with the distance between the undergraduate major and the discipline of English, you set out to take advantage of the new position as director.

Challenges and Obstacles

The challenge that serves as the basis for this essay involves instituting a peer tutoring program. The key challenge is one of process: How do you go about initiating a peer tutoring program in a Writing Center? The obstacles toward such a goal are both far-reaching and reasonable.

Within your key challenge, there are other, overlapping challenges. First, there are problems already inherent in the suspicions surrounding (a) what writing centers do and (b) the exacerbation of these suspicions by the proposed presence of undergraduate peer tutors in your Writing Center. Second, there are problems that are more or less local to undergraduate peer tutors—problems that are "unique" to peer tutors.

Problem-Solving Process

The problem-solving process in this chapter is comprised of three stages:

1. presentation and approval of the idea;
2. selection and training of the peer tutors; and
3. implementation of the peer tutoring program.

Although no solutions to these problems will be offered (these issues are discussed in the case commentary located at the end of this essay), it should be clear that without successful negotiation of the early stages, there will be no later stages. As a result, the problem-solving here is cumulative and progressive.

From the beginning, the Writing Center must answer to the charge that the tutors are somehow doing more than helping the writing process and facilitating the students' own work. Those who do not allow their students to bring their course work to a writing center often make that decision as a result of a fear that the student papers are being written for the student by the tutor, that the student sits passively while the tutor makes "suggestions" that result in the students no longer being the rightful authors of the paper.

> How do you fight this misconception?
>
> What sorts of strategies might you employ to allay these fears, and how might you change such a climate?

However, my experience suggests that a corollary to this misguided view is the view that the writing center is counterproductively sympathetic—that the writing center listens to and accepts student complaints about the poor quality of the instruction being received in a course, and that the writing center staff will sit in judgment of any professor's writing pedagogy. This suspicion is no doubt heightened by the uncertainty that many teachers who have no training or confidence toward their abilities to teach writing feel as they are increasingly asked to do so. The increasing prevalence of writing across the curriculum furthers this uncertainty, just as it increases the numbers of teachers outside of English or the humanities in general who are asked to teach writing.

> Should you institute a "wider" training program for teachers with doubts about their own writing pedagogy? What would such a program include? How might such a program influence your ultimate goal of initiating peer tutoring?

In making the proposal for a peer tutor program, you must first come to terms with how the following problem will be solved. That undergraduates work together (or seek and receive assistance from other undergraduates) in a way that would make an instructor uncomfortable is a given. Whether it is on the dorm floor or in the apartment building, students' friends often have too great a hand in the writing of a student paper. Undergraduates often develop a "lifeboat" mentality that encourages a sharing of services—"I will help you with your English paper if you help me next week on the calculus assignment." And certainly the students will be quick to sympathize with the complaints of other undergraduates. Therefore, given the perceived propensity of undergraduates to offer assistance that many teachers would feel crosses the line, how are undergraduates to be trusted as writing center tutors?

> Must you try to revise the overall perception of both Writing Centers and peer tutors?

Closely related to the question of "too much help" is the question of basic ability—of authority and experience. Such concerns are in many ways valid, but also stem from fundamental misunderstandings of undergraduate ability and aptitude. In general, I have found that undergraduates will respond to challenges put forth. Such a response is certainly characteristic of our strongest undergraduates. However, faith in the undergraduates counts little in terms of a proposal because of the considerable competition the university faces.

This competition comes from several areas. Creighton University is fifty miles north of the University of Nebraska at Lincoln, and also competes locally with neighbor University of Nebraska at Omaha. Because Creighton's tuition is more than double that of its closest competitors, and because our student population is largely regional, Creighton must work hard to demonstrate that its tuition is worth paying. In short, Creighton must establish that it is "twice as good" as its competition.

A perceived problem with very large state schools such as the University of Nebraska is an overreliance on teaching assistants. Creighton aggressively advertises that its students will have regular contact with Ph.D.-holding faculty, even in its lower-division courses. Creighton lives up to its promises in this regard. Course assignments take into consideration that even the most senior faculty should be teaching the lowest-level courses as part of a regular rotation. To see a tenured, full professor near retirement teaching first-year rhetoric and composition is not unusual, nor is seeing those students interacting freely with that same professor outside of class.

Key Challenge

One of the largest obstacles that you face during the proposal phase is the philosophy of "no teaching assistants." Since you argue for non-B.A. holding undergraduates to assume important teaching positions, you might be perceived as transgressing this philosophy in an extreme way. The success of your own undergraduate peer tutoring program and the success of several other such programs around the country might seem testimony enough to the possibilities of peer tutoring. But perhaps even a successful peer tutoring program would itself be seen as a failure, since it would by design work directly against one of the tenets of Creighton's mission statement and its promotional and actual positions.

> What sort of proposal might have the best chance of addressing the concerns that any administration might reasonably have in this regard? What angles might this proposal take?
>
> How might you employ other aspects of a mission statement toward your goals?
>
> What is the current state of the research on non-Ph.D. teaching success?

Key Charges

You will need to be prepared for a good-natured struggle. In my experience, the art of the proposal is largely a matter of timing and climate. Timing and climate are in many ways inseparable. You need to be aware of the context into which your proposal will be made. Thus, the proposal phase will end once you have answered the following questions:

> Have you ascertained the "reputation" of the Writing Center as it currently exists?
>
> Do you understand and sympathize with the fears surrounding Writing Centers in general and peer tutoring programs in particular?
>
> Does your proposal address those fears in a convincing way?
>
> Is it the "right time" to submit your proposal?

If these questions are addressed with care, you will have the greatest chance to reach the second phase of initiating a peer tutoring program.

Once your proposal has been approved, the selection and training stage is the most important, since it includes to some extent the implementation. After all, if the selection and training stage is successful, a successful implementation is more likely.

AUTHOR'S CASE COMMENTARY

Key questions that surround peer tutor selection include the following:

> Should students from all majors be invited to apply?
>
> How much say should the writing center director have in the decision process?
>
> Should the applications be by selective invitation only?

Should there even be an application process, or should the director simply choose potential peer tutors based on other available criteria?

What are the qualities of a successful tutor?

How might such qualities be measured or assessed?

The selection and training phase is largely comprised of pedagogical concerns. While the relationship between student and teacher within the shared writing classroom is local on one level, teaching undergraduates to become tutors in a university writing center has implications that reach from the biology course to the literature course—from Einstein's atom to world literature. These implications are most informative about the anticipated differences in teacher and student responsibilities between writing classroom (where the relationship between student and teacher is direct) and writing center (where the tutor's main task is to assess what the client and the client's professor want, and to respond accordingly as a surrogate or "third party").

Thus, once committed to initiating a peer tutoring program in a writing center, you need to reconsider your pedagogy as it moves from writing instructions for undergraduates to teaching undergraduates how to teach writing.

You might particularly consider those components of your writing pedagogy that were designed to facilitate transition in your first-year writers. For example, since I stressed in my writing classes that the students' writing was now their own, and that as such they had complete responsibility for it, should I offer such responsibility to students' pedagogies?

What do you want peer tutors to lean about tutoring? Might a prioritized list be of help? What sorts of priorities would be the highest?

What were the implications of risk in relation to growth?

How could one facilitate a uniformity of excellence that would no doubt be as different as the tutors themselves?

What elements of your classroom pedagogy are more likely to work in your tutor-training pedagogy? What elements are less likely to work?

How long should your orientation be?

What sorts of exercises might you use?

It might help to locate answers to such questions in ways that suggest that teaching writing is not different than teaching teaching. Remember, your experience in the classroom will be of use to you as you design and implement your training program. Once you have come to some working conclusions about the answers to the above questions, your training sessions are likely to be both enjoyable and productive.

Implementation is mostly the "follow through" of the strong foundation you have laid during your proposal and selection and training phases. However, implementation carries with it challenges of its own, many of which are derived from early challenges. Consider the following questions:

> Remembering any strategies that you employed to "ready" your climate for your proposal, what sorts of strategies might you employ toward maintenance? How might you continue to "spread the good word?"

> What are the areas of the previous two phases that still need work? How might you address these areas during the implementation phase?

Finally, successful implementation requires an eye on the future. In order to work toward continued and greater success, you might address the following:

> Where do you see your peer tutoring program in five years?

> What steps might you take now to facilitate your five-year goals?

Although the challenges of initiating a peer tutoring program are sometimes trying, in my experience your dividends will exceed your investment several fold. Never losing sight of your dream and moving toward it one step at a time will provide you with the motivation you need to address these challenges.

Of many such anecdotes, I recall one that might be relevant here. As part of the implementation phase, I wanted to integrate our peer tutors into the professional dynamic of our department, so I requested that our peer tutors receive mailboxes amid the faculty mailboxes. At one tutor's graduation party, her mother informed me that this tutor was taking one memento with her as she went off to earn her Ph.D.: she took the name tag from her mailbox, presumably as a symbol of her entry into this profession. This tutor, now a Ph.D., plans to use this very book in her courses.

Suggested Reading

Aleamoni, Lawrence M., ed. *Techniques for Evaluating and Improving Instruction: New Directions for Teaching and Learning*, no. 31. San Francisco: Jossey-Bass, 1987.

Astin, Helen, and Carole Leland. *Women of Influence, Women of Vision*. San Francisco: Jossey-Bass, 1991.

Bazerman, Charles, and David R. Russell, eds. *Landmark Essays On Writing Across the Curriculum*. Davis, CA: Hermagoras Press, 1994.

Bean, John C. *Engaging Ideas: The Professor's Guide to Integrating Writing, Critical Thinking, and Active Learning in the Classroom*. San Francisco: Jossey-Bass, 1996.

Bennis, Warren, and Burt Nanus. *Leaders: The Strategies for Taking Charge*. New York: Harper and Row, 1985.

Bishop, Wendy. "Going up the Creek without a Canoe: Using Portfolios to Train New Teachers of College Writing." *Portfolios: Process and Product*. Ed. Pat Belanoff and Marcia Dickson. Portsmouth, NH: Boynton/Cook, 1991. 215–28.

Bleich, David. "Evaluation, Self-Evaluation, and Individualism." *ADE Bulletin 101* (Spring 1992): 9–14.

Braskamp, Larry A., Dale C. Brandenburg, and John C. Ory. *Evaluating Teaching Effectiveness: A Practical Guide*. Beverly Hills: Sage, 1984.

Clark, Irene L. *Writing in the Center: Teaching in a Writing Center Setting*. Dubuque, IA: Kendall/Hunt, 1992.

Computers and Composition. Ed. Cynthia Self. Michigan Technological University.

Conference on College Composition and Communication. (n.d.). *Scholarship in Composition: Guidelines for Faculty, Deans, and Department Chairs*.

Conference on College Composition and Communication. Committee on Professional Standards. "A Progress Report from the CCCC Committee on Professional Standards." *CCC* 42 (October 1991): 330–49.

Covey, Stephen. *Principle-Centered Leadership*. New York: Summit Books, 1991.

———. *The Seven Habits of Highly Effective People*. New York: Simon and Schuster, 1989.

Davis, Barbara Gross, Michael Scriven, and Susan Thomas. *The Evaluation of Composition Instruction*. 2nd ed. New York: Teachers College Press, 1987.

DePree, Max. *Leadership Is an Art*. New York: Dell, 1989.

Dykstra, Pamela D. "The Patterns of Language: Perspective on Teaching Writing." *Teaching English in the Two-Year College* 24 (1997): 136–44.

Edgerton, Russell, Patricia Hutchings, and Kathleen Quinlan. *The Teaching Portfolio: Capturing the Scholarship in Teaching.* Washington, DC: AAHE, 1991.

Fulwiler, Toby, and Art Young, eds. *Programs That Work: Models and Methods for Writing Across the Curriculum.* Portsmouth, NH: Boynton/Cook, 1990.

———. *Writing Across the Disciplines: Research into Practice.* Upper Montclair, NJ: Boynton/Cook, 1986.

Gardner, J. W. *On Leadership.* New York: The Free Press, 1990.

Grego, Rhonda, and Nancy Thompson. "Repositioning Remediation: Renegotiating Composition's Work in the Academy." *College Composition and Communication* 47 (1996): 62–84.

Hamp-Lyons, Liz. "The Challenges of Second-Language Writing Assessment." In *Assessment of Writing: Politics, Policies, Practices.* Ed. Edward M. White, William D. Lutz, and Sandra Kamusikiri. New York: MLA, 1996. 226–40.

Healy, Dave. "A Defense of Dualism: The Writing Center and the Classroom." *The Writing Center Journal* 14.1 (1993): 16–29.

Helling, Barbara. "Looking for Good Teaching: A Guide to Peer Observation." *Innovation Abstracts 3* (6 March 1981): 7.

Herrington, Anne, and Charles Moran, eds. *Writing, Teaching, and Learning in the Disciplines.* New York: MLA, 1992.

Holdstein, Deborah H. "Technology, Utility, and Amnesia." Review. *College English* 57.5 (September 1995): 587–98.

———. *Computers and Composition.* Englewood Cliffs, NJ: Prentice Hall, 1994.

Machlup, Fritz. "Poor Learning from Good Teachers." *Academe 65* (1979): 376–80.

McLeod, Susan H, ed. *Strengthening Programs for Writing Across the Curriculum.* San Francisco: Jossey-Bass, 1988.

National Council of Teachers of English, Commission on Composition. (n.d.) *Teaching Composition: A Position Statement.*

Peters, Thomas J., and Robert Waterman. *In Search of Excellence: Lessons from America's Best-Run Companies.* New York: Warner, 1982.

Powers, Judith K. "Rethinking Writing Center Conferencing Strategies for the ESL Writer." *The St. Martin's Sourcebook for Writing Tutors.* Ed. Christina Murphy and Steve Sherwood. New York: St. Martin's, 1995. 96–103.

Reigstad, Thomas, and Donald A. McAndrew. *Training Tutors for Writing Conferences.* Urbana, IL: NCTE and ERIC, 1984.

Roy, Alice. "ESL Concerns for Writing Program Administrators: Problems and Policies." *WPA: Writing Program Administration* 11.3 (1988): 17–28.

Seldin, Peter. *Successful Faculty Evaluation Programs: A Practical Guide to Improve Faculty Performance and Promotion/Tenure Decisions.* Crugers, NY: Coventry, 1980.

Shaughnessy, Mina. *Errors and Expectations: A Guide for the Teacher of Basic Writing.* New York: Oxford University Press, 1977.

Soliday, Mary. "From the Margins to the Mainstream: Reconceiving Remediation." *College Composition and Communication* 47 (1996): 85–100.

Sorcinelli, Mary Deane, and Peter Elbow, eds. *Writing to Learn: Strategies for Assigning and Responding to Writing Across the Disciplines.* San Francisco: Jossey-Bass, 1997.

Stay, Byron L., Christina Murphy, and Eric H. Hobson, eds. *Writing Center Perspectives.* Emmitsburg, MD: NWCA Press, 1995.

Tinberg, Howard B. *Border Talk: Writing and Knowing in the Two-Year College.* Urbana, IL: NCTE, 1997.

Walvoord, Barbara E., and Lucille P. McCarthy. *Thinking and Writing in College: A Naturalistic Study of Students in Four Disciplines.* Urbana, IL: NCTE, 1990.

Walvoord, Barbara E., et al. *In the Long Run: A Study of Faculty in Three Writing-Across-the-Curriculum Programs.* Urbana, IL: NCTE, 1997.

Weiser, Irwin. "Surveying New Teaching Assistants: Who They Are, What They Know, and What They Want to Know." *WPA: Writing Program Administration* 14.1-2 (1990): 63–71.

Writing Center Journal, The. Dave Healy, ed. Minneapolis: National Writing Centers Association.

Writing Lab Newsletter, The. Muriel Harris, ed. Lafayette, IN: Purdue University.

Yancey, Kathleen, and Michael Spooner. "Postings on a Genre of Email." *College Composition and Communication* 47 (1996): 252–78.

Works Cited

Bartholomae, David. "The Tidy House: Basic Writing in the American Curriculum." *Journal of Basic Writing* 12 (1993): 4–21.

Belanoff, Patricia, and Marcia Dixon. *Portfolio Grading: Process and Product.* Portsmouth, NH: Heinemann, 1991.

Belanoff, Patricia, and Peter Elbow. "Using Portfolios to Increase Collaboration and Community in a Writing Program." *WPA: Writing Program Administration* 9.3 (1986): 27–40.

Berlin, James A. *Rhetorics, Poetics, and Cultures: Refiguring College English Studies.* Urbana, IL: NCTE, 1996.

Birnbaum, Robert. *How Colleges Work: The Cybernetics of Academic Organization and Leadership.* San Francisco: Jossey-Bass, 1988.

Bishop, Wendy. "Designing a Writing Portfolio Evaluation System." *The English Record* 40 (1990): 21–25.

Blythe, Stuart. "Networked Computers + Writing Centers =? Thinking about Networked Computers in Writing Center Practice." *The Writing Center Journal* 17.2 (1997): 89–110.

Boyer, Ernest L. *Scholarship Reconsidered: Priorities of the Professoriate.* Princeton: The Carnegie Foundation for the Advancement of Teaching, 1990.

Cambourne, Brian, J. Turbill, and A. Butler. *Frameworks: A Whole Language Staff Development Program.* Stanley, NY: Wayne-Finger Lakes Board of Cooperative Educational Services, 1993.

Carino, Peter. "Early Writing Centers: Toward a History." *The Writing Center Journal* 15.2 (1995): 103–15.

Catalano, Timothy, et al. "TA Training in English: An Annotated Bibliography." *Writing Program Administration* 19 (1996): 36–54.

CCCC Committee on Assessment. "Post-secondary Writing Assessment: An Update on Practices and Procedures." (Spring 1988). Report to the Executive Committee of the Conference on College Composition and Communication.

Clausen, Christopher. "Part-Timers in the English Department: Some Problems and Some Solutions." *ADE Bulletin* 90 (Fall 1988): 4–6.

Conference on College Composition and Communication. (n.d.) *Scholarship in Composition: Guidelines for Faculty, Deans, and Department Chairs.*

Conference on College Composition and Communication. Committee on Professional Standards. "A Progress Report from the CCCC Committee on Professional Standards." *College Composition and Communication* 42 (1991): 330–49.

Conference on College Composition and Communication Executive Committee. "Statement of Principles and Standards for the Postsecondary Teaching of Writing." *College Composition and Communication* 40 (1989): 329-326.

Cooper, Charles R. "Holistic Evaluation of Writing." *Evaluating Writing: Describing, Measuring, Judging.* Ed. Charles R. Cooper and Lee Odell. Urbana, IL: NCTE, 1977. 3–31.

Cox, Bené Scanlon. "Priorities and Guidelines for the Development of Writing Centers: A Delphi Study." *Writing Centers Theory and Administration.* Ed. Gary A. Olson. Urbana, IL: NCTE, 1984. 77–84.

Crossley, Gay Lynn. "Not Only Assessment: Teachers Talk about Writing Portfolios." *Journal of Teaching Writing* 12.1 (1993): 33–55.

Despain, LaRene, and Thomas L. Hilgers. "Readers' Responses to the Rating of Non-Uniform Portfolios: Are There Limits on Portfolios' Utility?" *WPA: Writing Program Administration* 16.1-2 (1992): 24–37.

Dickson, Marcia. "Directing without Power: Adventures in Constructing a Model of Feminist Writing Program Administration." *Writing Ourselves into the Story: Unheard Voices from Composition Studies.* Ed. Sheryl I. Fontaine and Susan Hunter. Carbondale: Southern Illinois UP, 1993. 140–53.

Dykstra, Pamela D. "The Patterns of Language: Perspective on Teaching Writing." *Teaching English in the Two-Year College* 24.2 (1997): 136–44.

Elbow, Peter, and Pat Belanoff. "Portfolios as a Substitute for Proficiency Examinations." *College Composition and Communication* 37 (1986): 336–39.

Fairhurst, Gail T., and Robert A. Sarr. *The Art of Framing: Managing the Language of Leadership.* San Francisco: Jossey-Bass, 1996.

Fulwiler, Toby, and Art Young. Introduction. *Programs that Work: Models and Methods for Writing Across the Curriculum.* Eds. Fulwiler and Young. Portsmouth, NH: Boynton/Cook, 1990. 1–8.

Gameran, Adam, and Robert Dreeben. "Coupling and Control in Educational Organizations." *Schools and Society*, 2nd ed. Ed. Jeanne H. Ballantine. Mt. View, CA: Mayfield Publishing Co, 1989. 119–45.

Gappa, Judith M., and David W. Leslie. "Academe's Dual Labor Market." New Pathways: Working Paper Series. AAHE, 1996.

———. *The Invisible Faculty: Improving the Status of Part-Timers in Higher Education.* San Francisco: Jossey-Bass, 1993.

Gill, Judy. "Another Look at WAC and the Writing Center." *The Writing Center Journal* 16.2 (1996): 164–78.

Glau, Gregory R. "The 'Stretch Program': Arizona State University's New Model of University-level Basic Writing Instruction." *WPA* 20:1-2 (1996): 79–91.

Green, Madeleine F., and Sharon A. McDade. *Investing in Higher Education: A Handbook of Leadership Development*. Phoenix: American Council on Education/Oryx Press, 1994.

Greenberg, Karen. "Competency Testing: What Role Should Teachers of Composition Play?" *College Composition and Communication* 33 (1982): 366–76.

Greenberg, Karen, Harvey Wiener, and Richard Donovan, eds. *Writing Assessment: Issues and Strategies*. New York: Longman, 1986.

Grego, Rhonda, and Nancy Thompson. "Repositioning Remediation: Renegotiating Composition's Work in the Academy." *College Composition and Communication* 47 (1996): 62–94.

Grimm, Nancy. "The Regulatory Role of the Writing Center: Coming to Terms with a Loss of Innocence." *The Writing Center Journal* 17.1 (1996): 5–29.

Guskin, Alan E. "Facing the Future: The Change Process in Restructuring Universities." *Change* 28.4 (1996): 26–37.

Hamp-Lyons, Liz, and William Condon. "Questioning Assumptions about Portfolio-Based Assessment." *College Composition and Communication* 44 (1993): 176–90.

———. "Readers' Responses to Portfolios." CCCC Annual Meeting. Boston, March 1990.

Hansen, Kristine. "Face to Face with Part-Timers: Ethics and the Professionalization of Writing Faculties." *Resituating Writing: Constructing and Administering Writing Programs*. Ed. Joseph Janangelo and Kristine Hansen. Portsmouth: Boynton/Cook, 1995. 23–45.

Harris, Joseph. *A Teaching Subject: Composition Since 1966*. Upper Saddle River, NJ: Prentice Hall, 1997.

Healy, Dave. "A Defense of Dualism: The Writing Center and the Classroom." *The Writing Center Journal* 14.1 (1993): 16–29.

———. "The Deprofessionalization of the Writing Instructor." *WPA: Writing Program Administration* 16.1-2 (1992): 38–49.

———. "Writing Center Directors: An Emerging Portrait of the Profession." *WPA: Writing Program Administration* 18.3 (1995): 26–43.

Hemmeter, Thomas. "The 'Smack of Difference': The Language of Writing Center Discourse." *The Writing Center Journal* 11.1 (1990): 35–48.

Herzig, Carl. "Portfolio Assessment as Faculty Development: The Small-School Context." *Journal of Teaching Writing* 12.1 (1993): 25–31.

Hult, Christine. *Evaluating Teachers of Writing*. Urbana, IL: NCTE, 1994.

Hult, Christine, and the Portland Resolution Committee. "The Portland Resolution." *WPA: Writing Program Administration* 16.1-2 (1992): 88–94.

Huot, Brian. "Reliability, Validity, and Holistic Scoring: What We Know and What We Need to Know." *College Composition and Communication* 41 (1990): 201–213.

————. "Toward a New Theory of Writing Assessment." *College Composition and Communication* 47 (1996): 549–66.

Institute for Research on Higher Education. "The Landscape: The Academy in a Changing World: Restructuring in Higher Education." *Change* 27 (July/August 1995): 41–44.

Jolly, Peggy. "The Bottom Line: Financial Responsibility." *Writing Centers: Theory and Administration*. Ed. Gary A. Olson. Urbana, IL: NCTE, 1984. 101–14.

Kail, Harvey, and John Trimbur. "The Politics of Peer Tutoring." *WPA: Writing Program Administration* 11.1-2 (1987): 5–12.

Keller, George. *Academic Strategy: The Management Revolution in American Higher Education*. Baltimore: Johns Hopkins UP, 1983.

Lankard, Bettina A. "The Changing Work Forces: Trends and Issues Alerts." Eric Clearinghouse on Adult, Career, and Vocational Education, Columbus, Ohio, 1993.

McLeod, Susan, and Margot Soven, eds. *Writing Across the Curriculum: A Guide to Developing Programs*. Newbury Park, CA: Sage, 1992.

Meeks, Lynn. "Using the Condition of Learning at the College Level to Teach Teachers." *Frameworks Focus,* Summer, 1996.

Merrill, Robert, et al. "Symposium on the 1991 'Progress Report from the CCCC Committee on Professional Standards.'" *College Composition and Communication* 43 (1992): 154–75.

Murphy, Christina. "Writing Centers in Context: Responding to Current Educational Theory." *The Writing Center: New Directions*. Ed. Ray Wallace and Jeanne Simpson. New York: Garland, 1991. 276–88.

National Council of Teachers of English, Commission on Composition. (n.d.) "Teaching Composition: A Position Statement."

Oakeshott, Michael. "The Voice of Poetry in the Conversation of Mankind." *Rationalism in Politics and Other Essays*. New York: Basic Books, 1962.

Olson, Gary A. "Establishing and Maintaining a Writing Center in a Two-year College." *Writing Centers: Theory and Administration*. Ed. Gary A. Olson. Urbana, IL: NCTE, 1984.

Olson, Gary A., and Evelyn Ashton-Jones. "Writing Center Directors: The Search for Professional Status." *WPA: Writing Program Administration* 12.1-2 (1988): 19–28.

Peterson, Jane E. "Valuing Teaching: Assumptions, Problems, and Possibilities." *College Composition and Communication* 42 (1991): 25–35.

Phelps, Louise Wetherbee. "Becoming a Warrior: Lessons of the Feminist Workplace." *Feminine Principles and Women's Experience in American Composition and Rhetoric*. Ed. Louise Wetherbee Phelps and Janet Emig. Pittsburgh: U of Pittsburgh P, 1995. 289–339.

————. "The Institutional Logic of Writing Programs: Catalyst, Laboratory, and Pattern for Change." *The Politics of Writing Instruction:*

Postsecondary. Ed. Richard Bullock and John Trimbur. Portsmouth, NH: Boynton/Cook, 1991. 155–70.

Pratt, Mary Louise. "Arts of the Contact Zone." *Profession 91*. New York: MLA, 1991. 33–40.

Putnam, Robert. "Bowling Alone: America's Declining Social Capital." *Journal of Democracy* 6 (1995): 65–78. httpp://128.220.50.88/demo/journal_of_democracy/v006/putnam.html. 1997.

Rajagopal, Indhu, and William D. Farr. "The Political Economy of Part-Time Academic Work in Canada." *Higher Education* 18 (1989): 267–85.

Robertson, Linda R., and James Slevin. "The Status of Composition Faculty: Resolving Reforms." *Rhetoric Review* 5.2 (Spring 1987): 190–94.

Robinson, William S. "The CCCC Statement of Principles and Standards: A (Partly) Dissenting View." *College Composition and Communication* 42 (1991): 345–49.

Roemer, Marjorie, et al. "Portfolios and the Process of Change." *College Composition and Communication* 42 (1991): 455–68.

Rose, Mike. *Lives on the Boundary: The Struggles and Achievements of America's Underprepared*. New York: Free Press, 1989.

———. "Remedial Writing Courses: A Critique and A Proposal." *College English* 45 (1983): 109–28.

Roundtable, The Pew Higher Education. "To Dance with Change." *Policy Perspectives* 5 (1994): 1a–11a.

Schon, Donald A. *Educating the Reflective Practitioner: Toward a New Design for Teaching and Learning in the Professions*. San Francisco: Jossey-Bass, 1987.

Senge, Peter M. *The Fifth Discipline: The Art and Practice of the Learning Organization*. New York: Doubleday, 1990.

Simpson, Jeanne. "Perceptions, Realities, and Possibilities; Central Administration and Writing Centers." Paper presented at CCCC Annual Convention. Washington, D.C.: March 23–25, 1995.

Sledd, James. "Why the Wyoming Resolution Had to Be Emasculated: A History and a Quixotism." *Journal of Advanced Composition* 11 (1991): 269–81.

Slevin, James F. "Depoliticizing and Politicizing Composition Studies." *The Politics of Writing Instruction: Postsecondary*. Ed. Richard Bullock and John Trimbur. Portsmouth, NH: Heinemann, 1991. 1–21.

Smit, David. "Evaluating a Portfolio System." *WPA: Writing Program Administration* 14.1-2 (1990): 51–62.

Soliday, Mary. "From the Margins to the Mainstream: Reconceiving Remediation." *College Composition and Communication* 47 (1996): 85–100.

———. "Shifting Roles in Classroom Tutoring: Cultivating the Art of Boundary Crossing." *The Writing Center Journal* 16.1 (1995): 59–73.

Sommers, Jeffrey, et al. "The Challenges of Rating Portfolios: What WPAs Can Expect." *WPA: Writing Program Administration* 17.1-2 (1993): 7–29.

Strenski, Ellen. "Recruiting and Retraining Experienced Teachers: Balancing Game Plans in an Entrepreneurial Force-Field." *Resituating Writing: Constructing and Administering Writing Programs.* Ed. Joseph Janangelo and Kristine Hansen. Portsmouth, NH: Boynton/Cook, 1995. 82–99.

Trimbur, John. "Peer Tutoring: A Contradiction in Terms?" *The Writing Center Journal* 7.2 (1987): 21–28.

Tuman, Myron C. "Unfinished Business: Coming to Terms with the Wyoming Resolution." *College Composition and Communication* 42 (1991): 356–64.

Waldo, Mark L. "What Should the Relationship between the Writing Center and Writing Program Be?" *The Writing Center Journal* 11.1 (1990): 73–80.

Walvoord, Barbara. "Getting Started." *Writing Across the Curriculum: A Guide to Developing Programs.* Ed. Susan McLeod and Margot Soven. Newbury Park, CA: Sage, 1992. 12–31.

Weimer, Maryellen. *Improving College Teaching: Strategies for Developing Instructional Effectiveness.* San Francisco: Jossey-Bass, 1990.

White, Edward. "Language and Reality in Writing Assessment." *College Composition and Communication* 41 (1990): 187–200.

———. *Teaching and Assessing Writing.* San Francisco: Jossey-Bass, 1985.

Wingspread Group on Higher Education. *An American Imperative: Higher Expectations for Higher Education.* Racine, WI: The Johnson Foundation, 1993.

WPA Executive Committee. "Evaluating the Intellectual Work of Writing Program Administrators: A Draft." *WPA* 20.1-2 (1996): 92–103. WPA-L (Writing Program Administrators' listserv: LISTSERV@ASUACAD. BITNET).

Wyche-Smith, Susan, and Shirley K. Rose. "One Hundred Ways to Make the Wyoming Resolution a Reality: A Guide to Personal and Political Action." *College Composition and Communication* 41 (1990): 318–24.

Yancey, Kathleen Blake, ed. *Portfolios in the Writing Classroom: An Introduction.* Urbana, IL: NCTE, 1992.

Index

Northfield State University, 146
NWCA. *See* National Writing Centers
    Association

Oakeshott, Michael, 45
O'Hare, Frank, 239
Ohio State University Agricultural
    Technical Institute, 112–13
    mission of, 113–14
On Leadership (Gardner), 256
online services, setting up, 138
Online Writery, 141
"Online Writing Labs (OWLs)" (Harris
    and Pemberton), 140
online writing labs, 16, 181–82
    setting up, 141–45
Ory, John C., 255
OWL. *See* online writing labs

"Patterns of Language, The" (Dykstra),
    256
PD. *See* professional development
pedagogy, components, 252
peer collaboration teams, 197
peer consultants, 134
peer observation, of teaching assistants,
    196
peer tutoring, initiating, 248–50
peer tutors, 16, 17, 114, 231
    resume and business writing, 17
    selection of, 251
Pemberton, Michael, 140
Peters, Thomas J., 256
Peterson, Jane, 238
Phelps, Louise Wetherbee, xx, 94, 239
Pine, 142
placement testing, 161
Polanyi, Michael, vii
"Poor Learning from Good Teachers"
    (Machlup), 256
portfolio assessment, problems with,
    48–49
Portfolio Pilot, 45
    goals of, 46
portfolios, teaching, 198
"Postings on a Genre of Email" (Yancey
    and Spooner), 257
power, 209–10
Powers, Judith K., 256
Pratt, Mary Louise, 46
Principle-Centered Leadership (Covey), 255

"Priorities and Guidelines for the
    Development of Writing Centers"
    (Cox), 118
problems, assessment of administrative,
    100–108
problem solving, xviii, 210–11
    process of, 248–49
processes, work, 86, 92–93
professional development, 87, 88–90
program business, accessibility of, 89
program coordinators, 93
Programs That Work (Fulwiler and
    Young), 256
public relations, 177–78
Purdue University Writing Lab, 14
    OWL of, 141, 143, 144
Putnam, Robert, 86

Quinlan, Kathleen, 256

Rajagopal, Indhu, 245 n 3
reading courses, 113
Reigstad, Thomas, 256
"Repositioning Remediation" (Grego
    and Thompson), 256
research, Internet, 136
Research Writing, 31
resources,
    financial, 89
    human, 82–84, 89
    moral limits of, 95–5
"Rethinking Writing Center
    Conferencing Strategies for the ESL
    Writer" (Powers), 256
revision, 129
Rickly, Rebecca, 197
Robinson, William, 243
roles, work, 86, 92–93
Rose, Mike, 154–55, 219
Roy, Alice, 257
Russell, David R., 255

scholars, writing instructors should be,
    236–37
scholarship,
    definition of, 237–39
    encouraging, 239–41
Scholarship in Composition (CCCC), 255
Scholarship Reconsidered (Boyer), 237
Scriven, Michael, 255

Editor

Linda Myers-Breslin is assistant professor at Texas Tech University, where she directs the composition and rhetoric program. She has presented her pedagogical research and ideas at national and international conferences. She edited *Approaches to Computer Classrooms: Learning from Practical Experience* and has published articles and book reviews in journals such as *The Journal of Advanced Composition, Computers and Writing,* and *Freshman English News.* Current work includes "Complex Networking between Students, Writing, and Technology" in *Complexity in the Classroom* (edited by John Harmon); and "Technology, Distance, and Collaboration: Where Are These Pedagogies Taking Composition?" in *Writing the Wrongs: Reforming College Composition* (edited by Ray Wallace, Alan Jackson, and Susan Lewis).

Contributors

Paul Bodmer is associate professor of English and chair of the arts and communications department at Bismarck State College, a comprehensive two-year college in Bismarck, North Dakota. He teaches first-year composition, American Literature, and Western American Fiction. He is a former chair of the Two-Year College English Association of NCTE, and a member of the Conference on College Composition and Communication and TYCA-Midwest.

Richard Bullock directs the writing programs at Wright State University. He has edited or co-edited three books: *Seeing for Ourselves: Case-Study Research by Teachers of Writing, Why Workshop? Changing Course in 7–12 English,* and *The Politics of Writing Instruction: Postsecondary,* which won the 1993 *CCC* Outstanding Book Award.

Allene Cooper, formerly the writing director at Boise State University, is a lecturer at Arizona State University. She has written *Thinking and Writing by Design: A Cross-Disciplinary Rhetoric and Reader* and several articles in composition, writing across the curriculum, program administration, and American literature.

Robert S. Dornsife, associate professor at Creighton University, earned the school's highest teaching honor, the Robert F. Kennedy Student Award for Excellence in Teaching, in 1996. In 1997 and 1998 he won the Greek Award for "commitment to students." Dornsife is the Director of Graduate Study and the Director of the Writing Center. He has published in *The Journal of Advanced Composition, Computer-Assisted Composition Journal, The Writing Lab Newsletter, The National Teaching and Learning Forum, The Teaching Professor,* and other publications.

Lisa Gerrard holds a Ph.D. in comparative literature from the University of California, Berkeley, and has been a lecturer in UCLA Writing Programs since 1980. She has published books, articles, and software in several fields, including women and literature, foreign language composition, and computers and writing. Her most recent work is "Modem Butterfly and Her Cybersysters: Feminism and the Rhetoric of Women's Websites" in *Women on the Web* (Ed. Sue Webb, in press).

Muriel Harris, professor of English at Purdue University, founded and continues to direct the Purdue University Writing Lab and founded and continues to serve as editor of the *Writing Lab Newsletter.* She also initiated and continues to oversee the Purdue OWL. As Writing Lab Director, she oversees three staffs of tutors and trains and assists with the selection of the graduate students who work with writers from any course in the university and peer tutors who work with the writers in the developmental writing program.

Carol Peterson Haviland is associate professor of English and Director of the Writing Center, California State University, San Bernardino. She teaches undergraduate and graduate composition courses and focuses her work on writing centers, writing across the curriculum, intellectual property, feminism, and composition theory. In the spring of 1998, Haviland published *Weaving Knowledge Together: Writing Centers and Collaboration*, co-edited with Maria Notarangelo, Lene Whitley-Putz, and Thia Wolf.

Dave Healy directed the Writing Center at the University of Minnesota's General College from 1988 to 1997. Before that he served as director of the Writing Center at Bethel College in St. Paul, Minnesota. From 1994 to 1997 Healy was editor of *The Writing Center Journal*, and from 1992 to 1994 he served as Chair of the Midwest Writing Centers Association. Currently he works as a freelance editor and writer.

Douglas D. Hesse is President of the Council of Writing Program Administrators. From 1994 to 1998 he edited *WPA: Writing Program Administration*. He has published articles in *CCC*, *JAC*, *RR*, *WOE*, and *The New England Journal of Medicine*, and chapters in *Passions, Politics, and 21st Century Technologies; Writing Theory and Critical Theory; Academic Advancement in Composition Studies; Essays on the Essay; Narrative and Argument; Literary Nonfiction*; among others. He teaches at Illinois State University.

Deborah H. Holdstein is professor of English and rhetoric at Governors State University, where she previously directed the writing program and co-ordinated the program in English. She has published widely in a number of fields within composition and English studies; in addition to several books, her essays have appeared in such journals as *CCC*, *WPA*, and *College English*. In addition to her work as co-director of the WPA Consultant-Evaluator service, Holdstein has served on the MLA publications committee and is presently on the executive committee of the MLA Division of Teaching Writing.

Linda S. Houston is the Coordinator of Communication Skills and the Writing Center at the Ohio State Agricultural Technical Institute in Wooster, Ohio. She holds a B.S. degree and an M.S. degree from Syracuse University. She teaches developmental English, first-year composition, technical and business writing, and speech. She also teaches a writing course in Current Issues in Agriculture. She is past chair of what is now TYCA-Midwest; she has presented at NCTE and CCCC Annual Conventions; and she has published in several national journals.

Christine A. Hult is professor of English and Associate Department Head at Utah State University. Her research interests include computers in writing, and program and teacher evaluation, as reflected in recent publications including *The New Century Handbook* (with Tom Huckin) and *Evaluating Teachers of Writing*. She has published books and articles on a range of composition and administrative topics in various composition journals, including *WPA*, *JAC*, *Rhetoric Review*, and *Computers and Composition*, along with a series of WAC textbooks.

Sara E. Kimball is associate professor in the Division of Rhetoric and Composition and the Department of English at the University of Texas at Austin. She directs the Undergraduate Writing Center, which she started in 1993. Her research includes work on historical linguistics and Indo-European, lexicography, and literacy, ancient and modern.

Barry M. Maid is professor of rhetoric and writing at the University of Arkansas at Little Rock. In addition to teaching, he has served as director of the Writing Center, Director of Freshman Composition, and Chair of the Department of English. His current professional interests include technical communication, program administration, personality theory, and computer-mediated communication.

Rita Malenczyk is assistant professor of English and Director of the University Writing Program at Eastern Connecticut State University, where she teaches writing, composition theory, rhetorical theory, and literature. Her scholarly interests include writing program administration, nineteenth-century women's literature, and the role of undergraduate peer tutors in the evolution of composition theory.

Ben W. McClelland is professor of English and holder of the Ottillie Schillig Chair of English Composition at the University of Mississippi. He directs the university's comprehensive writing program and center. McClelland earned his M.A. and Ph.D. degrees in English at Indiana University. Under NEH fellowships, he completed postdoctoral study in composition studies at the University of Pittsburgh and in rhetoric at Carnegie-Mellon University. Among his book publications are a freshman English textbook and three professional books. McClelland is past president of the Council of Writing Program Administrators and the director of its Consultant-Evaluator Board.

Lynn Langer Meeks is associate professor of English and director of the Writing Program at Utah State University, Logan. Prior to that she was the language arts coordinator for the State of Idaho Department of Education and prior to that she taught high school English in Scottsdale, Arizona.

Joan A. Mullin, Director of WAC and the Writing Center at the University of Toledo, started both programs in 1987. She publishes in various journals across the disciplines. Her co-edited collection, *Intersections: Theory-Practice in the Writing Center* won the 1994 National Writing Center Association Award for Outstanding Scholarship, and her recent co-authored book, *ARTiculations: Teaching Writing in a Visual Culture* indicates her interest in visuals across the curriculum. Past president of the National Writing Centers Association, she co-edits *The Writing Center Journal.*

Louise Wetherbee Phelps is professor of writing and English and former director of the Writing Program at Syracuse University, where she currently directs graduate studies in composition and cultural rhetoric. Recent publications include *Feminine Principles and Women's Experience in American Composition and Rhetoric, Composition in Four Keys,* and essays on composition theory, teaching, and administrative practice. A consultant on writing program administration, she is working on book projects in feminism, design of writing assignments, and graduate pedagogy.

A graduate of UCLA and Brandeis University, **Howard Tinberg** is currently professor of English at Bristol Community College in Fall River, MA, where he serves as director of the college's writing lab. He has authored *Border Talk: Writing and Knowing in the Two-Year College* as well as articles published in a variety of journals, including *College English, College Composition and Communication, The Journal of Basic Writing, Teaching English in the Two-Year College,* and *the Writing Lab Newsletter.*

Edward M. White is professor emeritus of English at California State University, San Bernardino, where he has served as English department chair and coordinator of the university writing program, and a visiting professor at the University of Arizona. Statewide in California, he has been coordinator of the CSU Writing Skills Improvement Program and was director of the English Equivalency Examination program. On the national scene, he directed the consultant-evaluator service of WPA for six years and in 1993 was elected to a second term on the executive committee of CCCC. His publications include *Teaching and Assessing Writing, Developing Successful College Writing Programs,* and *Assigning, Responding, Evaluating.*

This book was typeset in Palatino and Helvetica by
Electronic Imaging.
The typeface used on the cover was Trajan.
The book was printed by Edwards Brothers, Inc.

CCCC and NCTE
The Best Minds in Composition and Rhetoric Meet Right Here . . .

The Conference on College Composition and Communication (CCCC) is a constituent organization of the National Council of Teachers of English (NCTE) whose main interest is the study and **teaching of reading and writing at the college level. This group provides a forum in which directors of composition programs, two-year college teachers, researchers, technical writers, graduate assistants, theorists, media specialists, and many others can share their special insights and concerns.**

Join Us. No matter where you are on your professional path, CCCC has the resources you need to connect with your colleagues on campuses across the nation. When you join CCCC, you'll have access to information that will keep you informed on the latest in our profession—all for less than 15¢ a day!

Membership in CCCC/NCTE Enriches Your Teaching and Scholarship!
With your membership you can:

➢ Have a comprehensive look at what's happening in our field with an annual subscription to *College Composition and Communication,* which provides a forum for critical work on the study and teaching of reading and writing at the college level. Some articles focus directly on teaching practices, others locate those practices in their historical and institutional contexts, still others relate current work in composition studies to that going on elsewhere in English and related fields.

➢ Share what you know by responding to **calls for submission of manuscripts for publication and program proposals for meetings.**

➢ Stay informed of important education news and **keep updated on professional development opportunities** with a year's subscription to *The Council Chronicle.*

➢ Learn about cutting-edge ideas from highly respected authors and scholars from across the country with **discounts of up to 30% on publications.**

➢ **Network with leaders** in the field and save up to 30% by using your member discount to register for conventions and conferences.

➢ Get answers when you need them with **24-hour access to the latest resources**, developments in teaching, and research available online at www.ncte.org.

Other Journal Options for the College Teacher-Scholar
➢ *College English*
Dedicates articles to literature, critical theory, language and applied linguistics, literacy, rhetoric, composition, and professional issues related to the teaching of English. *College English* also includes original poetry and nonfiction prose, review essays, and letters from readers.

➢ *Teaching English in the Two-Year College*
Includes reviews, news of interest, and practical features like "What Works for Me," a section devoted to the sharing of successful teaching practices for the two-year college English teacher.

➢ *Research in the Teaching of English*
Explores the relationship between language teaching and learning at all levels. Articles reflect a variety of methodologies and address issues of pedagogical relevance related to content, context, process, and evaluation of language learning.

Membership
CCCC/NCTE individual membership is only $48 per year. Other journal rates vary. Special discounts are available for students. *NCTE membership is required for membership in CCCC.*

Join CCCC and NCTE today!
Call toll-free 1-877-369-6283 or enroll online at www.ncte.org.

p-3141